Pay, Pack and Follow

PAY,
PACK
and
FOLLOW
Memoirs

Jane Ewart-Biggs

Weidenfeld and Nicolson
LONDON

First published in Great Britain by
George Weidenfeld & Nicolson Limited
91 Clapham High Street, London SW4 7TA
1984

ISBN 0 297 78535 4

Typeset and printed in Great Britain
at The Pitman Press, Bath

FOR
CHRISTOPHER
AND
HENRIETTA, ROBIN AND KATE

Contents

Contents

Illustrations

My brother and me on Scraps and Titbits
With two friends at Grenoble University
Christopher aged five
Middle East Centre for Arab Studies, 1950
The diplomatic staff of the British Embassy in Algiers
Henrietta in her pool, Club des Pins, Algeria
Christopher with Henrietta and Robin at Ellis Green
King Baudouin and Queen Fabiola at a court reception
Henrietta and Robin at Dunmow fête
Kate aged about eighteen months
The family with Konrad at Villereau in 1974
Signing the visitors book at Château Barton, Bordeaux
A Paris cocktail party with Françoise Giroud and Alex Grall
Christopher at Cavalaire
Jane and Christopher's last day at Villereau
Kate and Christopher after he had presented his credentials to the
    Irish President, July 1976
Launching the Christopher Ewart-Biggs Memorial Fund (*Guardian*)
Introduction to the House of Lords, June 1981 (*Keystone*)
Working on this book in Washington, summer 1983

Not by a radiant jewel, not by the sun nor by fire,
but by conciliation alone is dispelled
the darkness born of enmity.

Panchatantra, story 11

Foreword

The form this book has taken differs from the one I had originally planned. I had intended, by describing both my life as a diplomat's wife and the one forced upon me by the death of my husband Christopher, to illustrate how the threads of one life can be drawn together to provide the fabric for another. However, I became so engrossed in recounting our life in various embassies that I began to relive it and found that inevitably it dominated the book. The intended balance was, therefore, lost and the part which would have reflected the life which emerged in the wake of Christopher's death has been condensed into a postscript. Nevertheless, the new formula has the advantage of allowing me to distance myself from the intervening years and thereby recognize more clearly how the different stages in building a second life evolved.

I found reading and rereading Christopher's diaries a source of pain and of pleasure. These journals, which he typed meticulously with two fingers and maintained throughout his diplomatic career, had, I believe, several purposes. Firstly, they provided him with an accurate record of the current state of international affairs and the relations between his country and the one to which he was accredited. Secondly, they provided an innocent means of letting off steam about professional frustrations and personal disagreements or tensions. Lastly, I am sure he intended the diaries to provide the basis for a post-retirement literary project. I am sure he never wrote them *per se* for publication, so I have discriminated when quoting from them and avoided the parts which reflect the friction which naturally exists in the life of any embassy. I have, instead, focused on the parts which describe the problems which faced him as a diplomat, the humour he drew from the rather artificial life-style, and the satisfaction and absorbing interest he so often found in his work.

To complement the picture, I have written about how I adapted, as a wife and mother, to the unusual circumstances imposed on all members of a diplomatic family and the enjoyment I derived from being a hostess. I have, with affection, recollected the people who became our friends, the beautiful places we visited and the different houses which were our homes. I realized anew, as the book progressed, how intense a life the world of diplomacy offered, how very much part of it and committed to it Christopher and I were, and how through sharing so much it is right that diplomats of every country should call themselves 'one of the world's great freemasonries'.

Finally, in the postscript, I have tried to record – as frankly as I can – how devastating are the effects of bereavement on the survivor of a marriage and how hard is the path to recovery. I describe my overwhelming need to fill the void left by Christopher's death and to reassemble the ingredients of the life we shared so fully to enable me to build the foundations for a second one.

I am indebted to many people for their help and encouragement during the writing of this book. Lacking any literary experience, at the outset I asked the advice of my friends Dervla Murphy and Susan Crosland – both of whose work I admire – and their guidance was invaluable. I am grateful to Stephen Wall for his advice, to Maria Fairweather for allowing me to quote her, and to committee members of the Diplomatic Service Wives' Association for the information they gave me. I am also grateful to Mrs Wendy Stokes for information about Christopher's childhood, and to Robert Vaes, formerly Belgian Ambassador to London, for reminding me of so many facets of Belgian life and history. I am indebted to Alex MacCormick, my editor, without whose warm-hearted and kindly encouragement I might often have felt like giving up, and to Maria Ellis for typing the manuscript and showing so much heroism over deciphering my handwriting. I should like to thank my children for their forbearance towards a parent whose mind was continually wandering. Finally I am indebted to Kevin O'Sullivan, who, having contributed so much over recent years to the life and well-being of the whole family, has helped me believe in myself again sufficiently to write this book.

1

Cold Ash

Christopher was travelling with two companions in his chauffeur-driven ambassadorial car on the morning of 21 July 1976. They had turned out of the gates of the official residence of the British Ambassador to Ireland and were heading towards Dublin and the British Embassy. The car was specially designed to withstand attack, with reinforced bodywork and, inside, a panel of switches. One, if pressed, locked the steering. Christopher pointed this out to his passengers. 'Don't touch that,' he said to them. 'We're always telling the children not to. We call that the fatal switch.'

His light-hearted warning to the two passengers coincided exactly with the pressing of that other malevolent switch behind the hedge which was wired to the explosive lodged under the culvert over which the dark blue Jaguar was passing.

The force of the explosion shot the car high into the air, before it fell back heavily on its roof. Two of its occupants survived – the other two did not. This meant that Christopher was Britain's Ambassador to the Republic of Ireland for only twelve days.

On the same morning I was travelling from Liverpool to London. I had crossed from Dublin on the overnight ferry to collect some curtain material from the Department of the Environment to prepare for our first big embassy party. I was driving along Birdcage Walk with the car radio on when the programme was interrupted for an announcement. 'The British

3

Ambassador to Dublin has been killed this morning – his car was blown up.'

I first met Christopher in his parents' house in Kent. He was wearing a dark-grey flannel suit and was reading *The Times*. People considered him the stereotype of the British diplomat, almost a caricature. He was tall, angular, well-dressed and wore a black monocle to cover the loss of his right eye as the result of a war wound. But he didn't much like this image and often told the story of how once, when on holiday in the south of France, he had been approached by another holiday-maker who asked: 'Excuse me, but in order to satisfy a bet would you mind telling me if you are a British diplomat?' Christopher answered – or said he did – by saying: 'No, I don't mind your asking, but in return and merely to satisfy my curiosity would you mind telling me if you are a Greek shipowner?'

When we met I must have been about twenty-five and was working as a secretary to one of the directors of the Savoy Hotel. Mollie and Henry Ewart-Biggs had kindly invited my current boyfriend, who was a friend of theirs, and I to use their house in Leeds, near Maidstone, as a rather distant base for our expedition to the opera at Glyndebourne.

I can remember the exact circumstances of that first meeting with Christopher. I had changed into a party dress for the opera and was walking down the stairs when I saw him sitting in the little hall below. He looked up at me and smiled, introducing himself. I felt drawn towards the tall, distinguished looking person whose teeth stuck out a bit (the brace expensively acquired by his mother in his formative years had spent more time in his pocket than in his mouth). He was then married to his first wife, Gavrelle. She was tall, fair, very pretty and the mother of four children from previous marriages. They were both in their mid-thirties, she a few years older then he.

Looking back, I suppose my youthful, carefree image must have appealed to a man with the responsibility of being a stepfather to four children. Indeed my own background was very different from his. Ours was an incomplete family and I was conscious of it. My father, Basil FitzHerbert Randall – whom I never knew – was a major in an Indian Army cavalry regiment known as 'Skinner's Horse', and he died when I was only a few months old. It was his idea to call me

Felicity and so was I christened, but it didn't take long for the dour expression on my small, sombre face to persuade my parents to change it to Jane.

I never knew much about my father, because my mother seldom spoke of him, and as he had been an only child, we had no uncles and aunts to tell us about him. But from the little I gleaned he was obviously a gentle, charming person, never attracting enmity and with a wonderful gift for sympathy. His death was a dramatic one. Unaware of his heart condition, he played a great deal of polo – this was part of the life of a cavalry officer attached to Government House – and during one strenuous match he had suffered a severe heart attack and died instantly. My mother, after only seven years of what apparently had been a very happy marriage, was left widowed with two children, a small Indian Army pension, and a few polo ponies to her name. She returned by sea to England with my brother and me, and the courage and determination which characterized her whole personality helped her to start again. She was very pretty – still is, although now a very old lady – with a lovely skin and green eyes. She had a quick wit and, to my great admiration, always found the right word to inject humour into conversation. She mourned my father long and hard, which was presumably the reason she never married again. I meanwhile craved for the demonstrative affection she found difficult to give and often thought nostalgically of how, had my father lived, he might have cuddled me.

On her return to Britain she bought a little cottage called The Witches in Queen Camel, a village near Yeovil in Somerset, and that was where I spent most of my childhood. It was a pretty, little white stone house, with a tiled roof, set right in the middle of the village with two huge cedar trees in the front garden. The rooms were small with low ceilings and the bedroom I shared with my brother Dick had a stove which kept it cosy all the time.

I do not have a clear picture of the kind of child I must have appeared to others. My own recollections are primarily of extreme shyness: I always seemed to be the onlooker, the minority child. My shyness was so absolute that Dick answered for me when I was asked questions. I can remember vividly the sense of isolation brought on by my inability to communicate. But I had a pony – or rather a series of ponies – and I was happy enough with them. They were at the centre of our existence and also provided an entry into the lives of the more well-to-do Somerset families. My mother was not well off. Her Indian Army pension in no way allowed her to follow the lifestyle of the families in the social class to which she aspired, and in those pre-war days, when society was even more polarized than it is today, there was no natural social niche for us. So with great good sense she made her investment in what amounted to the passport to those circles: the horse.

She herself had a large chestnut called Lawless, which she rode sidesaddle to hounds, looking handsome in her dark blue habit, bowler hat and veil drawn tightly over her face. For us there was a series of ponies starting with a Shetland called Titbits, who almost immediately – and most conveniently – had a foal, Scraps. They used to wander into the small drawing-room of the cottage and slide around on the Indian rugs on the shiny wooden floor. These were followed by a succession of other ponies, each one larger than the one before. We took part in gymkhanas and hunter trials all over the county, though we didn't travel to these by horsebox accompanied by grooms like the others. Instead we used to lead our ponies from our bicycles sometimes for distances up to twenty miles in order to get them there feeling fresh enough to take part successfully in the jumping competitions, the bending races, the musical chairs, the showing events, etc. As we always had good ponies and had been taught well, we often returned home covered with rosettes and glory. However, even the successes did not bolster my ego sufficiently to overcome the embarrassment of the bicycle rides, and my constant fear of being overtaken as we panted along by a horsebox or smart car full of friends who would wave to us. To this day I cannot look at the grassy verge of a road without reliving the anguish of the hours spent grazing our ponies there to save the expense of oats and hay. My brother was a much more confident child and did not share my anxieties, although when it came to showing courage on our ponies I was usually the bolder of the two. Although we were so different in character and although we quarelled like most brothers and sisters, he and I were unusually close throughout our youth. His sudden death while I was still writing this book left me feeling bereft of my whole childhood.

Another clever idea of my mother's was to take on foreign girls to look after us; they were, in fact, the original version of the present-day au pair. In return for a little English conversation with her in the evenings, these French, German and Swiss girls looked after my brother and me and spoke either French or German to us. So, in our early childhood we spoke English, French and German all at the same time. This useful arrangement naturally came to an end in 1939; but only after my mother discovered us being lectured one day by Magda, our current German au pair, on the virtues of fascism and drilling us in the Nazi salute, to which we were responding enthusiastically.

During this period we went for our summer holidays to Brittany in order to speak French and because it was cheap. My mother had ingeniously discovered an old *abbaye* run by the nuns as a guest-house in a fishing village called St Jacquut-sur-Mer. It was primitive, but the garden stretched down to the sea. The nuns did all the work and the one who acted as head gardener used to chase us off her rosebeds and out of her vegetable garden. There was a minuscule chapel in the gardens almost filled by a particularly realistic crucifix, and when the nuns got themselves into a muddle – having, say, overbooked or found their vegetables overrun by Colorado beetle – they hurried off and prayed there for divine intervention. I remember how much the crude portrayal of Christ's death in that tiny chapel terrified me.

During the war years we moved to Studland Bay, near Bournemouth, where one of my uncles ran a riding-school, and the plan was for my mother to help him. My education at this time went through a dramatic phase. Up till then it had been scanty, mainly consisting of sharing governesses or being taught by my mother or the foreign girls. At one point I went with my mother to a family in Versailles, where I accompanied Marie Odette, the small daughter, to her convent school every day. This didn't last long, however, as very soon I succeeded in making myself ill to avoid going to school because the nuns – kind though they were – intimidated me. I never thought of telling my mother of my fears, but instead ended up a skeleton and we had to go home. At Studland it was decided I should share a governess with the Crossley children who lived on the other side of the moors, which were also at that time used for rifle practice. My mother, who obviously didn't believe in mollycoddling, sent me off each day across the moors alone on my pony. I was only ten years old, but it was left to me to turn back if the red flag was flying to indicate that rifle practice was actually in progress. On those days I didn't do any lessons, but instead just messed about with the ponies.

When I was thirteen I was sent to a boarding-school. The money was scraped together somehow and I was delivered, with my trunk, to Downe House, situated on top of a hill in a village named – rightly – Cold Ash, near Newbury. It was a school of two to three hundred girls and we wore a strange and unbecoming uniform consisting of a djibbah made of green sackcloth. This garment, which we much revered, was modelled on the lines of an ancient Greek tunic and, although no doubt suitable enough for its original purpose, did nothing for the bulging shapes of Britain's wartime girls.

Looking back on my time at Downe House, I now have no doubt that the school did its best to prepare us for life. The curriculum, as I remember it, was quite well balanced; and we were taught a lot of non-academic skills such as basket-making, pottery, carpentry, etc. The school had a reputation for music (indeed the teaching there provided the basis for future musicians such as Amaryllis Fleming), and each year there was a performance of a Shakespearian play in the school's Greek Theatre. We played lacrosse in the winter and netball and cricket in the summer, with a smattering of tennis. I can remember wondering at the time whether lacrosse was an appropriate sport for girls whose faces were to be an important asset in years to come: why allow their vital attribute to be a focus for hard rubber balls and swishing lacrosse sticks (I always felt 'cradling' to be a misnomer for the slashing, cutting movement)? Cricket, our other major sport, although much less physically hazardous, seemed an equally inappropriate talent for future years.

My recollections of those four years at Downe House are dominated by the memory of continued shyness and the onset of asthma. The burden which each of these afflictions adds to life is unimaginable to those who have not experienced them: how shyness brings in its wake a sense of failure, which in turn adds to the already strong feeling of inadequacy, which has given rise to it in the first place. A shy person feels locked in a prison made up of anxiety and self-denigration out of which no escape can be found. Although I had always been shy, it was only as a teenager that I really suffered and it brought in its wake a disproportionate need for friendship, which became my major preoccupation. I felt a positive craving for the comfort and security provided by the certainty of having friends.

I did very soon acquire two friends, to my great relief. They were both very pretty – one, Ann Baron, tiny, blue-eyed and extrovert, came from Nelson in Lancashire, and the other, tall, lithe, dark-curly-haired and popular, was called Robin Moody and lived in Somerset. They each possessed an acceptable and respected talent. Ann played the cello – it seemed as big as herself – and Robin was athletic and ran with infinite speed and beauty on the lacrosse field, transforming the ludicrous game into a contest of style and grace. She was also so attractive in looks and character that she positively magnetized affection.

My own achievements fell a long way short of theirs, and I was constantly anxious about retaining their friendship. I read avidly and was good at lessons, finding maths comprehensible, English and history interesting. French and German were well established by the au pairs' contribution in my early childhood. But because of the curious attitudes of that period (still, I fear, reflected in some English circles) any academic success was suspect and being 'too clever by half' – whatever that meant – was frowned on. So instead of achieving credit for often being top of my class I was judged rather on my looks, social skills, performance at games and in the field of music. At that time my looks were dramatically – and literally – overshadowed by the eleven stone resulting from a ravenous appetite, brought on by growing fast and accentuated by the cold of unheated buildings and the starch-dominated diet. My social attributes were severely undermined by my inability to say anything. Moreover, the asthma which afflicted me and for which there were then none of the present palliatives, seriously inhibited my success as an athlete. In lacrosse – my particular torment – a concession was made to my disability (although always described as 'Jane's silly wheeze', as my hay fever was 'Jane's tiresome sniffle') by putting me at Third Man: a defence position entailing the minimum amount of running. But nevertheless the short spurts of speed still necessary, and the effort required to move eleven stone through the mud, were enough to bring about paroxysms of gasping and wheezing which in today's kinder and more medically advanced world would have led to medication and bed.

My final hope of attaining glory was therefore through the medium of music, but there again, although my mother had generously paid for piano lessons and I had made regular attempts to be admitted to the Junior Choral Society, my musical sense was insufficiently acute. This left me with nothing to fall back on except the dubious glory of fainting on most Sundays in Chapel and an assurance from the headmistress – an elderly lady with a dominant personality called Miss Willis – that I had the ability to succeed in anything, but might find it difficult to identify what I really wanted. Until then, she advised me, I should try to mask my shyness, which transmitted itself in a sullen look, by smiling.

My schooldays came to an end when I was still only sixteen. I had done pretty well in my School Certificate with distinctions in five subjects, but there was no question of staying on to work towards a place at university. This was a typical example of discrimination against girls in higher education: my brother went to Oxford without any question. But my mother thought that for a girl staying on at school only meant 'helping to look after the little ones'. I wonder if things would have been different had my father been alive to exert some influence. Members of several generations of the Randall family had followed a scholarly tradition at Winchester and New College, Oxford, before going into the Church. My great-grandfather was Dean of Chichester and his distinguished old face had peered down at us throughout our childhood from a portrait hanging in the dining-room in Somerset. Perhaps my father might have intervened and I could have benefited from the opportunity I most resent having missed – a university education. Certainly my brain would have been better equipped to take on some of the work which has inadvertently come my way. In the end it was my marriage which took the place of any academic training and it was Christopher who did so much to fill the void created by my lack of formal education.

Nevertheless, my mother decided that in order 'to get over my shyness' I should go to Grenoble University to do a summer course. This rather daring experiment more or less worked, and after six months I returned home able in a modest way to take part in conversations;

but also – less welcome to my mother – heavily made up and smoking like a chimney. In order to increase my small post-war foreign allowance, my brother sent me tins of army cigarettes to trade with the *concierge* for French francs. One day I discovered the alternative use for them, and this started off that unattractive habit which continued through the birth of three children.

After my return home I went to Miss Judson's Secretarial College in Courtfield Gardens to do a shorthand and typing course – much despised. I was quite good at shorthand: like most people who are always in a hurry, I translated most of my life into shorthand anyway. But I didn't much like typing.

I then found myself earning a small wage as a secretary in the Foreign Office before I was even eighteen. When I say the job was in the Foreign Office, I really mean I *thought* it was in the Foreign Office.

My mother having pointed me in that direction, I went with another girl from my college for an interview in Whitehall. We were shown into a shabby office where rather a furtive-looking elderly gentleman welcomed us. First he discussed our secretarial qualifications and then, completely out of the blue, he launched his bombshell: 'I must now tell you that this is MI6. You are now members of the British Secret Service and bound by the Official Secrets Act, a copy of which you will find with your contract. It spells out the penalty for breaking your cover.' The other seventeen-year-old and I looked at each other speechlessly, and when I got home it only took about a second to break the Act by hysterically telling my mother what had happened.

However, pretty soon I found the work mundane, similar to many other secretarial jobs. My usefulness had its limitations: I worked in a large room full of girls, telephones and typewriters, but was never brave enough to answer a ringing telephone if I was the only person in the room.

After a couple of years I asked to be sent on a foreign posting. The British Mission in Bonn in those post-war years was the only one sufficiently large to incorporate a 'nanny service' for young secretaries. This had my mother's approval as my brother was in the Army at that time, stationed in Lüneburg, and could keep an eye on me. We were accommodated in military-style flats and taken each day to the office in buses. Soon I had a car – a black Volkswagen with red upholstery. I drove it with great confidence but little skill, since I had not been required to pass a driving test. Garrisons of the BAOR were often my destination. I filled the car with my girl friends and we set off northwards along the *autobahn* to Lüneburger Heide, Hanover or Hamburg, for a ball or a horse show organized by some smart regiment. For the first time I came into contact with the young male's primeval need to destroy, and with amazement watched the cavalry officers throwing glasses around after dinner, letting out great whoops of excitement. (It was only many years later that it dawned on me that such behaviour from the middle classes is termed 'high spirits', whereas when young working-class males break the place up it is called 'vandalism'.)

I made two discoveries about myself during my time in Germany. First I realized I was able to get things done quickly. This was brought home to me when my various bosses, complaining about my apparent idleness, discovered that I had long since finished the task set for me. This capacity for speed has never left me and, although often making me intolerant of other people's performance, has helped considerably with the administration of everyday life. But the second discovery was an even greater morale booster. To my utter amazement one day I overheard one of the officers of the Mission say, 'Of course Jane can charm the birds off the trees.' I couldn't believe it. I was so used to thinking of myself as shy that it made me exceptionally happy to realize that other people saw me as a person able to please them.

The reason for returning home after only two and a half years in Germany was that I had fallen in love and the object of my passion was a Fleet Street journalist. My love life up till then had been rather one-sided with a variety of suitors and one or two proposals of marriage, but my feelings had only once before been seriously aroused, by a skiing champion I met in Zermatt. However, my new attachment was strong enough to draw me back to London.

I was obliged to leave government service, having broken my three-year contract for the Bonn posting, and so I moved on to what was to be the first in a long succession of jobs. This was with the Savoy Hotel and my position was secretary/personal assistant to one of the company directors, John Hannay. He and I got on well together.

I was fascinated by the Savoy, and soon realized that a large hotel is a world of its own. With a hierarchical structure made up of people of so many nationalities – directors, managers, hall porters, head waiters, chefs, and, lower down, the commis-waiters, chambermaids, messenger boys, washers-up, etc – there are innumerable power bases with passions and jealousies abounding. Although each has his place in the hierarchy, the staff of a big hotel are nevertheless bound inexorably together by their hatred of the worst kind of guest: the guest who is rude only to those who are in no position to answer back.

Among all my jobs before marriage this was my favourite, and the two years spent in that mixed community probably contributed something to my overwhelming wish to see a more equal society. I saw that the way of achieving this depended so much on members of society inculcating a sense of fairness through their attitudes and behaviour one to another.

My romantic life during this period was active. My original romance had come to an end through the young journalist's inability to respond adequately to my affection, but he was soon replaced by a succession of friends who trooped through the flat I shared with a girl-friend near Marble Arch. I enjoyed myself but never shared with any of them the bond which, in my view, provides the most resilient link between two people: the bond brought about by shared sensitivities.

I was first convinced of this when I met Christopher – which happened at this particular time in my life and in the manner I have described. He and his wife called me 'Savoy Jane' and asked me to their parties.

I know relatively little about Christopher's childhood. He didn't seem to talk about it much, but I do know the manner in which his mother announced the prospective happy event to his father, an Army officer who was serving with his regiment in Constantinople at the time. She wrote in a style typical of that used by the young set in the early 1920s, and having started the letter 'Very darling Henry – You are the toppingest man in existence ...', she did not get round to telling the vital news until the postscript, written the next day: 'My own darling man – I've thought another night and still I don't know how to put it so I'll just tell you anyhow. You see, darling, next July about 20th we are going to have a baby. I hope it isn't a fearful shock to you and you aren't fearfully bored and think it a great bother. You see it's quite different for me – I love children and . . .' And on 5 August 1921 Christopher duly made his appearance.

Mollie Ewart-Biggs was attractive – tall, blonde and slim. Warm and generous by nature, she loved entertaining and possessed the gift of making her guests feel entirely at home from the moment they crossed her doorstep. During his childhood Christopher obviously felt close to his mother, for whom he had the greatest affection. However, she did not repeat the experience of childbirth, complaining that it had hurt too much, and so Christopher remained an only child. Fortunately for him, however, he did not have a lonely childhood as he was brought up with his aunt, Wendy, born the same year as himself, and with whom he seemingly shared an even closer friendship than that between real brothers and sisters. When he was up at Oxford he used to tell his friends about his aunt coming to visit him and watch their incredulous looks when the tall, attractive nineteen-year-old girl arrived. Christopher called her 'Clumper' because of the way she walked, and she called him Thomas. 'It's so difficult to say goodbye to you,' he said in the letter he wrote her when going off to the war. 'I can't write the ordinary things because I know you better than anyone else.'

Christopher's father Henry, a captain in the Royal Engineers, had seen active service in the First World War and came from a military background. Henry's father, also a Field Engineer, had a distinguished career in the Indian campaign and was awarded a DSO in 1898 for the part he played with the Tirah expeditionary force in India. Members of the Biggs family all seemed to have rather big noses set in distinguished faces. In about 1918, after Henry's maternal grandmother Mrs Ewart died, he assumed the name of Ewart-Biggs in order to keep alive her name.

During his father's service with his regiment, Christopher, with his mother, spent much of his childhood in his grandfather's home which was a big, handsome, part-Edwardian, part-Victorian house called Mockbeggar near Rochester in Kent. Grandfather Brice, through enterprise, determination and dogged hard work, built up his own firm called the Ham River Grit Company and it prospered. Indeed this

great pioneer of private enterprise succeeded in everything he undertook. Soon the fruit farm he had built up round Mockbeggar as a
hobby was selling the best Cox's Orange Pippins in the country. I have
learned from Wendy about his devotion to the family and how, in line
with those Victorian times, he treated them all with a mixture of love
and firmness. His wife, 'Little Granny', radiated love and comfort to
the children, all of whom she called 'Duckling'. One of her pleasures
in life was to have the occasional little 'flutter' on a horse and afterwards was the first to get her hands on the evening paper to see the
results.

Wendy's description of Christopher is of a matchstick child –
ridiculously thin with golden curly hair and extremely blue eyes. He –
but not she – was academically bright. They both hated hurting
things – small animals or even insects.

Christopher's spindly body made him physically uncoordinated
and poor at games, but the two children were carefully coached in
tennis and made an impressive pair. Wendy remembers how Christopher used to try to curb her bold play: 'Yours – but take care,' he
cautioned her during tournaments. Their childhood was surrounded
by warmth and love – and indeed also by the material comfort which
mine lacked. This may have been one of the reasons for Christopher's
future insouciance about money, for in years to come he showed a
greater wish to rid himself of it than to conserve it.

He had a conventional education – a preparatory school called
Wellesley House followed by Wellington College, where his father
and grandfather had preceded him. But its military setting was probably better suited to them than to Christopher who, with his particular idiosyncrasies, attracted more than the usual amount of
teasing and bullying. It was only during his last two years at school
that he was exempted from the torture of rugger and allowed to
pursue his academic interests, history and English. The vivid style of
writing which he used throughout his professional life started early.
There was proof of this, although in rather exaggerated form, in the
December 1939 publication of *The Wellingtonian*, which my own
son's housemaster came across and gave me when Robin was there in
the late 1970s. It was soon after Christopher's death and the housemaster had been struck – indeed shocked – by the tragic coincidence

of the subject for the essay which appeared in the magazine. It was called 'Thermidor' (the name given during the French Revolution to the eleventh month of the year in the Republican calendar):

He died violently, for fanaticism is the beginning and the depth of violence. With the hard, cold passion of the single mind he fashioned for himself a belief which armed him against the chaos of conflicting opinions, and which enabled him without reason but with a deep conviction to reject them; after that, the way became easy. Blinded by his own soul's light, he walked straight where other and wiser men would have paused to consider. With no crease in his coat, with no hair of his wig out of place, he sought his accusers. No army stood behind him, no force but his own fatal certainty; until choked with the blood of Danton, he screamed his last appeal to the plain. Then the cloak of the cold and authoritative leader was thrown aside, and the fierce passion of the fanatic lay beneath. Could the timorous lawyer from Arras have seen himself on the 9th of Thermidor 1794, he must have wondered at the disaster wrought in man by fanaticism, and doubted of the virtues of a single mind.

That same year he left Wellington with an open scholarship in history to University College, Oxford. His arrival there coincided with the start of the war and he realized that he would be called up before completing his degree. This perhaps contributed to his adopting a detached lifestyle during his sadly short stay of four or five terms. According to him he frequently took to the river and made a start on what was to become his major hobby: the telling of anecdotes. However, he left with the assurance of his generous tutor that, had he been allowed the opportunity of sitting his final exams, he would certainly have passed them with first-class honours; and even such a short time at Oxford provided a sound base for his future intellectual life.

A humiliating period at Sandhurst followed his call-up. During this short, intensive training preceding active service his athletic shortcomings together with his absent-mindedness counted against him. 'Get up off your knees, Biggs,' was the sergeant-major's unequivocal reaction to what Christopher felt to be his most aggressively military-style marching.

There was the embarrassing episode of the stolen gasmask. With two masks already inadvertently mislaid, he did not dare admit to the

Sandhurst authorities the loss of a third. Instead, after lunch with his mother at the Lansdowne Club one day, he found himself gazing longingly at rows of service gasmasks hanging round the walls of the gentlemen's cloakroom. No one, he thought, could be in such a vulnerable position as he with two losses behind him. Consoling himself in this way, he committed the only act of theft of his life and walked off with one of them hanging over his shoulder. God's punishment followed swiftly on. Next day came one of the routine air-raid practices. All cadets assembled in the parade-ground were, as usual, required to test out their gasmasks. Christopher, highly relieved to be in a position to do so, complied – only to find to his excruciating discomfort that his purloined mask was an entirely different model. It had a long tube attaching it to the case, presumably designed to allow bomber crews unimpeded movement around their huge aircraft. The act of putting his mask on therefore brought about the emergence of yards and yards of spiral rubber tube which fell in cascades round his feet, giving him an elephantine look quite out of keeping with the others'.

However, he adapted himself to his new military environment better than some of his friends, who like himself had been destined to be men of letters rather than men of war. For example, there was the evening when he and Alistair, a contemporary from Oxford and winner of a scholarship in English to Christ Church, were returning to Sandhurst from a day in London. As they walked from the station to the military academy they were stopped by the Commandant in his Bentley, who offered them a lift for the rest of the way. Christopher, who by that time had picked up the military style and knew what was expected of him, stood smartly to attention, lifted one foot high up in the air prior to bringing it down resoundingly beside the other, and saluted. Then, using the tones he had discovered were expected when addressing officers, he shouted, 'Thanky' verrmuchsurr', and got in. But Alistair was a much more genuine person – Christopher said when telling the story – and had not seen fit to adapt his behaviour to conform with his setting. He merely leant over towards the car window and said, 'Angel, bless you', and got in. As a result Alistair spent his war years in the Catering Corps.

On leaving Sandhurst, Christopher joined the Royal Kent Regiment which, since he lived in Kent, seemed to him appropriate, and was sent on active service. His mother and one of her high-powered military admirers came to see him off on the troopship taking them to an unknown destination. 'Good luck, my boy,' said the General, 'and look after the Regiment.' Christopher had not seen it quite that way, but did not dare admit that he had rather hoped the reverse might be the case, with the Regiment looking after him.

The part he played on active service, as he modestly described, was not very glorious. He maintained that in the first place he lacked sufficient moral courage to declare himself a conscientious objector, whilst in no way possessing enough physical courage to face up to danger. He considered war uncomfortable, degrading and frightening, and attached no glory whatsoever to it. His description of the only battle in which he took part seemed to bear out this attitude. It was at El Alamein and early on in the exchange he was wounded by an exploding shell. Traumatized by the noise, confusion and terror, he crawled under the shelter of an armoured car. He soon realized that he was not alone: '*Mamma mia*', muttered a voice a few feet away. Recognizing – but not reacting to – what could only be the voice of the enemy, he thought: well, that makes two of us.

However, this wound may well have indirectly saved his life for it brought about the loss of his right eye and his consequent removal from active service. Deeply affected by the physical disability, he decided to wear a black monocle in order to mask the contrast between the penetrating effect of a living eye and the blankness of an artificial one. This black monocle, which became his hallmark, also served to mislead people as to his character: the Bertie Wooster image which gave the lie to the truly radical thinking which lay beneath. The revulsion and horror which his experience at El Alamein caused him may have given root to the attitude towards violence which he held throughout his life and which he stated so clearly on the day before he himself fell victim to it. 'I have one prejudice,' he told a group of Irish pressmen gathered to find out more about the newly arrived, enigmatic Ambassador, '... a very distinct and strong prejudice against violence....'

Mercifully, having been withdrawn from the field of combat, he was transferred to Libya on an assignment he always described as the one which placed heavier responsibilities on him than any other in his life. His political diaries of that time testify to this fact. As Italy had withdrawn from the war, Libya was at that time under a British military administration, and Christopher, then aged twenty-three, was sent as a political officer to Jefren in Tripolitania. He showed considerably more talent as an administrator than as a warrior and, having taught himself Italian and some Arabic, succeeded so well that he was described by his boss, the Chief Administrator, as the most brilliant young officer under his command. Through his deep involvement and genuine interest in the life and culture of the community he built a circle of real friends among the local Arabs.

He remained there for a few years after the war, and then, recognizing that he had outgrown the wish to return to undergraduate life at Oxford, he was lucky enough to be awarded his BA. In 1949 he sat the Civil Service examination and passed into the Foreign Office in company with a small percentage of the candidates. Helped by the knowledge of Arabic acquired in Tripolitania, he was sent to the Middle East Centre for Arab Studies at Shemlan near Beirut.

He often told stories of his time there; of how he and his two particular friends – all three of them around six foot three – sat trying to absorb the difficult language whilst being distracted by the twinkling lights in the distance of the then glamorous Beirut. In the evenings they often succumbed to the lure and went to the Tabu nightclub, where they sat for hours over their one drink listening to the music. They chose this particular nightspot because one of the trio had fallen madly in love with its cabaret artiste – inevitably an English girl – called Veronica. They sat until the early hours of the morning, waiting for her to finish. Once liberated, Christopher's friend took her for drives to discuss the philosophy of life. His intentions towards her were entirely honourable and he placed – perhaps mistakenly – complete confidence in her own moral integrity. Although these nocturnal vigils did little for their progress in Arabic, 'La vie en rose' – the artiste's favourite song – was engraved for ever in their subconscious. It was the arrival, in the nick of time, of the pretty sister of one of the other students, with the subsequent transfer of affection away from the Tabu and sleepless nights, which saved them from humiliating failure in their exams.

Following this came his first Foreign Office posting as a Third Secretary to Bahrain. There he witnessed the passing of one of the last of the great British proconsuls, Sir Rupert Hay. Every morning at sunrise the British Resident in full diplomatic uniform arrived at the gates of the Embassy for the unfurling of the Union Jack. His entire staff were in attendance. After a while Christopher transferred to Qatar, where he became the political adviser to Sheikh Ali bin Abdullah al-Thani, the Emir. The major results of his influence over this oil-wealthy sheikh were, according to Christopher, to persuade him to abolish slavery and also to refrain, when sitting cross-legged on his priceless oriental carpet, from spitting on top of it but instead to lift one corner of it and deposit the spittle underneath.

During a home leave from Qatar he met and married Gavrelle Verschoyle and, as already described, I first met them on their return from the Gulf, when Christopher had been transferred to the Middle East Department of the Foreign Office. In 1956 Christopher and Gavrelle were posted to Manila, and I went to the United States, where I spent nearly two years. I had become restless at the Savoy and, succumbing to wanderlust, I joined the army of English girls who at that time were crossing the Atlantic to search for innovation and adventure. We lived not so much by our wits but by our voices, for employers were keen to have our inimitable British accents echo round their offices and answer their telephones. This, inexplicably, added cachet to their establishments. On my return to England in 1958 my mother said, 'What a relief, darling. I thought you'd come back talking with a dreadful American accent. But, if anything, you sound more British than when you left.'

For some months I worked as a secretary in part-time or temporary capacities to give me a chance to decide whether to go back to the States to get married. I had been through several romantic entanglements in New York, San Francisco and Aspen, Colorado, during my time as a ski-bum. But it only took one telephone conversation with Christopher – returned from Manila – to show me that the bond I had shared with my final American suitor was too fragile to justify marriage.

I knew there could be no thought of marriage with Christopher either, although we knew how happy we could have made each other.

He was not the sort of man to walk out on his wife, any more than I was the single-minded type of girl able to set about breaking up a marriage, especially one such as theirs which, although not helped by Gavrelle's serious depressions and a certain lack of compatability, involved a great deal of affection and concern one for the other. However, fate interceded and Gavrelle died suddenly in premature childbirth. Christopher and I did not see each other for some months.

I embarked on what turned out to be my last job – I became the secretary/assistant to a Tory MP. He was member for the Wycombe constituency and the tallest man in the House of Commons. I joined the throng of girls working in the – then – primitive setting of Westminster Hall, and if someone had at that time foreseen my return to the Palace of Westminster as a Peer of the Realm I would certainly have thought they had taken leave of their senses.

I went to join his campaign office in High Wycombe to help fight the 1959 General Election. For some reason, now forgotten, I kept a journal for those few weeks, and it shows that the experience certainly aroused my interest in party politics. Until then I had felt no more than a natural affinity with the underdog, but the job made me replace this emotional attitude with more structured socialist thinking.

The Conservative candidate won the election with an increased majority, and I can remember gloomily congratulating him after the results were announced. But, for me, there was more to it than that. Christopher, with whom by that time I had become deeply entangled, came down to the constituency to visit me from time to time, and joined me at some of my employer's political meetings. Since his university days he had been a committed socialist, but as an intellectual, his belief was governed by ideology, whereas my own commitment grew out of a compulsive and deeply rooted emotional need to help people. Moreover, I felt that by being a socialist I was somehow making a gigantic apologia to those born less fortunate than myself. Although at that time I naturally kept my political leanings to myself, Christopher did not feel the same inhibition and grumbled away at the back of the hall during the meetings, taking issue, under his breath – but only just – with some of the points my employer was making.

Anxious about my future employment prospects, I remonstrated
with him, saying he must either keep quiet or bear the consequences
of my losing my job. In the end he chose the second alternative and we
were married in the spring of the following year.

It was not a particularly orthodox affair. The engagement *was*
announced in *The Times* and I *did* have a ring – sapphire and dia-
monds chosen together at Garrards – but otherwise the arrangements
lacked the conventional structure. The importance seemed to lie in
our conviction that with each other we had found a haven. We knew
that the acute sensitivities we each held would be safe in the hands of
the other. We knew that the loneliness we had each often felt, in that
nebulous area made up of doubt, moderation, tolerance, was over, for
we would occupy it together. So it was other considerations which
caused the lack of impetus. For one thing, we could not decide *how* to
get married. An even mildly ostentatious ceremony seemed out of the
question as there had recently been so many deaths in Christopher's
family. Some three years before, his gentle, unassuming father – the
one who did all the jobs no one else felt like doing such as teaching all
the young generation how to drive – had died. It was as if he had
suffered an inner defeat. 'Henry just gave up,' they said; but it
sounded as if the real cause, had it been diagnosed, was lung cancer.
Then, eighteen months later, Gavrelle's death left Christopher with
four stepchildren but no child of his own. Finally, a few months later,
his mother Mollie, whom he had loved so much, ended her life in
exactly the way she would have chosen. For someone who was so
fearful of old age, what better way than to die instantaneously in a car
crash, while being driven home from a dance by a boy friend twenty
years her junior. Following this series of losses Christopher first experienced what he called the 'leprosy syndrome'. People used to avoid
him as if he had some contagious disease. A colleague advancing
towards him along an endless Foreign Office corridor would suddenly
disappear, having escaped through a side door to avoid having to
offer condolences. This was not through a lack of feeling but because
the Anglo-Saxon finds it difficult to talk about death – although he
can write about it with great eloquence. This was something I was to
learn sixteen years later.

Finally the decision was made and we were married in the tiny

Savoy Chapel. Neither of us were churchgoers or even practising Christians. Christopher was somewhere between an atheist and an agnostic, and I somewhere between an agnostic and a believer. However, the prebendary who carried out the marriage service swallowed this, but got his own back when, in his address, he reminded us that being married was rather like being in the Foreign Office – it was all to do with diplomacy. This gave Christopher a nasty shock.

I noted the day, 5 May, in my diary by a drawing of the sun with a smile on its face, and my memories of it remain vivid and happy. My friends who operated the garage beneath my mews flat off Gloucester Road were, for once, there to see me off. (The reason my departure normally made them melt away was their knowing only too well – and from experience – that my car would only start after being pushed.) Our drive to the Savoy Chapel was splendid because the London streets had been fully decorated for the wedding of Princess Margaret the following day. The small congregation in the chapel comprised members of each of our families. The only hitch came when an uncle by marriage of Christopher's (Wendy's husband) was roused from his comfortable seat in the congregation and invited to act as Best Man – at about two minutes' notice. Christopher had completely forgotten to ask him, and although his natural absent-mindedness was known and accepted by the family, the Admiral thought this was going too far.

The reception went smoothly and was in line with any other following a conventional middle-class wedding. Although it was held in the socially acceptable setting of one of the Gilbert and Sullivan rooms of the Savoy, the reason for the choice was really to include among the guests the friends I had made while working there. Not only our relatives and Christopher's Foreign Office colleagues and friends from the social set were asked, but also the waiters, commissionaires, chefs, etc., who had been my friends at the hotel.

The wedding over, I took off my dark blue Hardy Amies dress – to match my sapphire engagement ring – and my little shocking pink lacy head-dress and departed altogether from convention by putting on trousers and a sweater. We were spending the honeymoon first at Christopher's cottage at Ellis Green in Essex – an Elizabethan, rural delight which we had found together, with a thatched roof but no electricity or road. Then, as a contrast, we planned to move on to a hotel in St Germain-en-Laye, just outside Paris, originally a shooting lodge of Henry IV, which was reputed to be the most expensive and luxurious hotel in Europe.

In fact, we were nearly prevented from enjoying either part of our honeymoon as a result of Christopher's one intolerance. As we were driving through the outskirts of London on our way to Essex the taxi-driver behind us sounded his horn and overtook us. Unfortunately Christopher suffered from the paranoia which affects many male drivers, transforming a rational being into a madman once he is behind the steering-wheel and feels himself snubbed by another driver. I have never been able to work out why a man's ego is at its most vulnerable when driving a car and how even a person like Christopher, usually the model of self-control and self-discipline, should be overcome with uncontrollable passions when feeling slighted by a fellow road user. 'For whom does the taxi hoot – but for me,' he used to say whilst getting ready to give chase to the offending cab. In this particular case the chase took place in Leytonstone, and to my horror I watched the man whom I had just married, mainly for his gentleness and tolerance, become transformed with his face set in lines of hatred and fury, driving like a maniac and placing me and everyone else anywhere near us in the utmost danger. When I finally managed to attract his attention, he immediately resumed his usual calm demeanour and – noticing my ashen-white face – apologized for frightening me but would not admit that he had been in the wrong. This was my first experience of the single Jekyll and Hyde aspect of Christopher's character – but I fear it was by no means to be the last.

2

Wife of a Diplomat

As marriage meant being with Christopher I immediately took to it, but it did bring with it some lonely moments. I had been working since the age of seventeen and had moved from one job to another with few interruptions, each time benefiting from the conviviality of the group around me. I had by that time become a sociable sort of person, after the shyness and introspection of childhood. Then, all of a sudden, there I was alone for many hours each day in a house which did not even make me feel at home. It was an attractive but old-fashioned, uncomfortable house in Bloomfield Terrace, which had belonged to Gavrelle and where she and Christopher had lived during their periods in London. Pimlico had not at that time achieved its present fashionable status. Another disturbing factor for me, as a bride, was the presence of Christopher's eighteen-year-old step-daughter, Christina Hobhouse, who had recently gone up to Oxford. Gavrelle's son and other daughter had been reclaimed by their respective fathers on her death, but Christina, whose father, Christopher Hobhouse, the writer, had been killed in the war, had nowhere to go so of course remained with Christopher at Bloomfield Terrace. Hers and mine was a difficult relationship. She was tall, dark, attractive and extremely intelligent, but understandably traumatized by the death of her mother. I, at that time, hadn't even a vestige of the tact which to some degree I acquired later in life, and not unnaturally, I longed for the privacy which a newly-married wife normally enjoys. However, between the three of us we did not manage too badly and the only moments of real crisis came when Christina insisted on introducing me to her undergraduate friends as her 'stepmother', a status I did not feel suited me.

I soon discovered that I had little interest in housekeeping. My bachelor days had involved the minimum of housework and cooking, and neither held much charm for me. Nor was I good at budgeting. Christopher, entirely generous, would have given me whatever weekly housekeeping allowance I wanted, but after discussion we decided £12 per week was about right. With my lack of experience and inability to cook, combined with his taste for expensive food such as fillet steak and lobster, I naturally never managed to make ends meet. I would sooner have died than admit this to him, so it was only through subsidizing the housekeeping with the miniscule rent from my mews flat that I was saved from losing face and he escaped the shepherd's pie and stews which he hated and I was entirely unable to produce.

However, this initial period of marriage, when I could have found time for myself but did not know how to use it, was short-lived. Just under a year after our wedding Henrietta was born, and five months later we were posted to Algiers. There was no doubt about the name for the baby. From the first moment, with her red hair and delicacy of bone structure, she represented a tiny replica of her paternal grandfather. Christopher, like the men of that African tribe who go into hiding at the time of their children's birth, showed every sign of extreme shock. This came out in an unfortunate way when a close friend telephoned with congratulations and asked what name had been chosen for the baby. 'Henrietta,' said Christopher. 'We think it is as attractive a name for a girl as Henry is an awful one for a boy.' The silence at the other end of the telephone surprised him until he remembered that he had been talking to our friend Henry Villiers.

The news of our posting came when Henrietta was still only about two months old. This is the pattern of things in the Diplomatic Service. Invariably, just at the point when the wife is well and truly settled at home, or alternatively has finally found her feet in a foreign posting, and possibly even just had a baby which is lying peacefully in a cot beside her, the telephone will ring. Her husband, at the other end of the line, using a particularly disembodied voice reserved for such occasions, will then say, 'Darling, there's news.' Such an announcement in a diplomatic family can only mean one thing – that the bedouin-style life once again requires her to move the tent on to some unknown destination. All kinds of thoughts may flash through her mind. She may with nostalgia remember the nice young man permanently entrenched in a job in the City, who had paid her court. She may, looking at the sleeping infant beside her, think, 'But it's far too small to move.' On the other hand, she may visualize the great bonus that goes with some diplomatic postings – a cleaning lady. Or she may, as is increasingly the case today, wonder how as a graduate in medicine she will replace her fascinating research job if the posting turns out to be to Moscow or suchlike.

Whatever thoughts may come to her, the knowledge that to refuse one posting is just about acceptable but to do so twice is not will probably make her decide that that is the very place she has been longing to know.

For my own part, the news that we were to be posted to the Consulate-General in Algiers brought on a mixed reaction. In the first place, I had fully anticipated going abroad as, having married a member of the Diplomatic Service, a foreign posting seemed to be the natural order of things, and since I had no profession the move would not frustrate my own career. On the other hand, I was fully aware of the security situation in Algeria, where a savage war of independence was being fought, and the idea of putting my precious baby into such a dangerous setting filled me with horror.

Christopher's preoccupations were different. As there is a two-tier system within the Foreign Office, he was far from pleased by the idea of a consular job. At that time the only jobs acceptable to the elitists in that most elite of professions were political. Consular, economic and commercial posts were considered demeaning. (I am happy to say that the situation has now entirely changed and it is universally accepted that Britain's economic interests can be immeasurably assisted by her diplomatic representatives in embassies abroad.) So the post of HM Consul to Algiers did not at all correspond with his expectations. But, like many others in similar situations, he fell for the ruse the Foreign Office employs to make unattractive postings sound attractive; namely by describing them as 'challenging'. Now places like Paris or Rome don't need such a wrapping, but the fiercely ambitious and competitive young men of the Foreign Office will swallow anything if made to feel that their careers will thereby be advanced.

(This manoeuvre was carried to the extreme when a friend of ours, posted from Paris to the New Hebrides, remembered wryly the Foreign Office personnel department once telling him they had always known he would go far.)

Christopher was further mollified by the knowledge that he was being sent as an Arabist and also charged with the responsibility of transforming the Consulate General into an Embassy, which would be necessary on Algerian independence.

So we both, in entirely different ways, started to prepare for the move. Christopher began brushing up his Arabic and working on the history of the Maghreb, concentrating particularly on the traumatic Franco-Algerian relationship. I, from a domestic point of view, read the Post Report to discover the general circumstances of everyday life, such as climate, shopping possibilities, schools, etc. Post reports are composed by the missions overseas and kept at the Foreign Office to help new embassy staff arrive well prepared. But as far as Algiers was concerned, the conditions of life were entirely influenced by the current political situation, and the Post Report could hardly be expected to remain in line with them and was consequently of minor assistance.

Of one thing there could be no doubt: we needed a nanny for Henrietta: someone who would help, guide and sometimes replace me. I advertised in the *Lady* and started interviewing the candidates. Women, young and less so, who were intrepid enough not to be deterred by the battleground of Algiers came forward. I found this new experience of conducting the interview, rather than the other way round, particularly daunting. I finally engaged a formidable lady, distinguished-looking with grey hair and piercing blue eyes, called Miss Swire. The choice was made in a negative fashion: she had been the one who had intimidated me most among all the candidates and I was consequently least able to turn her away. We soon realized that it was the lure of danger which attracted her, for soon after she joined us, while we were packing, she stormed into the drawing-room one evening, with blue eyes shining: 'I have just heard on the television', she said breathlessly, 'that one of our Consuls in Algiers was shot this morning.' Christopher – distinctly shaken – bravely said that perhaps shooting one British Consul would content them and this would ensure our own survival. We then waited for her to change her mind about coming, but she did nothing of the sort, and even appeared to be looking forward to our departure.

We had to find a tenant for the modest house in Chelsea to which we had moved from Bloomfield Terrace just before Henrietta's birth. The decision about a home base is a difficult one for diplomats. Either they find rented accommodation for their home postings or, as we did, invest in a property which they then let fully furnished when posted overseas. The house at 31 Radnor Walk had a pristine look – normal for a newly married, house-proud couple. Furthermore, in a moment of fantasy and in order to make it look more expansive, we had carpeted the drawing-room in white and put up a lot of gold-and-white wallpaper. It was a rather twee-looking little home crying out for careful tenants. However, Christopher's priorities were different. From his position of vantage in the African Department of the Foreign Office he had discovered that African diplomats in London were being discriminated against when looking for accommodation. His liberal soul was outraged, with the result that our house was specifically offered to and accepted by the Counsellor at the Ivory Coast Embassy. There was nothing equivocal about Mr Oga's ethnic origins, and when he stood, appreciative and utterly charming, in the glistening paleness of the drawing-room, I remember wondering whether something would have to give and the contrast lessened either by Mr Oga becoming paler or the setting becoming darker. (Two years later the estate agents charged with re-letting the house on Mr Oga's departure telephoned us in Algiers and in muted tones told us the second alternative had come about.)

Our preparations were finally complete. Konrad, our dog, was thoroughly injected against rabies and Henrietta acquired a passport with a photograph of her dribbling, four-month-old image, held firmly by a hand from behind. Early in November Christopher and I set off by car, taking the dog and leaving the baby to come by air with her steely matron. The journey through France was familiar – Christopher had decided the appropriate car for the Revolution was a white Jaguar and it swept us to Marseilles with a final visit to the Henri IV four-star establishment at St Germain-en-Laye on the way, and then through the Massif Central in the heartland of France and Provence to the ferry. It was then that the unfamiliar took over.

First, Konrad had the shock of his life when banished to the ship's kennel. The least comfortable niche he had previously ever occupied was a bedroom in SW3. Next, we learnt something of what was awaiting us in Algiers from sharing a table for dinner during the twenty-four-hour crossing with a colonel from the French Gendarmerie returning to his post. Colonel Chenu had spent his leave acquiring a new wife. He was taking her back to the Gendarmerie Fort on the edge of the Kasbah. She was a Corsican twenty years younger than he: sleek, brown and silent.

He told us of the difficulties facing the security forces in Algeria. The French Army, although then numbering nearly three quarters of a million, could not defeat the FLN (the Front de Libération Nationale, formed in 1954 to carry out the Algerian rebellion against the French, were fighting a guerrilla-style war from the mountains with the support or fearful acquiescence of the nine million Algerian population). On the other hand the French government knew only too well that any movement to grant independence would bring on the full fury and aggression of the one million white settlers, who were separated from the Moslem Algerians by a wide gulf – religious, cultural and economic – and who were represented by the OAS (Organisation de l'Armée Sécrète, the European terrorist organization set up in March with the purpose of preventing any move towards independence and maintaining *l'Algérie Française*). The French authorities and security forces were therefore threatened from each side. He told us of this and much more, speaking quietly and moving his chair close to ours to avoid being overheard.

In a sober mood we retired to our cabin that night, and Christopher, fearful of forgetting what the colonel had told him, pieced together what he had learned that evening with what he already knew, and this became the first Algiers entry in his political journal:

The first thing to understand is that there are not only two communities in conflict, but three, equidistant from one another. First, the nine million Algerians whose allegiance is commanded through both fear and fervour by the FLN, second the Metropolitan French, representing Government and identified with General de Gaulle and then, quite separate from these

30

and ready to hang de Gaulle, are the 1 million Algerian French, the Pieds
Noirs (so called because it was they, the settlers, who first planted the
vines and their feet became black through trampling them), the focus of
whose desperation is the OAS. Many of these Pieds Noirs are French only
in their insistence that Algeria should remain so; they are the jetsam of the
Mediterranean, Spanish in Oran, Italian in Bône, a hedonistic,
opinionated, volatile, intensely provincial people, at present in the grip of
paranoia.

The French Government are thus caught between two rebellions, the
colonial war with the FLN which they are trying to bring to a negotiated end,
and the second, inner, rebellion of the OAS directed against any settlement
of the first.

At this point the possibility of a negotiation, and even of a successful
negotiation, between the French Government and the FLN, seems at last to
be within sight. The principle of independence has been accepted. The
French Government have finally reached the conclusion that in the end
there can only be two possible destinies for Algeria; an independence in
co-operation with France or independence in hostility and bitterness towards France. They see that any attempt by France to secure for herself
more than the first of these makes the second more likely. De Gaulle is
moving reluctantly towards meeting the insistence of the FLN that they
should be treated as the only *interlocateur valable* of the Algerian people,
though there will be the face-saving device of a referendum. That is the
central point. It is, as so often, a matter of *amour propre*.

But the Pieds Noirs will oppose any settlement. Their instrument, which
carries their wholesale support and all that remains of their hopes, is the
OAS. Its strength is that it is a weapon of last resort, that it unites the
Europeans in fear of the future. Like fascism – and it is essentially fascist
in spirit – its doctrines are metaphysically empty and born of despair. The
Pieds Noirs are confused about what they want, but they know what they
refuse. The OAS has no clear policy, its purposes are negative, destructive
and variable; some of its leaders would like to operate in Algeria independently of the situation in France, others are more concerned to use the
Algerian problem as a means of destroying the Fifth Republic. The only
constant is to prevent the country becoming independent under an Arab
Government. With their military code words, their elaborate system of
extorting funds, their accounts of explosives issued and expended, their
archives of suspects and intended victims, their postal service and their
solemn injunctions to beat saucepans, they are at once formidable and
infantile; they combine the habits of mind of the Stern Gang and the

Housewives' League. But they do not lack talent. Their leader Salan – or SOLEIL to the initiated – was the most decorated general in the French Army and some of his colonels are tougher than he is. Many of their killers and 'specialists' are recruited from deserters from the Foreign Legion. There may be some 2,500 Europeans in hiding from the authorities and under the orders of the OAS's operational command. They have the active complicity of many thousands more. They may be strong enough not only to hinder an Algerian settlement but to put into question the future of France herself.

Meanwhile, they keep the centre of the stage by nightly acts of fear. They have recently shifted their tactical emphasis from plastic explosions to plain murder.

The French Army is the crucial factor. There seem to be some elements, even whole units, whose loyalty is uncertain. Individual officers and men are certainly connected with the OAS; more are sympathetic. More still, the majority perhaps, would not like to see the leaders of the rebellion they have been fighting arrive in triumph in Algiers. This reluctance may not reach the level of treason. National servicemen from France have little time for the Pieds Noirs. But there would be serious difficulties about ordering French soldiers to fire on Frenchmen. In moving towards Algerian independence, de Gaulle cannot march too far in front of his troops. He must go at the pace at which they are ready to follow him. In dealing with the European opposition the Army is a weapon that could break in his hand.

After seven years of seeking to impose the wishes of the Europeans on the Moslems, the French Government is finding the opposite process of imposing the wishes of the Moslems on the Europeans no less agonizing. But now at least they are moving with the tide.

We got up early next morning to capture a first glimpse of Algiers as the ship steamed in. The town, cradled in steep hills green with pine and palm, was one of the pearls of French Mediterranean culture, and arriving in its beautiful bay, our eyes were blinded by the massed whiteness of the terraces climbing from the sea. It certainly deserved the name given to it – Alger la Blanche. High above the city, on one side, was perched Notre Dame d'Afrique – a Catholic shrine of prime sanctity for the Pieds Noirs. On another hill nestled the luxurious Hôtel Saint-Georges, and below it the Palais d'Été, a dazzling white Moorish mansion where the Governor-General resided in full

32

vice-regal splendour. In the centre, like a brown stain reaching up among the whiteness, was the Kasbah. This, the old Turkish quarter, contained in its rich, impenetrable confines, redolent with the odours of spice and oil of any Arab city and resounding with its ululating, a totally Moslem community. Abutting on the Kasbah to the other side of the city lay the European working-class tenements of Bab-el-Oued.

We took all this in, then searched the quayside for our Consul-General, Christopher's future boss, whom we knew would be there to meet us. For our friend of the night before, the colonel, there awaited an armoured car carrying a heavy machine-gun. We said goodbye to him; he wished us luck – although it seemed as though he was the one in greater need of it. Trefor Evans welcomed us, got us swiftly through customs, and set off with us to the official residence in his lumbering old Jaguar. He started talking to us expansively – with the lucidity and volubility of the Welshman he was. But I did not like it very much when suddenly, his voice becoming jerky and tense, he said, 'Well, you know they've got him.' Not understanding, Christopher asked whom he meant. The Consul-General explained that the police had yesterday arrested the man who had killed the Shipping Officer from the Consulate, as had been reported on the television and heard by Nanny in Radnor Walk. Freddie Fox had been a locally recruited officer and had, for reasons never discovered, fallen foul of the OAS. (During all the time we were in Algiers he was remembered by his colleagues and referred to sorrowfully as 'poor Freddie'.) I also did not much like it when on the way up I noticed, down a side street, a stationary car with a man leaning out of it: it was only when we were well past the scene that I realized that the position of the man, sprawling out of the window, could only have meant he was dead. I had never seen anyone dead before. The route between the port and the Residence gave us our first sight of the OAS slogans scrawled in black all over the white walls: 'L'OAS veuille', 'Vive Salan', 'De Gaulle au poteau', and then 'Vive la mort', an echo of the war-cry of the Spanish fascists.

However, our arrival at the handsome villa surrounded by Bougainvillaea and plumbago, and set on the side of the hill with a splendid view of the bay, together with the friendly welcome from the Consul-General's comfortable-looking Welsh wife, Nest, did something to restore a sense of normality. (Although the ingredients were there, the

33

conventional picture of diplomatic life comprising sun, servants and cocktail parties had not yet materialized.) She gave us some breakfast and told us about the guests coming to the party they were giving that evening. (Again I was grateful for the assurance that a setting did in reality exist for me to carry out my anticipated role as a diplomat's wife: that of wearing a pretty dress, making conversation in a discreet fashion and, above all, listening eagerly.) It was next decided that Christopher should go to the office and I would be taken by Nest to see our new abode.

The manner in which a diplomat and his family are accommodated on their arrival in a new post can come about in two different ways. Either they move straight into a Post Hiring which means, in the tradition of the tied cottage, a flat or house either owned or permanently rented by the Mission for the holders of certain posts within that Mission. Or, if the new arrival is not in that category, then he and his family are put into a hotel and, with the taxpayer back home in mind, the hotels selected are *not* luxurious places. The wife then starts house-hunting. Naturally the Post Hiring provides the most speedy way of setting up house, but there are disadvantages. The first most obvious one is that in order to make it really work a conformity in the size of the resident families is necessary, but even in the greatest bureaucracy, and the Foreign Office is a highly bureaucratic organization, this cannot always be assured. So, if the Department of the Environment, the authority at that time responsible for diplomats' accommodation, decide that the prototype Counsellor's family should comprise three teenage children, this will then determine the size of the Post Hiring for the person holding a Counsellor's job in the Mission. Furthermore, the system is such a hierarchical one that the rights of each officer are unequivocally tied to his rank. This rigid structure can produce anomalies. One such instance was when a Third Secretary arrived to take up his post in an embassy where his accommodation was provided. The rules laid down that Third Secretaries should be bachelors, but this young man's precocious youth had led him not only to marriage but also to parenthood. There was no question of the family fitting into the minuscule flat awaiting them. With a great deal of anguish the system was adapted and the new member of staff was put into a Second Secretary's house which happened to be vacant. The rank of Second Secretary, being more senior, carried with it the right to marriage and fatherhood. In this case all went well until the arrival of the Inspector. (Inspectors are appointed by the Foreign Office to do the balance-sheets, both human and economic, of each Mission every three or four years.) When inspecting the drawing-room carpet – due for renewal – he discovered to his infinite discomfort that a mere Third Secretary, who had the right to a carpet ending ten inches from the walls, was in fact benefiting from one which extended to six inches from the walls. The story, which might be thought apocryphal (but I wouldn't be so sure), recounts that the grey-faced civil servant resolved the dilemma by solemnly producing his scissors and cutting off the four offending inches round the edge of the carpet.

Thus, in spite of it being a longer process, house-hunting sometimes produces a home better suited to the family's needs, only, of course, after numerous disappointments due to the rigidly hierarchical system whereby the grade of the officer governs the rent allowance permitted. Time and again the wife, certain of having found the ideal home, will be told that its rent falls fairly and squarely within the category of the grade immediately superior to that of her husband.

The accommodation allocated to HM Consul, Algiers, comprised part of the former British Hospital. Between the wars there had been a sizeable British community in Algeria, drawn there by the mild winters. Many of the street names witnessed this: Chemin Macklay and so forth. In addition to the pretty Consulate-General building there was also a British church and hospital. The Consul occupied the central part of the hospital building, originally occupied by the doctor and nurses, whilst the outer wings had been converted into flats for members of the British community, deserving cases such as a couple of elderly retired missionaries who for years had striven manfully but totally unsuccessfully in the Kabyle region of Algeria to convert Moslems to Christianity.

I shall never forget the utter despair into which the sight of my new home plunged me. From outside it seemed a solid enough building with thick walls and high rooms. The pale blue shutters were peeling, but there was an attractive terraced entrance and a garden with orange trees, where an Arab gardener was working quietly among the flowers. But its interior decoration had been allowed to fall into abject disrepair. (This is quite often the case as the nearer a family get to being posted the less care and attention they will, understandably, devote to the house they are about to leave.) Stunned, I walked round behind Nest, gloomily taking in the faded walls bearing the marks of our predecessors' pictures, the flaking paint from the ceilings fluttering down like snowflakes, the bathroom door swinging disconsolately from one hinge. In the entrance hall there was a gaping wound in the ceiling through which pipes and wires sagged like intestines. So what with all that and the fact that the furniture looked as if it had come from a service canteen, by the time Christopher came to pick me up for lunch the tears were streaming down my face.

He, in contrast, felt buoyed up, having spent a fascinating morning learning about his new job. His predecessor, staying on for a couple of days' overlap, had been filling him in, and I could see from the glint in his single eye that he had been busy collecting the ingredients for the second instalment of his political journal. It was then that I began to realize that the major problems arising from our nomadic life were going to affect me rather than him, and that the same circumstances creating political interest for him would make my life especially difficult. I started to see the picture of the husband after each move making a dash for his new office – where the pattern of work would be little different from the previous one – saying, 'Good luck, darling, with the house-hunting – or unpacking – or finding a maid – or deciding on the children's schools – or learning Spanish – or – or ...'

That evening the Consul-General and Nest gave a party whose dual purpose was to bid farewell to our predecessors whilst welcoming us. But there was an unforeseen prelude. Since we were staying at the Consul-General's residence until our predecessors departed, I had left Konrad there whilst I inspected our new home. He had wasted no time. For a while the preparers of the cocktail eats could not work out why there were always a few gaps in the symmetrically arranged plates of canapés, which through a lack of table space had been laid out ready on each step of the back stairs. Konrad's extremely bloated appearance eventually gave him away and, whilst apologizing profusely, I felt it was unfair of him to have made a bad beginning even worse for us. Nest took it quite well. She had a curious habit – used in

36

moments of crisis – of plumping herself down on the sofa with an exhalation of '*Eh, voilà!*' in a faulty French accent. She did it then, having said, unconvincingly, that what Konrad had done didn't matter at all.

The guests started to arrive – they consisted of a handful of French Government servants, putting in an appearance out of politeness to a foreign Consul; the rest of the consular corps, well versed in the game of entertaining one another at their governments' expense, and a large number of the richer and more 'respectable' Pieds Noirs – the wine merchants, the businessmen – for whom Algeria provided a much higher return than the same abilities could have commanded in France. The only Algerian present was serving the drinks. The party then took on a certain pattern – which was to become familiar in the following years. Because the ceiling of the drawing-room was too low, the voices ricocheted round the walls and the room was soon full of cigarette smoke.

A spectacular lady was introduced to us. We started talking to her, but first Christopher's interest had been distinctly aroused by the fact that the parts of her not dressed in Paris had been done to a turn at the beach club. She positively shone with elegance and had a soft, low voice which, fairly soon in the conversation and to my absolute horror, I heard saying, 'You see, there are nine million Arabs and one million of us. Well, I am ready to kill my nine Arabs.' As if to add credence to her words, from the town below the first of the evening's plastic bombs could be heard together with the start of the casserole concert. Da-da-da *dong-dong*, Al-gé-rie *Fran-çaise*, the whole town beating its saucepans in unison. '*Ça commence,*' she said with satisfaction.

Retreating from the sinister lady, we then met a member of the French Administration. Gerard l'Hôte, their Liaison Officer, only had one arm and he enjoyed telling members of the British Consulate-General that British troops had shot it off in Syria. He worked in the Prefecture in the town – not in the French Government offices at Rocher Noir, where the French central administration had retreated for security reasons and, isolated behind barbed wire, were striving to control events by telephone forty kilometres from the capital. L'Hôte's exposed position and his honesty, which became reckless with drink, put him in great danger from the OAS. At the top of his voice, he expressed his loathing for the Pieds Noirs and then obligingly fed Christopher with information ideal for the next instalment of his political journal. All the guests left together – the Pieds Noirs because they had no permits to stay out after the curfew hour, and the members of the French administration and security forces because, though they had permits, they had other things to do. We soon took our leave from the Consul-General and his wife in order to muse in a stunned fashion over the first day of our new life. Before he forgot, Christopher wrote up notes for his journal, the entry for which eventually took the following form:

In Algiers, as in Oran, murder is the order of the day. They are towns without law. Although the French forces could perhaps deal with any mass movement, they do not ensure the safety of the streets. Whatever the good intentions of those at the top, the administration and security forces, riddled in their lower echelons by the OAS, are demonstrably impotent. A new offensive against the OAS has been decided. Special police, taking their orders only from Paris, have been drafted in to deal with the OAS by its own methods. But this has yet to show results. The OAS is still able, more or less with impunity, to disfigure the town, to issue directives to the European population and punish disobedience to them, to carry out executions, to levy wholesale taxation. It arrogates to itself some, at least, of the powers of government. The FLN with its wide military and political networks does the same for the Moslem population. Both have lately stepped up the tempo of violence.

A few weeks ago there was an air of expectation. The Moslems looked towards a negotiated independence, the Europeans towards a *putsch*. Today, though both these possibilities are still in the offing, expectations are tempered by a vicious despair. The Moslems are feeling robbed of the future as negotiations with the French government still hang fire. The Europeans still profess a frantic confidence and attachment to Algérie Française, but beneath it there is fear and confusion of purpose. Racial passions are flowing black and ugly. There is, they say, no colour bar in Algeria; it is merely that social relations between the communities are conducted by knife, bullet and grenade. De Gaulle broadcast last night. He had some forthright words to the address of the OAS – 'a criminal group of those in revolt, openly yesterday, today concentrating on blackmail and assassination'. He looked to the possibility of a negotiated settlement but left no doubt that in one way or other France must wash her hands of the Algerian problem. There was an undertone of Olympian resignation. The Pieds Noirs have greeted it with derision.

Henrietta was due to arrive in two days' time. With all my heart I looked forward to the moment at the Maison Carré airport when I would again see the precious little baby with her cap of red hair and round blue eyes. I also devoutly hoped that her arrival would bring with it some return to a feeling of normality which had been so thoroughly shattered by the events of the day before.

First there was her room to get ready and – even more important – Nanny's. My heart quailed at the thought of what Nanny would think or – even worse – say about the house. I knew that her genteel soul would be outraged by its peeling, faded appearance.

The central part of the sprawling hospital building which made up our home was compact enough. It comprised a small entrance hall with drawing-room to the left and dining-room and kitchens to the right, and then at the top of a longish marble staircase was a landing with four bedrooms and one bathroom arranged round it. A garden sloped down in front of the house with a huge fig tree growing in a position which obscured all light to the drawing-room. (We made the decision to cut down the fig tree to give light – but regretted its loss when the fruit season arrived.)

We apportioned the bedrooms: we occupied one overlooking the bay and the child the other. Nanny was to be next door to Henrietta, leaving the last bedroom as a spare room (although I did wonder if anyone would be intrepid enough to visit us). I did my best – with the help of the surly little *pied noir* maid who had been with our predecessors – to make it all look nice. As a first priority we moved what seemed the best of the Ministry of Works's furniture into Nanny's room. Every time I displaced something my unwilling helper protested, saying that its previous position had been perfectly all right for Madame. I realized that in all probability I would never become 'Madame' until after our departure. (This is one of the problems of taking on staff who have become attached to previous occupants for, although their help accelerates the installation, the unfavourable comparison they make between past and present masters is dispiriting.)

39

Next morning I ventured out shopping. The nearest shops, owned by both Europeans and Moslems, were at the Colonne Voirol, a modest column put up a long time ago, I was told, to commemorate a punitive expedition. Whilst in the *pied noir* grocery shop buying the French brand of baby food the Post Report had told me would be available (in these as in everything else the French showed their gastronomic supremacy), I noticed immediately the discrimination shown by the shopkeeper against her Arab customers. The fact that she made the veiled women wait until the last and addressed them with the familiar '*tu*' astonished me.

By this time I had put the house into a slightly better state to stand up to Nanny's withering look. I had borrowed a cot for Henrietta, rigorously sprayed everything against the hated fly, and there were rows and rows of bottles of Evian water to make the baby's bottles. The house was filled with Bougainvillaea and plumbago to mask its imperfections.

At dinner on the evening before their arrival we learnt more about the current situation. Invited by another member of the Consulate, the officer dealing with passport applications, we became more aware of the fact that there was no other topic of discussion but '*les événements*', as the war was euphemistically called. Our hosts, who had themselves spent their entire lives in Algeria and had been locally employed by the Consul-General, warned us of the danger of expressing pro-de Gaulle views or appearing enthusiastic about Algerian independence. There were OAS spies everywhere, they said – the slogan on the walls, '*l'OAS vous écoute*', was true. The price of attracting their disapproval could be a small charge of explosive under the windowsill or under the bumper of the car. In response to our incredulous looks they reminded us of the fate suffered by 'poor Freddie'.

That night the plastic bombs went off again – one seemed very close. The next morning at the Colonne Voirol I found the little *crêmerie* where I had bought my cheese the day before in ruins, with the old Kabyle owner crying quietly outside it. He who had been so careful to mind his own business now stooped ankle-deep in the fragments of what was left of his livelihood. The milk ran in the gutter. On enquiring why he had been singled out, I was told that he must have been working with the FLN – but to me he looked too old and decrepit to make a good terrorist, though he may have had a son in the mountains to revenge him.

Later that day we went to the airport for the eagerly awaited arrival. On the way I continued to try to piece together the geography of the town and its outskirts, first seen from our boat. Paradoxically, the names of the European quarters were Arab, whilst the Arab townships had French names. The heights of the city, where we lived, were called El Biar, and the choice European area of the Governor's Summer Palace and the Hôtel Saint-Georges, Mustafa. Bab-el-Oued – the poor white stronghold – was a colonnaded slum, rancid with prejudice and racialism, full of Communists turned Fascist and women in their curlers and dressing-gowns at midday. No Arab dared enter there and even the police went in armoured cars. On our way to the airport that day we drove through the Arab ghettos, the teeming, FLN-controlled encrustment of poverty in the valley which, with a blind irony, was called Climat de France, and then through the shanty towns bearing names like Belcourt, La Redoute, Le Ravin de la Femme Sauvage – names that were a kind of mockery of the Arab spirit, as if to show them that the realities of life were French.

The Air France plane yielded up the precious baby. She had changed even in one week – her hair had grown a little, she had become more composed. Guarding her charge in her usual scrupulous way, Nanny's morale was at its highest. She had been the focus of attention during the flight. She and Henrietta were incongruous passengers, as the only other visitors to Algiers at that time were members of the French security forces. As I had anticipated, my efforts in the house were little appreciated, and Nanny embarked on the relationship she was to relish with the *pied noir* maid, based on misunderstanding and bias.

The next important milestone in our lives was the arrival of our luggage. In spite of having sent it off in good time from London, we still had to wait several weeks for its arrival at the house. The huge wooden box – for some unknown reason officially called a fork lift – had been delayed at the docks, and considering the security situation we were lucky not to have had to wait longer. The importance of those personal effects – as they are described in civil service jargon – to the life of a diplomatic family cannot be overestimated. Unlike

that of most other countries, the policy of the British Government is
to house their diplomats in furnished accommodation; their calcula-
tions having proved that it is more beneficial to the Exchequer to do
this than to pay for the transport of their furniture round the world.
The system, therefore, requires the family to ask for estimates from
three removal companies to pack and transport the possessions they
wish to take with them. If they wish to include items of furniture they
risk exceeding the limit allowed, so instead they carry round with
them all those small personal items which they then scatter round
someone else's house in a vain effort to make it seem like their own. It
is as if those big cardboard boxes contain their very personalities: the
pictures – we had a particular favourite referred to as the '*faux*
Correggio*' (which it was) – which adorned many a different wall; the
cushions, the books, the china objects, the framed photographs, the
bric-à-brac, the trophies picked up on different postings round the
world, etc. These possessions – vulnerable to loss or damage on the
way – sometimes become shabby through the constant moves but
remain precious. In our case, although they have now taken up a
permanent position in our London home, I can still quite clearly see
the way a picture or silver candlestick looked in Paris, Algiers or
elsewhere.

Although my first reaction to the house had been one of gloom, we
quickly developed a great affection for it. Even though, after being
repainted and – eventually – acquiring some new furniture, it was
never exactly elegant, it did have a character of its own and, most
important, was in a relatively peaceful part of the town. Furthermore,
because of its garden Henrietta never had to leave the confines of the
home base, but would lie in her pram under the orange, tangerine and
lemon trees in the warm autumn sun. She was only affected by one
feature of the unsettled environment: the helicopters. The sky over
the city was never empty of one or more on the look-out for trouble,
and Henrietta developed a positive terror of these huge sky monsters
hovering over her small world in the garden. She let out piercing
shrieks and Nanny would rush out fulminating against the OAS, FLN,
French or whatever, to gather her up. She never acquired much
political discernment.

The house having acquired its moderately pristine look and with the New Year approaching, we thought we had better give a party both as a housewarming and to celebrate the coming year – although it could have been said there wasn't really much to celebrate. But I was determined to seize this opportunity of filling the conventional role of diplomat's wife, which I had always understood was to give elegant cocktail parties with a well-assorted guest list. I was determined to become a hostess. There was not a great deal of choice as far as the guest list was concerned – it would have to be on the same lines as the one given by the Consul-General to welcome us. But in addition to the French officials, consular colleagues, members of the security service, representatives from the business community and international journalist corps we added two Algerians: M. Rezoug of the RTF (Radio Télévision Française), and Mme Bourboune, Mayor of El Biar. (This courageous lady was soon after to be the victim of an OAS attack.) The thick invitation cards, symbolizing a more stable environment, with 'Mr and Mrs Christopher Ewart-Biggs have the pleasure to invite ...' engraved on them, were sent off, and I then started on the administrative arrangements. There was no need to worry about the drinks – crates containing every kind of alcoholic and non-alcoholic bottle had been purchased duty-free and delivered on our arrival. But there were glasses to rent, canapés to prepare and flowers to arrange. Having booked the services of Mme Devert – the professional *pied noir* canapé-maker – I went to do the shopping. I decided to venture for the first time to the central food market in the heart of the city. (By that time I had acquired a black beetle Morris, very ancient and soon only able to make the journeys down town, which somewhat diminished its usefulness.)

I arrived at the huge covered market and underwent the search necessary before being allowed to enter. (It was common practice at that time for women to have their bags and shopping-baskets searched and for men to undergo a body search before entering shops, restaurants and cinemas. In order to avoid the risk of someone planting a bomb in a cinema and then leaving, the doors would be locked until the end of the performance, making it quite impossible to leave in the middle of a bad movie.) As I started my shopping I almost immediately became the unconscious instigator of a racial drama. At the sudden cry of '*Voleur, voleur*', the housewife standing beside me said she had just seen an Arab youth trying to remove the wallet from my handbag. A few seconds later a hard-faced European dragged a fourteen- or fifteen-year-old boy towards me. I refused to identify the young Arab, saying I had not actually seen him trying to steal. The man, looking at me contemptuously, said: '*Eh bien, Madame, vous mettez encore un voleur au monde.*' Then, seemingly taking the law into his own sadistic hands, he started knocking the boy around with his fists. With an ineffectual cry of '*Laissez-le,*' I rushed away, sickened.

The general conversation at this, my first official diplomatic party, was not typical. To start with I talked to a major in the French Army; he was clearly very '*excité*'. (Thus were described the French who became sympathetic to the *pied noir* cause after having been sent over by the French Government to oppose it.) In vivid terms he was criticizing de Gaulle's policy of working towards a negotiated settlement for Algerian independence. Imagining a parallel situation of, say, a Welsh Guards officer railing against the Queen, I asked him if he felt he would be obliged to resign his commission. He looked at me, astonished at my naïvety, and with true French logic said, 'Not at all – the very contrary – I can sabotage those policies far better by staying in.'

The French Police Commissioner was there – the most vulnerable man in Algiers, under attack from each side. The *pied noir* guests were keeping clear of him, and he was standing on his own. He was a big, tough Corsican, but the strain was telling on him. He was taking in a lot of whisky and his hand was unsteady. I brought a member of the French Délégation Générale up to talk to him. Pulling himself together, he wished the other guest a happy New Year. In return came the ominous answer, 'And to you, M. le Préfet, I wish you *a* year.'

In an effort to return to normality I attached myself to a group consisting of the German Consul-General and a group of journalists. An earnest observer of the political scene, the German was painstakingly describing the current situation – meticulous to the point of referring to the Pieds Noirs as the 'black feets'. (It did make them sound less sinister.) One of the journalists listening to him was the doyen of the English-speaking reporters from the *Daily Telegraph* and, unlike most of its other reporters, shared its views. In the hot weather the drink seeped out of him, and he was improbably married, *in absentia*, to a Persian princess. He also had the curious habit of eating toothpaste and kept a tube of it for this purpose in the pocket of his crumpled linen coat. He, like all the other journalists sent to report the crises, lived in the Aletti, a hotel in the centre of the town, and operated mainly from its bar. The bar was a 'truce' zone, used by both sides for contact with the press, and many correspondents never set foot outside it. It was for her fearless habit of going out to look for news that our intrepid friend, Clare Hollingworth, reporter for the then *Manchester Guardian*, earned the name of the 'Kasbah Kid'.

But that evening at our party the *Daily Telegraph* reporter was busy telling the earnest German diplomat of the scene he had recently witnessed in the Aletti bar. He described how he had been sitting there quietly one afternoon, with a French officer at the other end of the bar, when two men came in and sat down. The reporter didn't much like the look of them and decided to leave, but he was turned back in the doorway by a third man who was standing guard there with a Lüger. The reporter apparently made himself as small as possible, which could not in fact have been very small, in the corner of the bar, and might well, at this point, have taken a lick of his toothpaste to quieten his nerves. He then heard the two men ask the officer to join the OAS. The officer refused. The two men then said that in that case they would kill him. The officer said they would be cowards to shoot him since he was unarmed. One of the killers, possibly a Sicilian, threw a pistol along the length of the bar to the officer. The second had his gun in his hand. The man with the Lüger in the doorway was ready too. The officer, prudently, did not take up the pistol from the bar: instead, he unbuttoned his tunic and held it open. '*Voilà*,' he said. 'Shoot me. There's nothing there but my heart. And there's nothing in my heart but France.' Whereupon the OAS killer became so moved that he started to cry, and with his two companions left the bar. The reporter then bought drinks for the French officer and himself.

I could see that the earnest German was torn between not believing the story and yielding to the temptation of rushing back to his Consulate-General to report it to his Ministry.

45

3

Under Siege

In the early months of 1962 the unrest continued and the conflict increased. Negotiations were known to be going on in Switzerland between the French Government and the GPRA (Gouvernement Provisoire de la République Algérienne, the FLN Government based in Tunisia). Christopher noted in his journal on 5 March:

> In the early morning one hundred and seventeen bombs exploded in the doorways and windows of Arab shops in Algiers. The OAS intended this as a reminder of their strength and presence. They knew of the secret negotiations in Switzerland, and wished to show both the French government and their own supporters that they were still in the game. The effect was impressive, particularly in the silence of the dawn. It sounded as if the town woke to find itself under bombardment. There were almost no casualties, but a number of small shopkeepers lost their livelihoods. In one house near the Kasbah a sleeping child had her face opened by flying glass.

And again on 15 March:

> The Social Centre at El Biar is, or rather was, a small, well-meaning exception to the rule of separation between the communities. Of the staff of educationalists, half were Algerian. Milous Faraoun, the Kabyle novelist, was one of them. With a gentle whimsicality he had described the privations of his childhood in the mountains. His tragedy now was that of moderation. He was a moderate in a situation in which only extremism was respectable. To conform it was necessary to hate.
>
> This morning, after the classes at the centre had started, a car stopped there. The men in the car were silent and swift. They carried guns and with these they forced the teachers, French and Algerian, out of the building. The children did not scream or weep. They watched. The men put the teachers against a wall, in the classical fashion, and shot them. Only when

the men had driven away did the yelling of the children start. In a clandestine broadcast, the OAS claimed that they had executed a group of left-wing supporters of the FLN. As soon as the news became known all Algerian schools closed in mourning.

The next three months proved to be the most critical of all and numerous difficulties affected day-to-day life. The OAS, fearful of the successful culmination of the secret negotiations, unleashed their most savage attack on the Moslem community. No Arab was safe in the European quarters. The OAS marksmen would gun them down to the rhythm of 'Algérie Française'. The objective of the renewed onslaught was to provoke the Arabs into retaliating and thereby halt the negotiations.

With the Algerian workforce no longer able to enter the European parts of the city came the cessation of many of the public services. Refuse was no longer collected: we started to burn our own. Basing our system on the principle of incineration, we piled the fat bags into iron dustbins, placed on bricks and with holes pierced underneath to create a draught and, well soused with spirit, set them alight. But it was extraordinary how some items refused to disappear and reappeared time and again. Other residents of El Biar were less conscientious and started dumping their refuse on the side of the road. A great mound appeared outside the gates of our home, with more being added every day; one morning saw a dead dog topping the pile. It was only through the coincidence of a particularly cool spring that epidemics were avoided. Nanny had taken the violence in her stride, but the flies attracted by the mountains of refuse were too much for her.

It was at this point that we took on another task for our country! To help the beleaguered Consulate-General with its communication problems arising from the breakdown of so many of the public services, the Foreign Office had sent out a spanking new telex machine together with an instruction book. The Consul-General's personal assistant was put in charge of it but, being of a reactionary nature, did not take to it, and whenever some message from London came rapping out she readily abandoned her post. Christopher, realizing that a crisis might occur, decided to train himself to become the operator. We went together one Saturday morning to confront the monster. Christopher, after careful perusal of the instruction book, started painstakingly tapping out a message to London. Immediately the beast responded, throwing out a reprimand. Once again, with the instruction book in one hand, he fingered the board. Once more the Foreign Office operator, thinking she had a complete moron at the other end, responded with a brusque correction. Christopher then firmly screwed his monocle in – a habit of his when determined to win – and brooking no interruption tapped out the following message: 'This is HM Consul operating the telex for the first time so please mind your manners.'

Although there remained not a single Arab face in the European quarters, there were in fact still two in our employ. Our old Algerian gardener continued to tend the flowers he loved so much – the faces of the dazzlingly bright zinnias seemed to smile when his gnarled hands touched them. He was so old that dying could not have been an issue for him any more. On arrival, realizing that we were likely to meet few Algerians, Christopher used to try out his Arabic on him. The gardener waited politely and patiently whilst the four minutes of gargling, representing a greeting in his language, went on before saying, 'Bonjour, monsieur.' But, without realizing it, he played an important role in the work of the Consulate. For Christopher, starved of political contacts, sometimes tried out a few ideas on him, and would then report back to London according to the tone of voice the old man used. The mornings he sounded bitter Christopher's report to the Foreign Office stated that Arab opinion was hardening.

Our *pied noir* maid, unhappy at the best of times, had found life in Algiers too traumatic and given in her notice. We advertised for someone else. A beautiful Algerian girl called Meriem responded. She had been working as a *modiste* in one of the smartest fashion shops in the rue Michelet, situated in the heart of the European area. Unable to stay there because of the OAS onslaught, she felt that a diplomatic house might afford her greater protection. She seemed distressed when she came for the interview, saying that if she did not find a job she would have to return to her home in far-off Tlemcen but she needed the money for her little boy. We took her on – although her qualifications as a *bonne-à-tout-faire* were non-existent. Soon she not only became a real friend but also helped me concoct meals out of the miserable amount of food I was then able to buy. As the transport drivers were all Moslem, provisions were no longer being brought into the town. On her days off – unable to show her face outside the house for fear of being shot – Christopher used to drive her down to the town to visit her former employers from the dress shop. He made her lie down on the floorboards in the back of the Jaguar, and then hustled her into the house of her friends.

She left us to return to her real work after independence, but our friendship was the sort of bonus which can come out of the unusual circumstances which existed in Algiers at that time. As for Nanny, I think she actually fell in love with the beautiful, gentle girl, and was inconsolable when she left.

I experienced my worst moments of anxiety during that difficult period when Christopher made the weekly journey to the airport to meet the Queen's Messenger. The life of a Queen's Messenger is not the glamorous one generally imagined. On the contrary the job, often held by a retired officer of the services, is exhausting. He is responsible for the transportation of confidential mail between the Foreign Office and foreign missions. He must never allow this confidential mail, enclosed in a bag, out of his sight. If his plane crashes and he survives, his first responsibility is to scrabble around in the wreckage to recover the bag. His life consists of catching aeroplanes or waiting at airports. Furthermore, embassy staff tend to be concerned about him only until they have exchanged bags with him. After that they may lose interest in the elderly and distinguished gentleman who is probably dying for a rest and a drink.

It was so arranged – and badly so – that the Queen's Messenger on the North African route arrived at Algiers after the curfew hour. The flight schedules between the Maghreb capitals meant this could not be avoided. Christopher found himself driving to the airport at around 11 p.m. every week to meet the Messenger and exchange diplomatic bags with him. The job could have been completed rapidly as his white Jaguar was capable of great speed. However, the French security forces insisted on providing an escort, requiring the Jaguar's mighty engine to turn over at the same speed as those of the lumbering armoured cars preceding and following it, thereby presenting an infinitely easier target for any FLN marksman. The French explained that they felt it vital to provide this protection since, were the Jaguar to come under fire, their armoured cars would be there to counter-attack. Christopher answered that, although he was grateful for the concern, the counter-attack would by that time be of purely academic interest to him personally. And for me, waiting at home for the return from these nocturnal journeys, the purr of the Jaguar's engine sliding into the garage was like music from heaven.

On 18 March the Évian Agreements were signed and the cease-fire became effective next day. It was more favourable to the Europeans than most people dared hope, for it guaranteed them the two things they wanted above all else: to remain French and to continue to live in Algeria. Christopher reported this momentous event in his journal:

> On the eve of the Évian Agreements both sides, for their different reasons, were stepping up the rate of murder, the OAS in order to provoke the Arabs into action and thus to engage the French Army against them, the FLN in order to show that they were not defeated. This mounting rhythm of violence was suddenly interrupted by the announcement of the cease-fire which threw Algeria into a state of unnatural and unexpected calm. Algiers caught its breath. On the orders of the OAS, the Europeans stayed at home, contenting themselves with a *concert des casseroles*. Public services ceased and the life of the town was paralysed. The Algerians, on the orders of the FLN, did not come out into the streets or wave flags. With Arab terrorism cut off completely, the Europeans behind closed doors and the Army thick in the streets, the level of violence fell miraculously.
>
> But not for long. As the life of the town began the next day to go back to normal, so also did terrorism resume, for that too was the normal pattern. The OAS on 20 March fired mortar shells into the crowded Place du Gouvernement, centre of the Arab area. They almost succeeded in their object of bringing an angry swarm out of the nearby Kasbah. But the FLN showed their extraordinary discipline. Working beside French officers, identifying themselves for the first time, they turned their people back. Only one European, caught in his car in a side street not long after the mortar bombs fell, was dragged out by a small crowd and pulled to pieces.

The first Sunday after the signing we decided to make a trip inland to the Bled, as the French Army called the outback, to see if the cease-fire was being honoured. We went with our great friends, the Italian Consul and his wife Alix. We all felt elated that the terms for independence had finally been agreed, for the sake of France, which would once again move with the tide of history, and Algeria, and also in the interests of our personal lives, which would naturally be fundamentally changed with the ending of the war. We drove along the empty roads towards the Kabylia, the beautiful mountainous region which in many ways could be called the Scotland of Algeria and is inhabited by Moslems of Berber stock who are amongst the oldest inhabitants of the country, still using a separate dialect. The Kabyles are imbued with intense national and regional pride, and their women, in contrast to Arab women, traditionally walk outside without the veil, in boldly coloured dresses often adorned with exquisite necklaces of silver and coral.

As we approached our destination, a group of villages called the Benni Yenni perched defiantly along the top of a range of mountains, we saw a single file of soldiers coming towards us. I paid little attention, taking them to be French, and was surprised when Christopher stopped the car abruptly, got out and crossed over towards the column of men. I was just within earshot and realized that his greeting was in Arabic. After returning the salutation they moved on and I then recognized the green flash on the arm of their battledress – the only thing which distinguished the ALN (Armée de Libération Nationale) from the French Army. I realized that I had seen the forces of the FLN for the first time. We drove on and arrived at the principal village of the Benni Yenni range and immediately attracted a great deal of attention: tourists were a forgotten thing. As we walked around the narrow streets and saw the beautiful Kabyle jewellery being made, we suddenly realized that our every movement was being closely followed by an ever-growing line of children – all, noticeably, under the age of seven or eight. It was not we who were causing the interest, but Konrad. It was the first time they had ever seen a dog; all the village dogs had been killed at the beginning of the war to prevent them giving the alarm when the ALN entered the village at night for provisions. Although Konrad was accustomed to adulation, he had never known anything like this before.

The villagers were all very friendly and treated us with that Arab courtesy which we had not yet encountered. Enormously heartened by the cease-fire, they were busily clearing away all the barbed wire and preparing themselves mentally for peace. The atmosphere of relief, even euphoria, was in direct contrast to the hysteria which had gripped the major cities – with their big European communities – following the Agreements.

There was a monastery of the order of the Pères Blancs in the village and they told us that one of the fathers was a Canadian and would like to see us. (The news of our arrival had gone round the village like wildfire.) Such religious missions as this, spread through the mountainous regions of Algeria, had endured a difficult seven years trying to preserve their neutrality in order to continue their work of teaching. One of their members had even been taken away during the war and had never been seen again. The Father Superior – a gentle old Frenchman – introduced us to the Canadian priest, but we sensed a certain embarrassment. Finally the Canadian told us that they had other visitors – a group of three ALN guerrillas – wishing to meet us. Christopher and Luigi, the Italian Consul, envisaging heaven-sent material for their next despatch home, accepted. The three warriors were lined up in the monastery refectory as if for a press conference, and they answered the questions Christopher put to them in his slightly self-conscious Arabic. (In point of fact the language he had so laboriously learnt at the Shemlan language school did not exactly conform to the Algerian version, which was heavily interspersed with French words.) The spokesman, an officer who looked almost smart in his battledress embellished by an FLN scarf tied neatly round his neck, was flanked by two ruffians with empty faces and rifles slung over their backs. Well rehearsed in the GPRA line, he answered our questions accordingly; yes, the French Army had observed the cease-fire; yes, he did want independence in co-operation with the French. All that the Algerians desired was peace, he said. We thanked them and said goodbye to the White Fathers. As we got into our car to return to Algiers, we saw the three guerrillas, surrounded by Algerian girls, being fêted as the triumphant warriors they in fact were.

A few weeks later Christopher and I made another journey. He wanted to visit our Honorary Vice-Consul in Oran to enquire about the situation there and try to bolster the morale of the beleaguered man. Oran, 300 miles away, is the second city of Algeria, and the only centre where the *pied noir* population – mainly of Spanish origin – are predominant. Before the war Oran had been the gayest spot in Algeria with a thriving night life, but now the racial tension was the most serious in the country, and as I walked in the streets window-shopping I was strongly reminded of the Oran of Albert Camus, himself an Oranais, who depicts this town with its back to the sea as that of *La Peste*, a town stricken by a pestilence, with its inhabitants living on the edge of hysteria, avoiding contact with each other, scanning the newspapers for the latest count of deaths, trying to preserve a thin façade of normality, and its authorities bewildered and anxious in the face of emergency. As I looked in the shop windows – having been woken that morning by the shots which killed the Director of the Postal Services on the way to his office – I sensed that the people around me did not wish to come too close to each other and that I felt uneasy with my back turned towards them.

Christopher reported the journey and the visit to the town in his journal:

> If Algeria is a sick man, the Oranie is his poisoned limb. It looks about as healthy as a case of gangrene – with the ALN unruly, the Europeans pulling out and concentrating in the townships, the OAS despite the blows they have received still riding high and sharpening their knives, the communities drawing away from one another, the officials trying to administer from behind barbed wire and a splendid grape harvest in jeopardy.
>
> The road was deserted. The only European cars we met were a convoy of about twenty-five escorted by the Military on their way to Oran to leave the country. We did not meet the ALN who keep off the main roads on which the French still have patrols. But the ALN have been harassing European farmers, making exorbitant demands for money and goods, pillaging and kidnapping and even murdering people, to a greater extent in the Oranie than elsewhere. Paradoxically the problem comes from the French security forces having done too well against the ALN. Before the whistle blew they had been reduced to a scattered and disorganized handful and this meant that after the cease fire *ad hoc* groups of ruffians, labelling themselves ALN but not properly controlled or officered, sprang into existence and began preying on all and sundry. The Europeans are abandoning the outlying areas and falling back on the townships. They

have moved mainly from fear of the Moslems, but they are also acting under the directives of the OAS who may be trying to create a network of strong points in an enclave round Oran with the idea of making this the last OAS grouping or the basis of *de facto* partition.

In Oran itself the state of affairs is still nightmarishly strained and artificial. The Moslems are completely shut off from the European centre of the town by the mutual fear of the two communities and in many cases physically with barbed wire and troops. There have been exchanges of fire from rooftops and verandahs across these frontiers. We drove through the debris of battle. Much of the violence is spontaneous and unorganized. The Hon. Vice-Consul, himself by no means antipathetic to the Europeans, said that gangs of youths, conducting '*ratonnades*' (rat hunts), are behaving like animals. He had seen four Arabs literally dismembered by a group of them. As we drive through the town we see, from the top of a building in a European sidestreet, what we hope is only the effigy of a Moslem hanging by the neck.

The French Prefecture gives the impression that it is reeling from the blows it has received. There are gaping holes in the outside walls. The Préfet says that his own flat at the top of the building has been raked by machine-gun fire the day after he arrived in it. The walls of the buildings opposite are pockmarked by the exchange of fire. The OAS are still strong enough to do a lot of damage but they no longer have the liberty of the streets. The Prefecture of Police have machine-guns trained even along the interior corridors of the city.

On the way back to Algiers we visited Tlemcen, and in a village outside it we marvelled at the wonderful Andalusian mosque of Sidi Boumeddine. The Europeans of these places were too few to assert themselves. Those who could not live with the Moslems were already dead or gone. But the Moslem community lamented the war, as it killed tourism – and for them tourism was a livelihood. On the deserted road back to Algiers we stopped at a petrol station for oil. The Algerian mechanic peered at the vast Jaguar engine and said incredulously, '*On dirait une soucoupe volante.*'

Paradoxically, during all this time of danger and tension, the morale of the Mission staff and their wives was high. It is indeed a surprising aspect of diplomatic life that there is often more unhappiness among the junior staff and wives of missions in big, sophisticated capitals

than in small or troubled ones. The reason for this is that the major
cause of unhappiness in foreign postings comes from a feeling of
alienation or loneliness. Difficulties and dangers which are shared
prevent that loneliness and create a common bond. In Algiers, for
example, we were all in the same boat with the same responsibilities
and difficulties, regardless of our rank. In their work at the Consulate-General the husbands were responsible for reporting to the
Foreign Office the final stages in the life of France's colony of Algeria, for safeguarding any remaining commercial links between the
two countries, for representing the interests of the British subjects
remaining in Algeria, and for maintaining close contact with the
beleaguered French administration. Their wives were responsible for
being as supportive as possible to their husbands in this work and
for keeping, so to speak, the home fires burning. So, although we all
worried a great deal about the safety of our husbands, this again had
the comfort of being a common worry. As Britain had never inter-
fered in the affairs of Algeria, we did not have to fear any reprisals,
but nevertheless there was the constant risk of a stray bullet – *la
balle perdue* – as the fighting became more and more desperate.

As in all overseas missions, there were some locally employed staff
– expatriate British who at some point had settled in Algeria and
were employed under less favourable conditions than the home-
based members – and these might unwittingly have attracted the
attention of the OAS, as indeed had been the case with Freddie Fox.
Frank Benham was another. He had first known Algeria as a member
of the British forces in the war years and had subsequently been
lured back there by the sun, the beauty of the country and the at-
tractions of a *pied noir* girl whom he eventually married. Frank was
the 'fixer'. All overseas missions have one and he was ours. Whatever
was needed in those difficult days, Frank could find it, whether it
was a ticket on an airline with a long waiting list, medicine for a
sick child when the chemists had long been empty, some fillet steak
for an important visitor when the rest of us queued for hours for
small amounts of stewing lamb, or a part for our car whose aristo-
cratic engine found it difficult to digest so much sand. Frank was
everyone's friend and a loyal servant of the Consulate, but we knew
the tension that he and his wife, Paulette, were going through during

those last agonizing months in the life of their beloved Algérie Française.

A cause for concern appeared through a strange coincidence, namely that Christopher shared two characteristics with one of the major OAS leaders. The killer – based in Bab-el-Oued – was called '*Monsieur le monocle noir*', for the obvious reason that he wore a black monocle. Also he drove a white Jaguar. Christopher came in one evening looking rather pale; I asked him what was the matter. 'They cheered me when I drove through Bab-el-Oued today,' he said shakily.

In those difficult times the British community did have a spiritual leader. The Reverend James Lee Warner was a venerable gentleman who had served his God and his parishioners in various Mediterranean cities, eventually to end up in Algiers. He had lost his wife and could not manage well on his own. Although he was undoubtedly in charge of our spiritual well-being, there was equally little doubt that it was we who were responsible for his physical survival. He lived in a small, rather damp room in a wing of the pretty church beside the Consulate-General, and the wives used to take it in turns to make sure he had enough square meals to keep body and soul together. I can remember the many occasions when I knocked at his door bearing either an invitation to a meal or the meal itself, wondering whether I would find the indomitable old gentleman still alive. But his political views caused us even more concern. He was an unshakeably loyal supporter of de Gaulle – and since the day the General made clear his intention of giving Algeria independence, the hatred of the betrayed Pieds Noirs knew no bounds. Christopher had warned the Padre – as we all called him – that his outspoken admiration might well end with a plastic bomb in his church. Many members of his flock in the British community, despite being of British origin, shared the unequivocal stand for keeping Algeria French. However, there was nothing for it and the stubborn old Padre used to go so far as to include General de Gaulle in the Sunday Service prayers. To the passage in the service which went, 'And let us now pray for the Queen, HRH the Duke of Edinburgh and all the Royal Family', he added, 'And Charles, President of the French Republic', and then was totally unrepentant when half his congregation walked out. Christopher, realizing that persuasion would get him nowhere, tried some logic by reminding him that the congregation was in fact an Anglo-American one. Thus if, as the vicar thought it right, he wished to include the French President in the prayers, it would only be logical to include Jack, President of the United States of America, as well. However, as the old Padre for some reason had no admiration for the Americans, he decided to our great relief to exclude any reference to either.

Events took a different turn in the months of May and June preceding Independence Day, set for 3 July. The OAS had been in such a dominant position that the realization of independence was unthinkable, but the beginning of May saw the turning-point when the FLN put into effect a policy which struck fear into the hearts of the Pieds Noirs. Eminent Europeans just disappeared, leaving no trace, not to be seen or heard of again – kidnapped. The Europeans recognized this as a sign of the Arab revenge they had every reason to anticipate, outnumbered as they were by nine to one. Furthermore, they recognized that they could expect no support from the French people who, in a referendum, had just voted overwhelmingly – by ninety per cent – in favour of self-determination for Algeria. Another major setback was that their leader, General Salan, had been arrested in April. Thus the last heartbreaking phase in the history of French Algeria was set in motion. First, the French Administration, recognizing the crumbling of morale among the Europeans, pressed home their advantage against the OAS. The FLN, feeling their new strength, launched an attack against Europeans in a café on 14 May, killing twenty-nine and wounding over forty. The OAS, in one of its many clandestine broadcasts, proposed negotiations with the FLN and the threat of their 'scorched earth policy' as the alternative (meaning that if they had to give up Algeria they would leave it in ruins).

On 17 June Christopher made one of the last pre-independence entries in his journal:

The Pieds Noirs, an odd mixture of the volatile and the materialistic, at a given moment, suddenly came to terms with reality. They swerved away from absolute immolation. Two forces brought this about. First the realization that, come what may, the process of independence was in train, was moving every day closer to its conclusion and could not be stopped. And secondly, a growing fear of the future and of what the Moslems could do when they took matters into their own hands and the protection of the French Army was removed. A fear born of a bad conscience. The corollary of it was a collapse of confidence in the capacity of the OAS to secure its previous objectives and to protect its supporters. These feelings led the Europeans to different directions. To a movement on one hand to try to reassure their position in an independent Algeria by coming to terms with the Moslems. And on the other to leave the country, among the more desperate, to destroy the heritage they could not keep. The OAS itself followed both these lines and in fact made the second the means of procuring the first. They not only gave the order to their followers to leave – a complete reversal of their previous position – but used the threat of exodus as the instrument of their negotiations with the Moslems. They threatened to reduce Algeria to the state in which they had found it in 1830. It was the final renunciation of Algérie Française and the beginning of the attempt to come to terms with the future. Chevallier [the liberal Mayor of Algiers] played the part of broker between the two parties. The OAS could represent themselves as having put their stamp on the Algerian settlement. The FLN allowed themselves within limits but unmistakably to be blackmailed. They saw no other way of preventing the departing Europeans from destroying the basic assets of the state – the oil wells, the port installations, the gas and electricity undertakings – and leaving them with an empty shell. They judged, rightly enough perhaps, that the French Army would not or could not stop this destruction.

The final count of departures was nearly half a million Pieds Noirs, who abandoned their homes and livelihoods to pour destitute into metropolitan France. Whatever one's feelings of distaste for them had been, one could not but be affected by their manner of leaving. The Moslems came out of the Kasbah and mockingly set up stalls on the pavements selling suitcases. At the airport and down at the harbours of Algiers and Oran there were the most heart-rending scenes. The Pieds Noirs, permitted only two suitcases each, queued day and night for a passage out of the country in which they had been born. Men, women and children waited in the hot June sun for a means of escape from what they most feared – the anger and revenge of the Arabs. Many burnt their possessions before departure rather than let 'them' take possession. Others abandoned their cars on the road to the airport – or in some cases handed over the keys to any European who happened to be around. The smart shops in the rue Michelet offered their entire stocks for sale at knock-down prices. 'Let's face it,' a senior French official told British journalists, 'the whole of Algeria is up for sale.'

The 1st of July saw the Referendum carried out in the entire country, asking the people to vote yes for independence, and, as scheduled, Independence Day came about on 3 July. It was a day of unparalleled jubilation. The beautiful Meriem took part in the celebrations and arrived back flushed and joyous. The streets of Oran and Algiers became a sea of white, green and red flags, filled with wildly cheering and chanting Moslems. Despite the total anarchy threatened by the sudden departure of the Europeans, the take-over was effected with almost miraculous smoothness. Disciplined troops arrived to assume point duty from French gendarmes; from somewhere technicians appeared who could maintain the essential services of gas, electricity, water and sewage that had been deserted by the Europeans. The tricolour was lowered in Algiers for the first time in 132 years as the French High Commissioner left for home, together with the 600,000 French troops also returning to the other side of the Mediterranean.

I remember, however, that apart from the relief we felt at the end of the war and the establishment of peace, our main concern that day was for our car. Many of the celebrators were daubing parts of the town with the country's national colours: red for the blood of their martyrs, green for their fertile lands and white for the purity of Islam. Our white Jaguar presented a perfect background; it only needed the symbolic blood and fertility added to make it a true symbol of Algerian independence. We hid it away.

4

The Battle is Over

The facts of life for Algeria in 1962 on the first day of independence were roughly as follows. Many important installations and buildings in the major Algerian cities had been destroyed. These included the town halls of Algiers, Oran and Bône, the control tower at Algiers airport; the oil pipeline and three oil wells had been damaged, as had numerous hospitals, schools, Algiers University library, and many other buildings housing public institutions. The vast majority of the European community had fled, leaving the rest cowering in their houses hoping and praying that the safeguards in the Évian Agreements might be honoured; these recognized the rights of 'French citizens' to a share on equal terms in the protection and privileges accorded to Algerians over a transitory period of three years. Among those who had left were leading industrialists, farmers, wine-growers, engineers, doctors, chemists, dentists: the people, in fact, who had kept the fabric of society together as well as run the giant infrastructure originally set up. The Europeans had never trained the Algerians to replace them, allowing them to carry out only the most menial tasks.

That first summer of the new Algeria was turbulent in the extreme, seeming to prove Albert Camus right when he said, on receiving his Nobel Prize in 1957, 'Liberty is dangerous, as hard to live with as it is exciting.' There was mutual recrimination among Moslem leaders and a battle over the political leadership; hostile groupings appeared within the army; Algerians accused of having worked for France were massacred; and warring cliques and bands marched and counter-marched across the prostrate body of the so recently jubilant country. With total civil war looming, the distraught population appealed to the warring factions. 'Seven years, that's enough,' they pleaded. Furthermore, during this period when Algeria had no government, diplomatic relations could not be established and the foreign missions were left in a state of limbo.

However, by September 1962 Ben Bella had established his ascendancy and became Prime Minister, and in April 1963 the first President of the Algerian Republic. He was a good-looking man with a charming smile, but out of touch with external reality after his long incarceration in a French prison. He veered increasingly towards measures of abstract socialism, authoritarianism and the 'cult of personality' – so alien to the aims of the revolution.

However, our own preoccupation – of a rather frivolous nature – in those first weeks of Algerian independence was to take possession of our newly acquired holiday villa at the Club des Pins. This was a weekend paradise created by the most well-to-do Pieds Noirs on a lovely stretch of beach about fifteen miles from Algiers. To say that it was exclusive would be the understatement of the millennium. We had acquired this villa in an unorthodox manner characteristic of those times. Many of the departing Pieds Noirs, in a final attempt to safeguard their abandoned property, had sought out safe neutral tenants before leaving, and Christopher had been approached by a *pied noir* acquaintance who offered him the beach villa at a nominal rent. Christopher accepted with alacrity and the key was handed over. However, taking possession was not such a simple matter, as the Club des Pins fell within the Algiers area over which Wilaya 4, the capricious army division, had taken control. We came to a policy decision. Taking Konrad to assume the unaccustomed role of guard dog, but leaving Henrietta behind in Algiers with Nanny, we drove to the Club des Pins and having identified our villa – a particularly beautiful one, dazzlingly white and surrounded by a garden brilliant with colour and filled with cooling fountains and ponds – we settled in. Christopher then carried out his plan of making an official call on the Commandant of the army post. The villainous-looking guerrilla just down from the mountains was somewhat taken aback by this *démarche* – the more so coming from the tall, distinguished, monocled figure presented by Christopher. However, having presumably accepted that this was part of the ritual of the society from which he had been cut off for so many years, he responded positively and returned the call during the evening. So the first in the long stream of visitors to the villa was a uniformed member of the victorious army – heavily and visibly armed and positively stinking of the *maquis*. (What the rightful owner of the villa would have thought of this intrusion goes beyond the realms of imagination.) Out of respect for Islamic abstinence we offered him a non-alcoholic drink, and as he and Christopher had not quite come to terms with each other's Arabic, we settled down to a somewhat stilted conversation in French. We did not have much in common, but he was considerate enough to ask me if I had any children. Proudly I said yes, a lovely little girl; only to feel crushed when he answered in terms of 'better luck next time'. Christopher's effort at extracting a bit of political information for his next despatch to the Foreign Office fell rather flat, and silence reigned until our military vistor decided that the bizarre charade should come to an end and took his leave – but not before he and Christopher had what sounded like a long gargle at each other in the true traditions of Arabic.

Next day we returned to Algiers to collect Henrietta and Nanny. Meanwhile the Consular Corps had been waiting eagerly to see if we had survived Wilaya 4, before proceeding to take possession of the villas for which they too had keys burning holes in their pockets. Before long there was a small, contented diplomatic community spending their weekends at the Club des Pins – feeling they deserved the luxury after the months or years of suffering physical and mental constriction within the agony of Algiers. Henrietta had a little pool all of her own and I can still see her sitting there trying to keep cool with her finger held over the fountain in the middle to make the jet of water spray all over her.

We decided to take a short leave before embarking in earnest on our new lives. Christopher didn't like flying – he thought it was dangerous – so we returned home by sea and road. The visit, designed to restore the composure lost during those months of tension, was not an unqualified success. Firstly, in this case, the sight of the walls of the French Lycée at South Kensington covered with 'L'OAS veuille', etc, nearly reduced us to gibbering mania. Secondly, the interest our friends showed at our survival was shortlived. Having listened to the accounts of some of our more horrific experiences, eyes glazed over and their interest was diverted to more personal facets of British life. So, all in all, I was quite ready to return to Algiers. I had become conditioned to the environment.

The following months saw Christopher setting up the Embassy and establishing diplomatic links between Britain and the new and important Arab state of Algeria. I was faced with the less fascinating job of finding a cook, overcoming the domestic problems created by the exodus of so many of those in charge of running things, and making arrangements for some official entertainment.

The structure of an embassy is essentially hierarchical. All have an ambassador at the top of the family tree, and he is treated as a god, but the number of people under him will depend very much on the size of the Mission. The diplomatic ranks below that of ambassador are minister, counsellor, first secretary, second secretary and third secretary, and to each rank is attached a grade which determines his salary level. The embassy itself is divided into sections each with a different function. The chancery carries out the political work; there are the economic, commercial, information and consular departments, and an administration department covering the whole embassy. Working alongside there are attachés from Whitehall ministries other than the Foreign Office. The number of these will depend on the importance of the embassy − as will the size of all the departments. For example, in our Washington Embassy − as relations with the USA are important to Britain − besides the air, naval and military attachés there are representatives serving there from the Treasury, the Ministry of Labour and the Departments of Energy and Trade. The overall strength of the Embassy is about 300.

Our Algiers Embassy was more modest. Christopher, a first secretary, was number two to the ambassador. This meant that when the ambassador was absent he replaced him as chargé d'affaires. Tony Hayday, already there, became the second secretary in chancery. (Tony had achieved fame when his car, parked outside the house where he was at a party some weeks prior to independence, was partly blown up by a plastic bomb. This was reported back to the FO. Instead of the anticipated reply containing sympathy and promised compensation came the wry message: 'Please congratulate Hayday on his lucky escape.') The economic first secretary was also already there and new appointees came to fill the commercial, information, consular and administration slots. The British Council, up till then an embryo presence, was also reinforced. (Working separately from the Embassy, the British Council, as well as promoting British culture, etc, also arranged English language classes. These turned out to be in very great demand by the Algerians, who recognized the importance of the language from a commercial point of view.)

It fell to Christopher to be the major architect of the new structure, and I remember the passion with which he involved himself. At the same time he set about making contact with the Algerians who were to be the country's new leaders among the politicians, civil servants, diplomats, businessmen, etc. Many of these had been imprisoned in French gaols for their part in the revolution and had only recently been released, while many others had been forced into exile during the war years. They responded positively to Christopher's approaches, recognizing his total commitment to and knowledge of Algerian affairs accumulated during his ten months in their country. Our first real friends came from among the young men of the Ministry of Foreign Affairs. Brilliantly clever, educated in France but nevertheless true sons of the revolution, they represented a conflict of cultures which made them fascinating companions. First there was Mohammed Ben Habyles, the first secretary-general of the Ministry of Foreign Affairs, nicknamed 'Socrates' by his juniors because of his great wisdom and age. He was thirty-four, but as the average age for their first run of ambassadors was about twenty-seven, this made him a true veteran. He had recently married. It was an arranged marriage and he had only met his bride a couple of times prior to the ceremony. There was Ahmed Djezairi, nicknamed 'le Colonial Office' by his colleagues because of his strikingly English looks and voice, both inherited from his English mother who – it was rumoured – called him Kenneth. He inherited the name of Djezairi – which is Arabic for Algeria – from his grandfather, General Abd-el-Kader, the legendary hero of resistance against the French. Then there was Aziz Hocene, a Kabyle with light brown eyes and hair, whose idiomatic English nearly put ours to shame and who was the only other customer besides Christopher at a laundry in the town that performed the little-needed service of starching stiff collars. And also Layachi Yaker, whose beautiful, very blonde German wife Annette became a close friend of mine.

Our ambassador, promoted from being the consul-general, presented his credentials to the president, Ben Bella. I have a photograph of the slightly incongruous scene. The ambassador and his officers, resplendent in full diplomatic uniform with plumed hats and swords, are walking past a platoon of astonished members of Algeria's revolutionary army. I have another photograph which is of Ben Bella and his ministers in conversation with the British diplomats. This one still brings a lump to my throat as I look at it, for it reflects the animated faces of two outstanding men who died violently: Ahmed Khemisti, Algerian Foreign Minister, killed by an assassin's bullet and Christopher by a terrorist bomb.

Meanwhile my domestic life had not been easy. Although I enjoyed meeting all our new contacts and taking part in the political discussions, I had many problems at home. Henrietta, by that time about sixteen months old, was intermittently running high temperatures. There was by that time only one child specialist left in Algiers and he was under very great pressure. I used to ring him up, giving the baby's symptoms. 'Could you possibly come and see her, she's not at all well,' I pleaded with him. An exhausted voice replied, 'I'll prescribe an antibiotic – have you got a pencil? No, I can't come – I'm too hard pressed – I only visit children who might die.' I then went to a chemist with the scribbled prescription and he, more often than not, might say he hadn't got the medicine, his stock having become so depleted during the troubles, but helpfully suggesting another similar antibiotic. The anxiety I felt throughout her illness, exacerbated by the lack of adequate medical help, was hard to bear. I kept wishing that the British Hospital, instead of having been turned into our home, had continued to carry out its original function. However, a little later the Americans established and ran a hospital staffed with an American doctor and some nurses and equipped with medical supplies. On several occasions we found desperately-needed help there.

After the beautiful Meriem had left us to return to her fashion world we decided that we should conform to the more orthodox pattern of domestic staff and advertised for a cook. A good looking young man called Mohammed immediately responded. He was a Kabyle, and I could see from the way he looked at me that his attitude towards women was no different from that of most Moslems, but I managed to summon up enough courage to ask him if he had a reference. The interview then took on a strange tone. 'No,' he said, astonished. 'Oh dear,' I said, 'but surely there is a previous employer who would give you one.' Patiently he said, 'It's not like that – you see, for the last five years I've been cooking for the ALN up in the mountains – and very good experience it was – but there weren't any references.' And he looked down at his damaged arm. Convinced by his logic, I took him on and that was the start of our very complex relationship. He upheld the Moslem belief in the inferiority of women and I fought to maintain the European tradition of a woman being mistress of the home.

We started to give parties – proper ones without the curfew overshadowing them, but entertaining in an Arab country has its complications. Arabs are themselves very hospitable people and treat their guests with the utmost generosity and respect. Indeed the lavishness of the Bedouin host is legendary. Christopher described the way the Gulf sheikhs entertained – offering whole sheep roasted on spits over charcoal fires built in a trench, with the eye going to the most honoured guest. The men sat cross-legged and were served by the women, who would themselves eat later. Christopher could never forget this superabundance of food, and during our whole marriage he never got over his worry about there being enough to eat at our parties. His look roamed anxiously over the dishes brought in, measuring them unhappily against the previous excess. Indeed the very magnificence of the Arab style of entertaining soared above the practical details of time and place; with the desert providing the place, and the position of the sun the time, such considerations were meaningless. So we fully realized that the European habit of sending little stiff white invitation cards summoning guests to an appointed place at an appointed time on an appointed day might bring unexpected results. Either, mindful of European etiquette, the answer would arrive promptly, or it would not. Another hazard was that the guests might turn up extremely late, or – and this could be treated as a compliment – a guest might bring various members of his family with him in anticipation of a really good party. Anyhow, whichever variation the guest chose apart from the conventional one caused a newly married wife such as myself a great deal of anguish. Furthermore, our amiable 'terrorist' in the kitchen proved not always to be a pillar of support. One evening we were giving a dinner party; it was the sit-down kind (although later we resorted to buffets). The guests had arrived more or less on time – within an hour or so anyway – and in more or less the right numbers. (Pre-dinner drinks involved an elaborate deception. Many of our guests had departed from the Islamic law of abstinence during their years as students in the *quartier latin* of Paris and were keen to have a drink, but did not wish to be seen openly disobeying Allah. We hit on a way to accommodate them, which was to circulate trays of drinks, including some genuine fruit juices and others laced with gin or vodka, but all looking the same.) We then proceeded into the pretty white dining-room with a high ceiling and a glass door leading out on to the terrace. (The Department of the Environment had done us proud with a new grey carpet finishing at the required distance from the wall, peacock-coloured curtains and chairs covered in a tangerine-coloured material.) The table was decorated with various trophies inherited from Christopher's grandfather: two very tall silver candelabras (had we used them in our Chelsea house the candles would have tickled the ceiling), Crown Derby side-plates, Victorian silver forks and spoons, and a cut-glass rose bowl in the centre containing, not roses, but the beautiful, luminous zinnias from the garden. The placing for the guests had been carefully worked out according to protocol (but more of that anon), and Lakhdar (the waiter engaged for dinner parties) had distributed the plates for the first course. I felt quite pleased about it all. But this complacency was to be shortlived, for no sooner were Grandfather Brice's plates before us than to my horror I saw the 'terrorist' storming in from the kitchen to remove them all again, unfortunately before we had been given the opportunity of eating anything off them. I guessed what had happened. We possessed two sets of plates suitable for the hors-d'œuvre course. Lakhdar had chosen the plainer ones but I knew that Mohammed very much admired the other ones, painted with fish or game fowl in the true Victorian tradition, and was

obviously determined we should have them. The two of them were at
that very moment wrangling in the kitchen. Now diplomats learn
pretty soon that, at times like that, panic is to be avoided. Such
administrative hiccups must above all not be allowed to intrude on the
guests' enjoyment. Instead the host should imply that whatever has
happened is in fact synonymous with a particular facet of British life.
So when Mohammed reappeared and triumphantly placed one of
Grandpa Brice's best fish and fowl plates before each one of us, I
implied that we had just been through a very normal British ritual
which was to show off as much as possible of the very fine porcelain
made in Britain. And, of course, the further away one was from home
the better the chance of success.

The conversations at these parties were very different from those at
pre-independence occasions. Our Algerian guests, coming from the
civil service, the government, and business circles, were of very high
intelligence and all of them totally committed to helping the country
function again. One of their major problems was a lack of trained and
qualified Algerians. I remember at that particular evening Ben Habyles
was our principal guest and was sitting on my right. We were discussing
the lack of doctors; the *pied noir* ones having departed and there being
an insufficient number of qualified Algerian doctors to replace them. I
had heard that the Bulgarian government, wishing to assist Algeria,
had sent some of their doctors to help bear the load in the countryside –
the Bled – where there was the greatest shortage of medical assistance. I
asked him how the experiment was working out as there must, presumably, be an insuperable language problem. He agreed this was
indeed so and that there had been many cases of misunderstandings
over prescriptions, such as *swallowing* suppositories, plastic covering
and all. Then, with the whimsical smile which characterized his sensitive, aquiline features, he said, 'If only they had sent vets instead of
doctors, there wouldn't have been the same problem.'

In those early days of Algerian independence the wives of Algerian
officials didn't quite know where they stood. Neither Prime Minister
Ben Bella nor the Minister for Foreign Affairs, Mohammed Boute-
flicka, were married so there was no first lady to set the pattern
and create an example for the others to follow. Sometimes the husbands, just to be on the safe side, left their wives at home on such social

occasions. One day at the French Embassy I saw Layachi Yaker alone and asked him where his wife was. 'Oh, she had no one for the children,' he said. The next time I saw her – she was a graduate from a German university and an interpreter – I said how sorry I had been not to have seen her at the French party. Not one bit pleased, she remarked, 'But Layachi told me it was a men only occasion.' Layachi, out of fear of doing the wrong thing, had misled everyone.

I became very close to some of these young wives and we used to have long discussions about the place of women in Algerian society. Indeed, although the Algerian woman held a dominant position in the home, she still had a long way to go in establishing herself outside it. A large proportion of women in the streets were still veiled. It was said that many of them favoured retaining the veil for reasons of coquetry. Although the white veil held tightly across the bridge of the nose caused various nasal problems, it undoubtedly set off beautiful dark eyes to best advantage. But I remember being perplexed as to the actual degree of modesty which the veil represented when I saw two young Algerian women arrive at an only *fairly* secluded part of the beach at the Club des Pins and start discarding one layer of veiling after the other until they stood in their bikinis. They then took to the sea with shrill cries of excitement. There was a charming story about a journalist who, on learning that an Englishwoman had been living in the Kasbah for the last thirty years, went to interview her for his paper. He came across the heavily-veiled lady and asked her if she had become accustomed to Arab ways. 'Well, one thing I've never got used to', she said with a strong cockney accent, 'is this bloody 'aybag', and immediately pulled off the offending veil, uncovering strong Anglo-Saxon features.

That autumn in 1962 brought two surprises. I realized one day in November that everything had taken on a greenish look, and when that happens then it can only mean one thing, and that is a baby. I felt rather put out by this development, having just decided to start learning Arabic. Christopher had even found me a teacher. But I decided that contending both with nausea and one of the most difficult languages in the world at the same time would be too much; so I just concentrated on being pregnant.

Christopher's surprise was an OBE. He had been told of this

honour, to be announced in the New Year's honours list, about a month or so beforehand. Officer of the Order of the British Empire could be seen as rather inappropriate in a country which had just gone through the most savage struggle to rid itself of its colonial yoke, but that couldn't be helped. An OBE is reserved for officers of the grade of First Secretary who have conducted themselves with courage in a place of danger. Frank Benham, the Embassy 'fixer', was awarded the MBE in the same list. This was the appropriate award for his rank. I think that, on the whole, people are rather unkind about the award of honours to civil servants – the Queen's dogs wear her collars. I feel a servant of the Crown deserves a few compensations. He works for the government, giving an equal commitment to whichever political party is in power. It is true that his pay and conditions of service have for the moment become more secure whilst those of his equals in the private sector have become less so, but to set against these qualified advantages are a whole string of disadvantages such as the health hazards brought on by serving in alien climates; the hellish inconvenience of being perpetually on the move, and often at very short notice; the pressures on family life and so on. But I will return to this later.

Christopher's own reaction to the news of his honour was atypical. He was not one bit pleased. He was at that time anxiously awaiting his promotion from First Secretary to the next rank of Counsellor. This promotion was due and the climb up the ladder is tough, all the more so as he had entered the service immediately after the war in company with the excessive number of other young candidates, all of whom were very able, ambitious, and jockeying for position. The arrival of the letter bearing what should have been such good news merely filled him with panic that the medal was in lieu of promotion. However, he enjoyed the letters of congratulations. (Eventually his fears proved to be without foundation as his promotion followed a few months later.)

Meanwhile the new Algerian leaders were striving to make an impression internationally. Ben Bella, with his addiction to the cult of personality, went on missions abroad to proclaim the triumphant ending of the struggle against imperialist domination and the setting up of their Islamic socialist state. In return many foreign heads of state and parliamentarians were invited to Algiers. There was the Chinese Foreign Minister, Chou En-lai (the French pronunciation of this name was 'cabbage in milk'); Che Guevara, the Cuban revolutionary hero (in my view the most devastatingly attractive male I have ever felt moved by); President Tito from Yugoslavia, with his old face heavily made up and his majestic French wife beside him – and many others. Evening receptions were given in their honour at the Palais du Peuple (erstwhile Palais d'Été). These started at 10.30 in the evening, with Ben Bella receiving his guests. I can still feel the touch of his soft welcoming handshake and the warmth of his charming smile before we circulated with our glasses of fruit juice to talk to the other guests. On the edge of these gatherings, either talking to the Chinese or Cuban diplomats or standing alone, there was Colonel Boumédienne, chief of the Algerian Army. With his caramel-coloured eyes and mid-brown hair, and smart, military-style, perfectly creased trousers of cavalry twill, he was in no way a typical-looking Arab. He was called *'numéro un bis'* rather than the number two, and guests at these parties laughingly used to say, 'Look, there is Boumédienne plotting to overthrow Ben Bella.' (This actually happened soon after we left Algeria in 1965, when Ben Bella was arrested by his own army and returned to prison, but this time an Algerian one.) Boumédienne's brooding, silent presence injected a somewhat forbidding atmosphere into these affairs. One evening Christopher took on a bet from one of his colleagues that he would not succeed in engaging Boumédienne in conversation. Bravely Christopher went up to him and stubbornly tried to draw him out in a discussion about the Arabic language. (Boumédienne was a great scholar, whereas Ben Bella with his French education often used French words rather than Arabic ones in his speeches.) But Christopher lost his bet, for Boumédienne, having listened to him for a moment, turned on his heel and resumed his place, alone and brooding, on the periphery of the party.

Members of the British Labour Party were among the official guests to the new Republic of Algeria. In July 1963 we gave a lunch party for two of them: Fenner Brockway and Maurice Edelman. I had had a last-minute worry, having belatedly discovered that Fenner was a vegetarian – I should have guessed. However, I got my own back when during lunch, noticing my swollen figure, he said in his usual kindly way, 'Well, my dear, when's the happy event?' and became most alarmed when I said, 'The day before yesterday.'

Professor Balogh was invited to advise President Ben Bella on agrarian reform and never forgave him for ignoring this advice. And there was the visit of Barbara Castle – marvellously pretty and beautifully dressed, but in a rumbustious mood, which brought on an amusing incident. Christopher and I were among the guests at the supper party arranged for her by the Ministry of Foreign Affairs at a highly attractive restaurant specializing in local dishes. Our friends Socrates, 'le Colonial Office', Aziz Hocene, his stiff collar done to a turn, and many others were there, and also the interpreter designated to help Mrs Castle, whose very basic French was in no way sufficient to carry on a conversation in spite of the bravado which she injected. However, she felt she did not need him and entirely excluded him. (I remember how hurt be looked.) The incident started by Barbara snubbing Christopher. This happened at the beginning of the meal when we were all making our selection from the long list of North African specialities on the menu. Barbara asked Christopher for some clarification on a particular point in the Évian Agreements. He answered, having in his usual way carefully thought out what he was to say, but prefaced his reply with, 'I think ...'. Before he could go on there was an outburst from the lady, who snapped, 'Diplomats are not paid to think, they are paid to know.' Our Algerian friends, who had already observed the interpreter's resigned look, felt it was time to intercede after the snubbing of their friend Christopher. They decided deliberately to misunderstand when she started talking about Algerian oil, calling it 'huile'. (This dangerous practice of assuming that similar words in each of the languages have a similar meaning is described as 'faux amis' by the French.) 'But, Madame le Ministre, you must of course know that Algeria has no "huile". Were we discussing Tunisia – for whom it is a major export – then of course it would be quite different.' Infuriated, the fiery British politician said, 'What can you be talking about; everyone in the world knows that not one single drop of "huile" has ever been found in Tunisia.' With their tongues positively dislodging their cheekbones, they continued this charade until both the disposed interpreter and discomfited British diplomat had been suitably revenged, and then with a great deal of charm and profuse apologies they explained that they now realized that she had been discussing crude oil whereas they had been referring to olive oil, and they were '*désolés*' about the misunderstanding.

However, very soon these highly cultivated young men from the Ministry of Foreign Affairs were themselves to pass through an embarrassing period. The Algerian and Moroccan governments had become locked in conflict over an old Saharan dispute, and threatening noises were coming from each side. President Ben Bella, whose military sensitivities were still very acute after the seven-year Franco-Algerian war, felt he must prove himself to be in earnest and ordered his parliamentarians and civil servants into uniform as a proof of his intent. This brought on the incongruous sight of the cream of Algeria's intelligentsia – the young diplomats – appearing at public functions in battle fatigues. Aziz Hocene's stiff collar had to go by the board. Their embarrassed looks topping the camouflaged khaki battledress and baggy trousers added to the farce. We teased them unmercifully and then gradually, little by little, small refinements in their outfits started to appear. First a silk scarf knotted round the neck, then a shirt, then a collar and tie; to be followed by the replacement of the shapeless Baba-like horrors with highly-creased trousers. The 'war' then came to an end and they were allowed to put aside the whole gear.

There were unexpected repercussions from another official visit. These came with the arrival of a ship of the Indian Navy in the port of Algiers. This ship had been a British destroyer previously. The Algerians, who had been looking forward to comparing notes with these brother revolutionaries who, like themselves, had thrown off the yoke of colonialism, welcomed the captain and his crew eagerly but expressed shocked surprise when they noticed that the Indian naval officers and other ranks were wearing the same uniform as that of their erstwhile oppressors. The Indians disappointed them even further by saying that there had been no reason for changing the Royal Navy design, as it was such a practical one. But there was even worse to come. The Algerian authorities overwhelmed their visitors – their comrades in arms as they saw them – with invitations and hospitality, but were finally forced to recognize that the captain and his officers were focusing their attention wholly on the British ambassador's whisky and the British embassy secretaries. And the sailors were busy exploring the town's shadiest dives, in a way far removed from the moral behaviour of sons of the Revolution.

Even the Indian ambassador's dinner party in their honour nearly ended in disaster. Sheila Sen, the ambassadress, had an English mother and an Indian father. They had four children, two of whom were at the Dragon School in Oxford. (When Sheila arrived in Algiers soon after independence her sari had attracted the attention of her taxi driver, who asked if she was from '*le metropole*'. She did not realize this meant mainland France, and flew into a rage with him, thinking he was accusing her of being a nightclub singer.) They entertained lavishly. Her arrangements included one innovation which was to use different coloured napkins – red, yellow, green, mauve, etc. – to designate the guests' places at the table. Her guests that particular evening came from the Algerian government, from Foreign Affairs, and the Ghanaian ambassador and his wife from the diplomatic corps. Our sari-clad hostess, elegant and tiny, ushered us into the dining-room and started to allocate the places. She bent over her plan and without really looking up said to one guest, 'You're green', and then to another, 'You're lilac', and so on. It was somehow inevitable that when she came to the flamboyantly attired, dusky Ghanaian ambassadress she would launch herself straight on to the rocks. 'And you're b . . .', she stuttered, just averting disaster.

Meanwhile the Ewart-Biggs domestic scene was not exactly free of problems. The birth of my son was a dramatic one. I had determined to have my baby in Algiers, against the advice of many, rather than go home or to the American hospital in nearby southern Spain. The last remaining gynaecologist, a particularly rude and aggressive Frenchman, had been looking after me. It was generally thought that he was very good at delivering babies, and every time I saw him I checked that he was not planning to join the general *Pied Noir* exodus of that time. Many of the safeguards for the rights of the European community, laid down in the Évian Agreements, had not been honoured. Property if found empty was requisitioned by the authorities. In fact at one point it only took the time required by a family to go to the movies for their flat to be declared a '*bien vacant*' and requisitioned. Many departed to southern France and Corsica under cover of night, in order to avoid settling their tax debts. But *le professeur* Ezes assured me he had no intention of going.

The day arrived – or rather the night, as babies make a habit of entering this world during the early hours – and Christopher, returning from one of the Palais du Peuple rave-ups, said, 'Are you sure?' I said, 'Yes', and we drove down the deserted dark streets of Algiers to the Clinique Laverne, where a bed had been reserved for the birth. The porter, half asleep at the entrance, asked the name of my doctor. '*Le professeur* Ezes,' I said, remembering gratefully that he was meant to be good at delivering babies. '*Parti*,' said the porter happily. Christopher, keeping a grip on himself, asked who was replacing him. '*Personne*' – even more happily. The midwife then gave Christopher a list of doctors who, she said, might be persuaded to rouse themselves and come and deliver, but she was sure there was no point in telephoning them. Christopher set off in his Jaguar through the deserted streets. His face was as white as his car. There was no answer at the first address on his list so he rushed on to the next. This was a huge block of flats and the entrance door was shut and locked. He rang and rang, but nothing happened. Completely losing his grip on himself, Christopher took off one of his shoes and frenziedly hammered the door with it. Windows started to open everywhere with exasperated Pieds Noirs leaning out and telling him to shut up. He shouted out the name of the doctor he had been given and eventually a very surly, unshaven, possibly slightly drunk man appeared at the front door, struggling into his rather grimy shirt, and declared himself to be the doctor. Without any preamble whatsoever Christopher manhandled him into the back of the car and drove off at such a high speed, skidding round each corner, that the doctor was visibly shaken on his arrival at the clinic. But – as it happened – his arrival exactly coincided with that of our son. By then I had reached the point of not caring about anything any more, with one exception. This was when, lying resigned and with my eyes closed, I had felt the little Algerian nurse lifting up my left hand and heard her saying pensively, '*Quelles jolies bagues.*' In spite of the imminent arrival of the baby, I sat bolt upright and snatched my hand away.

However, the trauma of the birth was soon forgotten and Christopher happily added a spirited, highly exaggerated account of it to his list of anecdotes. But I knew that I owed my son to the Algerian revolution. Had I not benefited from the natural phenomenon of wars bringing in their wake a compensating surplus of male infants?

However, the baby – soon to be christened Robin Thomas Fitzherbert by the old Padre in his little church – turned out to be a true son of the revolution in more ways than one. Its spirit was deeply embedded in him and he voiced it – very loudly – throughout most of the day and night. (Mohammed flinched at the noise and he made a resolve there and then never to get married.) As I became more and more exhausted, my delight at his birth was somewhat diminished. The nights without enough sleep, the August heat, together with the debilitating effect of a breast infection contracted soon after his birth, single out that period as one of despairing physical weariness. My one aim was to get sufficient rest each day – a modest but all-consuming ambition.

Of course this difficult period would have been resolved with the help of a nanny. The problem arose because we had replaced the old, pre-independence Nanny Swire too hastily on a flying visit to London. From among the candidates we chose a girl who was a trained nurse – a priceless asset in medically starved Algeria – and our concentration on this qualification blinded us to the girl's empty eyes and loose mouth combined with the non-committal reference from her matron. However, although we had not been alert, Henrietta certainly was. On our return to Algeria, whenever the small two-year-old sighted the SRN, she would open her mouth and let out blood-curdling cries whilst cramponing herself on to me as if her very life depended on it. We thought this would pass, but it didn't. There were terrible scenes. 'Oh, darling, here's nice Margaret come to take you for a lovely walk.' Scream, scream, scream. 'Well, I don't know – I'm sure – what I've ever done to her.' 'No, no, Margaret, of course you haven't done *anything*. She's just being silly.'

Things were pretty bad, but we thought we could stick it out until after the birth – due any minute – and then review the position. However, a sinister development took matters out of our hands. I found her, one morning, in tears – not at all characteristic of the steely girl. 'What's wrong, Margaret?' I asked. 'I've lost my passport.' 'Well, that's certainly a nuisance, but it's not the end of the world. Do you know where you lost it?' The weeping increased: 'I didn't lose it, it was stolen.' A small alarm bell went off somewhere inside me. 'Oh, have you any idea by whom?' 'Yes, by a chap who said he was in the KGB.' With the alarm bell now clanging madly I said, 'But where on earth did you meet him?' Final bombshell: 'Jenny [the naval attaché's au pair] and I were picked up by him and another man in the rue Michelet and went back to their flat with them.'

I said I had better ring my husband. I was feeling distinctly weak. 'Oh, darling, are you busy – there's trouble at home.' 'Well, yes, I am in the middle of something, but what is it?' 'Margaret's lost her passport.' 'Surely that can wait until this evening.' 'But she says it was the KGB who took it.' Pause – new voice: 'I'll be home in a minute.'

The whole sordid little story was pieced together following a long cross-examination, and it transpired that the two girls, regular solicitors in the main street of Algiers on their day off, had on this occasion gone with a couple of men to a nearby flat, and whilst Margaret was busily engaged with one of them in the bedroom her passport was removed from her handbag. We realized the likelihood of the two men having posed as KGB agents to impress the girls, but as the incident coincided exactly with the aftermath of the John Vassall episode and directives had been circulated madly round embassies urging members of the staff to increase their vigilance concerning security matters, no risks could be taken. The two girls were therefore immediately dispatched by air, with a bowler-hatted MI5 representative meeting them at Heathrow to give them an extensive grilling. Margaret departed without a word and with the same impassive, empty look in her eyes, and we never knew if the whole thing had been a hoax or not. But we could be certain of one thing: it was only Henrietta who recognized the girl's deep psychopathic tendency and it wasn't the child's fault that we wouldn't listen.

Another drama was the kidnapping of Konrad. I had been out shopping one day with him as usual sitting on the back seat of my new Deux Chevaux. When I reached home I parked the car in the garage and opened the back door to let him out. My heart stood still when I saw the empty back seat. Realizing he must have escaped out of the open window, I raced back to the junction just below the old Consulate building and asked the policeman on point duty if he had seen a spaniel. 'Yes,' he said, continuing to direct the traffic, '*un petit cocker rouge* who jumped out of your car and was picked up by another passing car.' He then became visibly concerned when he saw me starting to cry. 'I might be able to help you find him,' he said promptly and, deserting his rostrum, leaving the traffic to organize itself, he got into my car. I wondered how he could possibly know but trustingly obeyed his directions. We drove on and on towards what had been Bellecourt (although it and many other street names had been changed since independence; and it was even said that Place Anatole France in Oran had become Place Anatole Algérie). My companion, who was looking more and more excited, finally called a halt in a sordid little street and said, '*Voilà la voiture*,' pointing to a parked car. I ran over to it and there, tied down on the floor by the back seat, was poor Konrad. He looked a distinctly different animal from his usual adored, cosseted self. My friend and I peered in at him and in a moment the owner of the car appeared. 'You've got my dog,' I told him, wondering whether by reclaiming him I was about to deprive the man of his '*déjeuner*'. However, without any demur he untied Konrad and handed him back, saying he had merely wished to save '*le joli petit cocker*' from being run over. I thanked my friend profusely and drove him back to his rostrum, where the undirected traffic had by that time come to a standstill. From then on Konrad's '*enlèvement*' became one of Christopher's favourite dinner-party stories.

Once the domestic scene had settled down again with the help of the newly arrived, slightly rounded and very warm-hearted Alison – the replacement for Margaret – I was liberated to take part in activities outside the home. We had by that time built up a wide circle of friends: people drawn from Algerian circles, the other embassies, the press corps, the British community and the French *coopérants* arrived since independence to work in co-operation with the Algerians to build the country up again. We liked to think of them all as friends, but of course the truth is that diplomats end up with only a few real friends in a very wide circle of acquaintances. I remember deciding the main criterion of a friend as someone I felt able to telephone in the morning with an invitation to dinner the same evening – replacing a guest who had fallen out – without giving offence. However, the conditions of life in newly independent Algeria in themselves provided a particular binding quality with some lasting friendships. Among the '*chers collègues*' (as diplomats of other missions are described) Luigi and Alix Fontana Giusti of the Italian embassy were our closest friends. Luigi possessed that priceless gift of mimicry and produced a perfect rendering of the *pied noir* voice which had us all in fits of laughter. (Indeed it was those very same intonations which were to tell me many years later, when I answered my telephone in Radnor Walk, that he and Alix had been posted to London. There is no news that gladdens a diplomatic heart more than the news that he or she is about to recross paths with cronies from some previous posting.) Alix herself had needed all the composure she could summon when, at the height of the OAS saga prior to independence, she gave birth to twin boys. Francesco was safely delivered, and while we all clustered round Luigi in the hospital waiting-room smothering him with congratulations the doctor arrived from the delivery room with a startled look on his face and said, '*Mais il y en a encore un autre.*' And that was Ranieri.

Christopher's opposite number in the American embassy was called John Root, and he and his wife Louise seemed to have a lot of children. Poor John had to make a difficult decision whilst she was away having the last of them in the American hospital in the south of Spain (following Christopher's harrowing experience over the birth of our son in Algiers, many expectant diplomatic wives were sent off to the security of this hospital). A group of children including his and some from our embassy had been playing with a dog who was subsequently suspected of having rabies. There was no proof whatsoever that the dog really was rabid or that the children had been in sufficiently close physical proximity to the dog's jaws to be in any danger. Moreover – at that time – the series of injections necessary to give immunization against the disease were extremely painful. About eighteen doses had to be injected into the stomach and no one would wish such an ordeal on to their worst enemy. In spite of many assurances that the children were only running a minor risk, John decided that his children had better undergo the treatment. 'Because you see I really couldn't have Louise coming back to find all the children down with rabies,' he said rather apologetically.

The position of doyen of the diplomatic corps was held by the

French ambassador, George Gorse, a politician. He and his Lebanese wife, both intelligent, cultivated and amusing, resided in Les Oliviers, the beautiful mansion reserved for the French representative, and they entertained lavishly. Their chef upheld the great French culinary tradition, and I can still remember the elaborate and exquisite dishes served there to the accompaniment of beautiful rose-coloured champagne. (I think M. Gorse was keen on me so we were quite often invited there.) One evening we went to their farewell party for the ambassador from one of the South American countries. He was a soldier by profession who was returning home to take command of the national army. Our host made a speech; the guests assembled in the garden surrounded by walls of Bougainvillaea and hedges of pink geraniums. 'We are here today', he said, 'to say goodbye to M. l'Ambassadeur and wish him well. But what can one wish the General of an army? For my part I would like to wish him peace, but what sort of future could that possibly present to one of his profession – and yet, to wish him the reverse ...'

The absurdly good-looking young couple, Michel and Corinne de la Perrière, stood out among our *pied noir* friends. Corinne's father, Jacques Chevallier, Mayor of Algiers, had previously worked very hard to negotiate an end to OAS hostilities, and Michel and Corinne had committed themselves to the future of Algeria by taking out Algerian nationality. There were also two Algerian girls whom we knew well and admired: Leila Hocene, holding a responsible position in the Ministry of Health, and Meriem Belmihoub, a lawyer, had taken their places among the smallish group of emancipated women, determined to work for the future both of Algeria and Algerian women.

At the embassy there was the newly arrived military attaché, most fittingly named Colonel Slingsby, and his marvellously pretty green-eyed wife Sally. She with extraordinary energy and enthusiasm contributed so much to embassy life and he carried out his important task of liaising with the Algerian army headed by the inscrutable Boumédienne. Laurence spoke perfect French, contrary to one's expectations of British army officers. Indeed it was said that he expressed himself more cogently in that language than his own, as French prevented him from including his usual flow of 'ums', 'actuallys' and 'you knows'.

There were no lack of romance among the members of the diplomatic corps. First, there was the engagement between Stephanie Carter, Second Secretary at our Embassy, and the Counsellor at the Danish Embassy, who delighted in the name of Bengt Pontopiddan. Then Michael Frost, a young Third Secretary in the administrative department of our embassy, married one of the highly attractive and likeable nurses at the American hospital. (My joy and surprise, years later, knew no bounds when, on a lecture tour of the west coast of America aimed at dissuading potential funders of the IRA, there at Seattle Airport was Michael Frost, HM Consul, smiling all over his face.)

And of course there were many, many more people we knew and admired – people who made up an important part of our lives and with whom the bonds of friendship were strong enough to stand up to the passage of time. The arrival of peace enabled us all to make a serious exploration of the country. We went on trips along the beautiful coastal strip, the rich fertile plains of the Matidja and down towards and into the mighty Sahara. Algeria's inheritance of Roman civilization is enormous. The beautifully conserved Roman town of Tipaza, set on the seashore some fifty miles south of Algiers, provided a perfect bit of Sunday tourism; as did Timgad, a Roman military garrison with its lofty pillars still standing high and intact, although on our first visit our eyes would not believe the desecration scrawled on the immortal stone: 'L'OAS vous écoute'. And there was the desert oasis of Bou-Saada. But perhaps Ghardaia, the mysterious Mozabite city, was the most memorable. Travelling south along about 500 miles of perfect French road from Algiers, the visitor felt himself taken in and folded into the inner warmth of the town.

On two occasions Christopher and I left the children with their dependable and much-loved Alison and went on short holidays, first to Tunisia and then to Morocco. These were countries which had experienced quite different colonial histories and whose people had little affection for their Algerian neighbours whom they found to be both alien and alienating. We visited our ambassador to Tunisia in the marvellous British residence just outside Carthage. This splendid mansion, which had originally been a present from the Bey to the British Crown, even had a private railway station at the end of the

enormous garden. Its drawing room was so vast that the fitted carpet
was reputed to be the largest to come off the Department of the
Environment loom. There we met our old friends the Davidsons. Alan
was the first secretary at the embassy and had just written a book on
Mediterranean fish. Christopher, with all the arrogance of the author
of two novels, asked him who was publishing it. 'The embassy
Roneo machine,' Alan answered. We went to El Djem and, having
travelled along the long straight road leading to this perfectly pre-
served Roman amphitheatre standing alone, aloof, scorning any
attendant presence, we were left without words and in awe of its lone
and majestic beauty.

In Morocco we first visited Fez, and Christopher settled down
happily in the great luxury of the Hotel Palais Jamai. I took this
opportunity of saying that it seemed strange to me that we always
stayed in top-grade hotels, remembering my own money-conscious
childhood. 'But any other hotels in this part of the world are nothing
better than doss-houses,' he said. I was not convinced, so when we got
to Marrakesh, with a much put-upon, resigned look, Christopher
booked into a second-class hotel. Next morning he failed to conceal
his triumph and satisfaction when I got up having had an excrucia-
tingly uncomfortable night scratching.

We left Algiers on 1 May 1965 – Labour Day. There were demonstrations going on in the town and we had to take a roundabout route to
avoid being held up. Sitting beside Christopher in the embassy car –
the white Jaguar having been taken down to the port ready for
embarkation the night before – I was silently weeping. Memories
passed through my mind as we went by all the familiar places. First,
just below our old hospital building, the Hôtel Saint-Georges, where
we had had our first lunch and whose elegance had become dulled and
fly-ridden; then the old consulate building and neighbouring church,
now bereft of the old Padre; just below the *carrefour* the Palais du
Peuple, scene of so many government receptions, and the memory of
Ben Bella's soft handshake; then down the rue Michelet past
Meriem's dress shop; and the central food market where I had
witnessed the brutal scene early after our arrival; and near by the
expensive French-owned *boulangerie* where I had always bought the

special bread for cocktail-party sandwiches. Finally the Aletti Hotel, home of the news-hungry journalists, and right at the bottom the old French *amirauté*, set in the beautiful old port of Algiers, where we had once gone to an exhibition given by an amateur artist in the French Navy and bought a picture which has ever since hung in Robin's room to remind him of the country of his birth. Finally, as we approached the *quai* along the seafront road, I was reminded – almost physically – of the day I had narrowly missed meeting head on an angry crowd from the Kasbah hell-bent on finding a European on whom to take revenge for some OAS atrocity.

All these were places and incidents which had formed part of my life, experiences which had drawn out of me a whole new range of sensitivities and had, I knew, transformed the person I had been on arrival at those very same docks three and a half years ago, experiences which had given birth to new tolerances and new intolerances. I had acquired a far better ability to deal with difficulties and upheavals, but also a deeply held revulsion towards brutality and violence, a revulsion which has manifested itself through emotional, mental and physical reactions.

The sheer misery brought on by departure was harder to rationalize. After all, it had been a difficult posting with many worrying and unhappy moments. The pressure put on our marriage had been considerable. My worries about the small children's health and welfare had in some ways isolated me from Christopher's preoccupations. He, in turn, had felt excluded by my concentration on the children. So why the tears after so many imperfections? Perhaps because it had been the very difficulties and demands of the place which made it so hard to leave. Verlaine rightly described departures in his famous lines: '*Partir c'est mourir un peu – c'est laisser un peu de soi-même dans chaque lieu, dans chaque endroit.*'

The attachment was so strong that many years later I went back there with the children for a holiday – but that was another life.

When we arrived at the steamer which was to take us away, we found a lot of friends who had come to see us off. Some of them had brought farewell presents. A Kabyle bracelet, two small white Algerian rugs with the children's initials woven in the corners, a box of fresh dates, and so on. Frank Benham was the last to say goodbye.

He had made all the arrangements for the journey and wanted to give us some final advice. He warned Christopher to keep a very watchful eye on his Jaguar when it was disembarked at Marseilles. He explained that the *pied noir* dockers – so many congregated there, close to their beloved Algeria – identified cars with Arabic number-plates and would gleefully cry out, '*Ah, voilà, le spaghetti,*' and possibly drop those particular cars into the water when swinging them from the ship's hold to the quayside. Their feelings towards independent Algeria remained bitter and vindictive.

The last wave – the last tear – and that was the end of Algeria for us.

5

Quarantine

The return to a home posting is sometimes quite a let-down for a diplomat and his family. Logically speaking, the reverse should be true for whereas an overseas posting presents him with the unknown, returning home should restore the safe and familiar. But the truth of the matter is that the slot abroad can be an easier one for him to fill than the rather ambiguous one that he, as a foreign servant, finds at home. The return often brings with it a sense of everything having changed beyond recognition, when in reality it is the traveller who has become a different person. The struggle to adapt to circumstances in a foreign setting is natural, but the same struggle on returning to base is not. Again, the feeling of being an onlooker, just outside the circle, is acceptable when abroad but deeply disturbing when surrounded by your own countrymen. Finally, as is usually the case, the difficulties of readaptation fall more heavily on the wife and children than on the husband. He will take up his new job at the Foreign Office, which, although more draining, is the same kind of work, while she will in many ways have to start again from scratch as regards children's schools, setting up house and finding herself something to do.

But our initial concern on returning home in early May 1965 was for Konrad. The thought of parting from him for the necessary six months was weighing heavily during the whole journey home, and the arrangements for putting him into quarantine already took up a thick file. Any wild thought we might have had of smuggling him through customs – under a rug on the back seat, in the boot heavily drugged – were abandoned when we realized that he had become the centre of attention not only on the boat between Algiers and Marseilles but to an

85

even greater extent between Calais and Dover. We had gone to a great
deal of trouble to track down the best kennels and, after obtaining a
list in the London area – accessible for visiting – we had even persuaded our contact in the Ministry of Agriculture to go against his
professional ethics and put a small, discreet cross against the ones
with the best reputations. We finally settled for an establishment in
Mill Hill, having followed much the same system as for selecting
boarding-schools for children. But getting him there was not at all
simple. The quarantine regulations are so strict that even before the
dog sets foot on British soil the authorities must take him in charge.
This is to counter the dangers of his becoming rabid within moments
of arrival. We had, therefore, made arrangements for Konrad's transportation to Mill Hill. (This turned out to cost about the same as
having a child returned to its boarding-school by helicopter.) When
the ferry arrived at Dover, all the other cars and passengers disembarked and we were left sitting in the Jaguar alone in the hold of the boat.
Konrad had obviously had a premonition of what was to happen: he
lay on the floor with his head on his paws, wearing his tragic spaniel
look. Then suddenly a black London taxi arrived, and on its back seat
was an ominous-looking wooden box with bars down one side. There
could be no doubt as to its purpose. Konrad was lowered gently into
the box with a bowl of water and his familiar rug. But the most
poignant moment was when he rejected the After Eight chocolates I
put beside him. The lid of the box was then closed and the taxi
rumbled off the ferry, leaving Christopher and myself feeling
distinctly disembodied.

Some people might question the strict necessity of the British quarantine regulations; the vast majority of countries are satisfied if
visiting dogs and cats have an up-to-date inoculation certificate. But
the British authorities – advised by the veterinary profession (who,
incidentally, own and run most of the highly profitable quarantine
kennels) – maintain that to make quite sure that rabies never threat-
ens the wild life of Britain an incubation period of six months is the
only safeguard. No doubt they are right, but the major sufferers are
those who work abroad, as not many visitors would be foolish
enough to bring their pets with them knowing of these regulations.

Initially the decision must be made as to whether to try to retain the animal's affection, during the six months' separation, by constant visiting or to leave it strictly alone and hope for the best when it returns home. We favoured the first course and, after allowing for the three weeks we had been told he would need to settle down, we (or rather I) started the weekly visits to Mill Hill. The first visit was very disturbing – Konrad was altogether out of sorts: coat staring and a dismal look. His kennel maid, who, like most people who met him, had become an ardent admirer, said he had been pining but would soon get used to the new routine. The circumstances of these weekly visits were rather bizarre, and only to be encountered in Britain. On the arrival of the owner, the kennel maid went to fetch the dog from his personal kennel and put him in an exercise pen measuring about six yards by four. (No physical contact was allowed between dogs in case one developed the disease and gave it to another.) The owner was then ushered into the pen, given a chair to sit on and unceremoniously locked in. This was to prevent a demented owner from making a dash for it with his dog. To begin with, feeling foolish, I used to stay only for about fifteen minutes, ample time for a quick word, a bit of brushing and combing and presentation of chocolate drops. However, the kennel maid, entirely concerned for Konrad's well-being, said that these short visits upset Konrad, who would then bellow for hours after my departure and upset all the other inmates. I must stay for a minimum of half an hour, she said. It was important not to reflect too closely on the sight one presented on these visits; for, after all, most of us want to keep what reputation we can for a semblance of sanity. The sight of a seemingly conventional human being sitting under lock and key talking to his or her pet – and on a rainy day doing it all under an umbrella – was surely beyond the limits of credibility. I was never sure whether the fact that the same charade was going on in the neighbouring pen made it better or worse. Some visits were less calm than others. When the children were there Konrad, jubilant, would jump at them (they were too short to be jumped *up* at) and topple them over to the accompaniment of howls of protest.

The day of deliverance finally came, and when we arrived to collect Konrad we found him posing for his kennel maid to take a last photograph. That done, he happily jumped into the back of the car, as if the previous six months had never happened, and resumed his former highly priviliged life. But I wondered if those particular kennels ever again accepted a dog coming from North Africa, because of the fleas. Not only did that particularly virulent brand refuse to be dislodged from his own person, they even succeeded in spreading themselves over every other dog in the kennels.

Our own re-entry into British life – although mercifully we did not have to endure such an extreme form of acclimatization – was not entirely dissimilar. We felt we were on the fringe, as if our country-men were occupying the citadel surrounded by a moat, and we were outside it. All our efforts to throw out bridges to cross the moat and enter the citadel seemed to fail. It was as if we were having to undergo a similar process of integration as in a foreign country. Often a family will have been away for about six years, as it is usual – although in no way a rule – that diplomatic officers serve two postings abroad to one at home. We were returning after only one overseas posting at our own request, having specifically asked to come back to London. I remember feeling the need to be engulfed by the security of British institutions after the irregularities of life in Algeria. In many cases diplomatic service families prefer to have a higher proportion of overseas postings because their pay and conditions abroad are better than those at home, and it is only during that time that they make a few savings to tide them over the spartan home postings. The extra allowances they receive when overseas are spent on creating a good image only for the sake of Britain's image. Thus the national image would suffer if Britain's representative lived in a garret abroad, whereas what he does at home is of no significance. Our arrival at the house in Radnor Walk was more traumatic. Although we had seen it a couple of times on visits home, we were in no way prepared for the shock. It looked drab and uncared for, much smaller than we remembered, and, worst of all, it looked like somebody else's house. I had fondly imagined the homecoming, but there was nothing familiar about 31 Radnor Walk: it was just like arriving at any old house – anywhere. It was a bitter anticlimax. I felt as despondent as when first inspecting our hospital home in Algiers, in fact rather worse, because my expectations in Algiers had focused on a house, while 31 Radnor

Walk was after all our home. In some ways the disappointment was irrational as the little house anyway would have lost its pristine look and grown a little shabby during those three and a half years; but in this case it seemed to have grown away from us by taking on the contours of all the tenants who had occupied it. First, Mr Oga and his extended family had left their mark, then the American couple, and finally the German diplomatic family who characteristically had restored order – but in rather a clinical way. Of one thing there could be no doubt: our own imprint on the house had disappeared.

Henrietta and Robin, then aged just four and nearly two, arrived by air with Alison and they too looked taken aback by the house; they had become accustomed to big rooms, high ceilings and a garden, and their new setting had none of these. It was the first serious readaptation they had to make as Henrietta had been too young on arrival in Algiers to be affected.

Perhaps I should at this stage try to describe how profoundly are the lives of diplomatic children affected by their father's profession. There is a myth that diplomatic life – with all the travelling, new places, new faces, etc. – is attractive and exciting for children, but I believe nothing could be further from the truth. To start with and above all, the circumstances of their lives deprive them of the essential sense of security which the same four walls provide. They have to change houses, schools, friends, food, languages, etc., every few years and at the same time accept that their parents have many preoccupations besides them. They are forced to share their home with a constant flow of visitors, whilst they instinctively recognize that these visitors are not real friends of their parents. They finally accept that the intrusion is an inexplicable part of their father's profession. The sense of insecurity of the nomadic life sometimes creates a strong sense of nationalism within them. It is not unusual for a child to become quite emotional at the sight of a British car, be it in Baghdad, Vienna, Mexico City or wherever. Likewise a glimpse of the Union Jack may unusually stir the emotions. The child might, as was the case with our youngest daughter in Paris, refuse to learn the local language. 'English is good enough for me,' she said. But I think it was Robin, our son, who expressed his need for a national base in the most poignant way. We were in Brussels and he was about four. One of those unctuous grown-ups, the kind who

wish to ingratiate themselves with small children, bent over him
solicitously to talk to him and asked what he was going to do when he
grew up. Robin looked up doubtfully and then, deciding he had
grasped the meaning of this peculiar question, answered, 'Live in
England.' Other small boys might have set their sights on being a
policeman, a train driver, or a spy, but Robin had got no further than
aiming to turn his sporadic visits to Britain into a full-time occupation.

Some friends of ours *en poste* in Nicaragua decided to send their
seven-year-old son home to boarding-school. His first evening there
the matron, wishing to do her best for the small, bewildered-looking
boy who had travelled all the way from Central America by himself,
said she hoped he did not feel homesick. The question perplexed him.
He realized that homesickness was meant to convey a yearning for
home, but in his case he did not know precisely where to direct the
yearning. Home for him, after all, had meant the big, rambling house
with a few cockroaches in Nicaragua, or previously the fifth-floor flat
in urban Paris, or the rented house near Camberley in England. So
where did she mean when she asked him if he was missing home?

There was also the little girl being driven along by her mother
somewhere in cosmopolitan Rome. Noticing the statue of a Madonna
through the car window, she asked her mother what it was. The mother
said it represented a Mummy, not wishing at that moment to become
immersed in a theological explanation. The girl then wanted to know
why the Mummy had a saucer behind her head and was told that this
meant she was a very good Mummy. The child understood
immediately. 'Oh, you mean the sort of Mummy who goes to hardly
any cocktail parties,' she said. The reason that children feel particularly hostile towards cocktail parties is obvious: their timing coincides
exactly with the most important part of their day – the time for
homework, supper and being read to in bed.

All this leads to the fact that the most difficult decision facing a
diplomatic couple is about the children's education. This is easier for
some than others, for certain parents are convinced there is nothing to
touch the British system of boarding-school education. Some fathers
have no doubt whatsoever that what was good for them must be
equally good for their sons. But it is often hard for mothers and
especially for non-British mothers to accept that the system of sending

boys of seven or eight away from home is the right one. (For obvious reasons there are a great number of foreign wives in the service, and I can remember so clearly the heartbroken Italian, Spanish, German or Scandinavian mothers, lacking the discipline imposed by tradition, mourning the departure of their small sons.) However, Christopher and I shared a less chauvinistic approach. Neither of us had found any joy or satisfaction in Britain's boarding-schools, and this, together with a genuine open-mindedness towards other countries' systems of education, made us decide to keep our children with us to be educated locally.

The financial arrangements for children's education are pretty generous. The boarding-school allowance is worked out by taking the average of a variety of school fees, and day-school fees abroad are paid as long as the school is on the embassy-approved list. However, if parents decide to move their children to a private day school when they are in a home posting those fees are not met from public funds, whilst boarding-school fees are. The system is worked out to help keep a continuity of education for these roving children. In the bad old days holiday fares for boarding-school children to join their parents were only paid once a year, but now – after an energetic campaign – the Diplomatic Service Wives' Association (DSWA) have achieved a second annual fare for all children, and a third for all children of a family bar the eldest.

However, to return yet again to our own homecoming in 1965, we found, paradoxically, that it can be harder to build up a circle of friends at home than abroad. A diplomat arriving at an overseas posting has an automatic right to make contact with the civil servants, parliamentarians, journalists, businessmen, etc., with whom his job at the embassy will involve him. After all, these are the people he will be working with and upon whom he will spend his entertainment allowance. Some of these professional contacts may develop into friends, but the majority of them will form part of the vast collection of acquaintances diplomats accumulate. However, on his return home he will find no natural framework for making friends. There will, of course, be all the foreign diplomats who in their turn will be pursuing him for information and heaping him with invitations. But he cannot count on many of his own countrymen showing much interest in him.

We decided to concentrate our own efforts initially on those old buddies with whom we had been exchanging Christmas cards year after year. Ours had reached them from remote places bearing exotic stamps and containing an entreaty to come and visit us. We had been receiving theirs – sent to us care of the Foreign Office for onward transmission by bag – from safe-sounding places like Moat Farm in Kent, or suchlike. Theirs had contained a synopsis of family news, details of any additions to the family, ending with a plea to let them know the minute we returned home. So that, of course, was exactly what we did. However, like so many things, the reality did not exactly measure up to the expectation. For example, the telephone, having rung for quite a few minutes in Moat Farm, would finally be answered by an excessively British voice (actually on first returning all voices sound exaggeratedly British until you get used to them again). The conversation might then go more or less like this. 'Oh, hullo, is that Daphne?' 'Ye-es.' Then, rather nervously, 'Oh, hullo, how absolutely lovely to hear you again, this is Jane. We're back.' This would be followed by an infinitesimal hesitation from Moat Farm, before, 'No, I can't believe it. How wonderful – welcome home. How was it all?' (But I knew that when saying 'how' Daphne really meant 'where'.) Trying to sound natural and calm, I then said, 'Well, it was all right – very interesting, of course, but a bit harrowing. There's lots to tell you when we have time. But how's it been with you? We're longing to see you both again.' Moat Farm, clearly relieved at not being subjected to a long dissertation on the forgotten place, says, 'Oh, yes, and we're longing to hear all about it and exchange news, but this week things are a bit frantic. All the children are at home and I've got no help in the house – not like you lucky people in embassies, ha, ha. And Roger has a tricky week at the bank; things in England aren't quite as easy as when you left, you know. But anyway, you *must* come and have supper soon – we'll be in touch – *lovely* that you're back and *longing* to see you.' My mind during this had been filled with memories of Christopher's curfew trips to the airport, the plastic bombs, working the telex machine, frightened children, hatred and violence. But, after all, it is important to recognize that anxieties and problems are entirely relative, so Roger's tricky week at the bank represented as great a worry for them as the complexities of life in Algiers had for us.

After a little while, however, things settle into place again and the returning traveller finds a niche for himself; but often feeling happier among the foreign community – the diplomatic corps, foreign journalists, etc. with whom he has so much in common. Indeed I think it is true to say that diplomats of all countries have a problem of identification when they return home. Many members of the business community, in all countries seem to harbour an irrational suspicion of their foreign servants. The diplomat himself might interpret this as envy of the proverbial comfort of embassy life and the advantages that go with it.

Speaking more generally it is true that, until now at any rate, too high a proportion of graduates with excellent degrees, mainly from Oxford and Cambridge, go into either the Treasury or the Foreign Office. This gives the Foreign Office an aura of élitism, which in turn arouses suspicion. British diplomats have gained a reputation for intellectual arrogance, and I now find myself in a better position to judge whether this accusation is justifiable or not. Although I know I may get myself into trouble with erstwhile colleagues, I do now recognize a certain degree of arrogance among members of the profession, and the alienating effect this has on others. The hostility evoked then manifests itself in different ways. Individual members of the Foreign Office tend to be blamed for errors in foreign policy. (I was startled and shocked by the near venom poured out against the Foreign Office over the Falkland Islands affair. It was as if the public seized this as an opportunity to express their disapproval of their diplomatic service; although the problem clearly had a political origin.) It is also inferred that diplomats do very well out of their allowances. They are not accused of actually cheating but the suggestion is that they do very nicely, thank you, and it's about time they returned to face up to the harsh facts of British life. The tone of voice used is sometimes sneering. Added to this, many people believe, perhaps correctly, that home-based civil servants are much more influential in the life of the community.

The diplomat finds these accusations and innuendoes difficult to swallow. From an economic viewpoint, he knows that, in a good year, the stockbroker presently haranguing him will make infinitely more than he could ever dream of earning. Moreover, he finds it unfair that the so-called perks of his profession are held against him when the disadvantages of his life far outweigh any such advantages. He rejects the accusation of intellectual arrogance regarding his style of expression as emanating from the nature of his work. This involves political analysis, negotiation, the composition of telegrams and despatches reflecting all the arguments and counter-arguments – in themselves intellectual exercises. Diplomacy has been loftily described as 'the application of intelligence and tact to the relations between countries', and, more cynically, as 'lying abroad for your country'.

My own interpretation, drawn from having now been on both sides of the fence, is that the sense of apartness usually results from misunderstanding. The purpose of a diplomat's work – his very *raison d'être* – is little known at home. After all, the benefit which members of the community derive from other professions – bankers, doctors, solicitors, teachers, etc. – is unequivocal, whereas the contribution, say, that the head of chancery in our Tokyo embassy is making to the life of the nation is unknown (in any case the significance of his very title is unknown). On the other hand the diplomat and his wife, through the circumstances of their lives, become cut off from what is going on in their own country. Indeed, how can they remain in tune with the way ordinary people are living and the current problems and difficulties afflicting them? Diplomats tend to become enclosed within the esoteric contours of their own life's circumstances, which in turn insulate them from the reality of British life and its changing social trends. I was made aware of this when I joined the lecture circuit a few years after my return to England in 1976. This led me to parts of the country I had never before visited, and made me realize how little I had known about the people of the very country I was trying to represent during those years. Conversely, since the lecture they liked best was the one called 'The Wife of a Diplomat', I also realized how little the members of the various groups I spoke to knew about my previous life.

Looking back, I suppose Christopher found the job awaiting him in London the one he least enjoyed during all those years in the Foreign Office. He was the head of the Permanent Under-Secretary's Department, responsible for liaising between the Foreign Office and the Intelligence Departments. This was outside his previous area of experience in the Arab world (specialists do not serve their whole careers within the same particular area) but although never as fascinated as he had been by previous jobs, he became absorbed in it, although the sensitive nature of the appointment created a great deal of strain and worry for him. Indeed it was at this time that the migraines which had started in Algeria, and continued to plague him periodically for the rest of his life, started in earnest. However, one of the major compensations was meeting up again with his old friend Denis Greenhill, who was the Assistant Under-Secretary for the department. Denis and Christopher, in spite of the difference in seniority, had always been great friends and part of the bond came through a shared sense of the ridiculous. They were both convinced that a light-hearted approach to life's disasters was the only way to survive them. Indeed Denis was to refer to this many years later when he gave the Address at Christopher's memorial service in St Margaret's Chapel.

Meanwhile I was going through the only really domesticated period of my life. My husband, my children and our home became my whole world. I have always recognized the importance of a well-run home, but had never before enjoyed cooking, shopping, housework, etc. Furthermore, I had never – and now even less – liked just being at home, unless for some purpose such as looking after everyone, eating, sleeping, etc. Yet, through the limitations of my life during those three years, I was nearer to achieving an inner peace than at any other time.

Henrietta needed to go to school. We chose one called the Garden House, which was within walking distance of home. She was delighted with her pretty uniform, a blue herringbone overcoat with matching velvet beret and grey skirt, blue sweater and blouse. She looked enchanting. However, only a week or so after the start of that Lent term it became obvious that she was ailing. The periodic fevers which had never been diagnosed in Algiers continued. She became listless, thin and withdrawn. Our family doctor came to the conclusion that she had a possible kidney infection – most certainly contracted in Algiers – and that she should have tests. We took the little girl, now weighing only twenty-eight pounds and looking like a delicate piece of Dresden china, to the Hospital for Sick Children at Great Ormond Street. The days that followed were filled with worry. I tried so hard to remain calm during my children's illnesses, but in fact never succeeded. It was only Christopher, holding the sick child with his long fingers almost closing round the small torso, who had a soothing influence. In this particular case not only was I traumatized at the thought of her illness – and the sight of the other children in the ward were proof of its seriousness – but the separation each evening brought in its wake paroxysms of despair from the child. Fortunately the results of the tests showed that our worst fears had *not* been realized, and she was released but, when we got the frail little creature home, it took many years for her to regain her full health, and this was later to be a determining factor in our lives.

The cottage at Ellis Green had come into its own during this period. The two children ran wild in the garden and Christopher found it a perfect setting to write his third novel, called *The Minority Man*, based on the time he had spent in Libya. But the cottage needed much attention. The absence of a road and electricity had been all very well during our courting period and honeymoon, but the romantic quality wears off when lugging carrycots across muddy fields. We needed 300 yards of road to join us to the state network. This was eventually carried out by 'Sammy', a small, dark green steam roller, and cost us £300. The hard core came from the runway of a neighbouring civil airport which was being closed down, and the Biggs Highway still provides us with an excellent service today. The decision to install electricity was harder to make. Not only did oil lamps reflect the most becoming light for those low-ceilinged, beamed rooms, but also produced a certain amount of much-needed warmth. Moreover, Christopher had decided that complete absorption in the mechanics of survival was the best therapy for his office anxieties. He spent most of the weekend trimming the lamps, filling them with fuel, mowing the lawn, cutting wood, lighting the fires, etc. But the problem remained of how to heat the empty house during the week. When we got down there on Friday evenings we measured its temperature with our breath; and it was a sad truth that it took until around Sunday evening for our breath to become invisible. We finally came to a decision and rows of telegraph posts were put up to bring us the service. After that Christopher's book progressed much more quickly and the 'breath test' was a thing of the past.

Around the beginning of 1967 – just when we were anticipating news of a posting – I became pregnant. I reacted with surprise and secret pleasure, while Christopher with surprise and horror, due to his natural fear concerning childbirth. Moreover, he was convinced we already had a well-balanced family – quite enough to cope with for someone like him who was a bit shy with small children. 'There's no communication,' he muttered gloomily. However, having elicited a promise that – depending on its sex – the child's name would be either Ultimo or Ultima, he resigned himself to a swelling wife and the jaundiced look which, sadly for both of us, accompanied all my pregnancies. However, when Ultima appeared on 16 November, his joy was unparalleled and, although enormously fond and proud of all his children, he quickly formed a relaxed relationship with Kate. But her looks came as something of a surprise to us all. Her ink-black hair contrasted dramatically with her golden-haired sister and ash-blond brother. Indeed her beauty was in some doubt until she opened her eyes; they were so huge that the tiny face was transformed. She soon acquired a greater equilibrium than the rest of us put together and lay in her cot silently beaming and revelling in the adulation. She never cried during the night and made no attempt to crawl or walk. She was as placid as Robin had been temperamental and I felt quite justified in having prayed for a girl.

For the first few months I was lucky enough to have Debbie – a student nanny – to help me. But she soon left to go abroad and we started on a long succession of au pair girls, the last of which passed under our bridge only a couple of years ago. Danes, Swiss and Germans – the turnover was rapid, but as they only helped during the evening my days were entirely taken up with domesticity. Henrietta had to be taken to school and back. This was mostly done on foot because for some reason, now forgotten, the dear old white Jaguar of Algiers days wended its way to the Foreign Office each day. Robin had by that time moved on from the neighbouring playgroup, which had given him a good grounding: I remember asking if his writing was getting on all right and being told yes, now that he had eventually decided which hand to use. He then went to the Holy Trinity Primary School near Sloane Square, which was an excellent little school teaching a wide variety of children, including a smattering of foreign diplomat's children. But, like wildfire, the Cockney accent spread to them all and whatever their differences they came together in calling what they had for pudding 'c-oi-ke'. Robin took to the school like a duck to water on all counts but one: he refused to have lunch there. His refusal was not for gastronomic reasons, but merely because of his need to return to base in the middle of the day to check up on things. He refused to leave the house in the morning before extracting a promise that he would be collected at lunchtime. If the promise was not forthcoming, he lay on the floor limp and inanimate. Once, when he was coerced into the car before getting the promise, he waited until the car was moving and then opened the door and got out. There was nothing to be done against such Gandhi-style passive resistance. This meant that I had to make the return journey to Sloane Square, pushing a pram and leading Konrad, three times a day. However, it was Miss Smith, the headmistress, who persuaded him in the end. Large and reassuring, she characterized everything that is good in a teacher and mentor of young children. She noticed my exhausted look bringing the triumphant little boy back after lunch one day, and she approached him that afternoon. 'Come on, Robin,' she said, 'why don't you bring your bob along tomorrow – like the others – and give it a try.' Next morning Robin demanded his bob as if it were the most natural thing in the world, and that was the end of the problem.

Although physically exhausting and mentally unstimulating, that particular stage in my life had a glorious simplicity about it and a complete inevitability. But, looking back, it must have been the time that Christopher found me the least stimulating both mentally and physically, which in my view proves that children can sometimes lead to the break-up of a marriage rather than act as the seal.

While at home we were not exactly inundated with social events (diplomats are not required to entertain others on a home posting), but there were a few and I remember one occasion clearly. We had been invited to a reception following a big dinner at No. 10 and on the way there in the taxi Christopher, thinking of his problem in remembering names, said, 'You wait, I'm going to get everything right this evening and introduce people left, right and centre getting every single name correct.' Soon after we arrived I saw him busily chatting to a distinguished-looking gentleman but standing somewhat on the periphery of the party. A little later Christopher rejoined me, rather crestfallen. 'Who was that? He looked nice,' I asked him. 'Well, noticing he looked rather out of things on the edge of the party I thought I'd try and draw him in. I knew I had seen him before and thought he was probably a newly arrived ambassador. It took my nearly half an hour to discover he isn't an ambassador at all, but is overseeing the catering for the evening. I was right about knowing him though, because he *used* to be the catering manager of my club. Oh, dear ..., well now I'll try again.' This time I stayed with him only to hear a lady greeting him in a challenging voice, 'Oh, hullo, Christopher.' Blank, worried look. She resumed with a less friendly tone, 'You don't really look as if you remember who I am.' 'I'm awfully sorry, no, I'm afraid I don't,' said Christopher, thinking he couldn't go through a whole voyage of discovery again. She turned out to be the wife – he had always been terrified of her – of his previous boss in the Foreign Office. He didn't award himself many points that evening for diplomatic prowess.

One day when Kate was only about six months old, the telephone rang and Christopher in his most sombre voice announced the news. The Foreign Office wanted to send him to Bahrain as the Number Two. It was happening all over again. My mind went back to 1961 when I had heard of the Algiers appointment with a new baby asleep beside me: Algiers which represented conflict and danger. And now, with another new baby sleeping quietly beside me, I was being told we were to go to one of the worst climates in the world, a place renowned for its unbearable heat and humidity, where English children who arrive with pink cheeks rapidly take on that yellowish tinge common to the tropics. My gloom was matched by Christopher's. He, in addition, felt the injustice of being sent for a second time to the Gulf. There is after all an unwritten law within the Service that all its members take the rough with the smooth. He felt acutely that Algiers followed by Bahrain represented too big a quota of rough, meaning there must be people somewhere getting too much smooth.

When Christopher came back that evening I felt low, but gratefully noticed the look in his single eye which indicated resistance. It is sometimes a characteristic of those who not only believe strongly in the principle of tolerance, but also put it into practice, to be very stubborn and stand firm on certain rare occasions. He was like that. He put up with all sorts of things which the rest of us would certainly not have done. Then, suddenly, something was said or something happened to break the tolerance. I knew the warning signs. With a steely look coming into his good eye, he would screw his monocle firmly into his bad one and become obstinate. It was like that over the posting to Bahrain. He knew the disadvantages only too well. He knew that the health of his children might suffer and he knew that the narrowness of the lifestyle imposed on us there would provide little stimulation, but in particular he resented the injustice of being sent there for a second time.

However, as I have already said, turning down postings in the Foreign Service is hazardous. The reasons for it going down badly with the personnel department are obvious. If one officer refuses a posting, a log jam is immediately set up, whereby the person designated to replace him is blocked and the one he himself is designated to replace cannot move on. The only excusable reasons for creating the blockage must be based on compassionate grounds. These usually arise from the health of a member of the family or responsibility for an aged parent. So, to cut a long story short, in the end it was Henrietta's kidneys which saved us. Although recovered from her original illness, she was still delicate and a letter from the Treasury doctor (the medical adviser for the whole of the Civil Service) confirmed this. This got us off the hook. I asked Christopher whom he thought would go in our place. 'Michael Weir,' he said. (Michael was an Arabist a few years junior to Christopher, who had uncannily followed him in various postings already.) The telephone rang a few days later. Michael's voice said 'hullo'. (He had a lugubrious voice; I mean the kind which conveyed a sufficient degree of hopelessness to make it ideal for recording the message on the answering-machine of EXIT.) Feeling apprehensive, I asked him if there was anything new. 'I've been posted to Bahrain,' he said. I couldn't think of anything much to say.

Finally, following about six months of uncertainty, we were told of the Brussels posting. Christopher was to be the Counsellor at the embassy. There are three British Missions in Brussels; the other two are delegations attached to the EEC and NATO. The news did not exactly fill our hearts with joy. The balance-sheet was roughly as follows: credit side, proximity; very appropriate for three small children; political interest generated by the negotiations for British entry to the EEC; the fact that we knew John and Diana Beith, the ambassador and his wife, who were great friends of ours; and (apparently) a nice house. Debit side: the year's time lag before going (Christopher had already had enough of his PUS job); the political interest Anglo-Belgian relations represented did not seem great; and the general risk that the job might turn out to be as lacking in stimulation as the Algiers one had proved challenging. But of course the most telling factor was the lack of choice. A second rejection was unthinkable. So philosophically we faced the irony of having over a year to prepare for the move to the capital nearest London.

6

Women and Wives

This chapter – something of a digression – is intended to reflect some of the circumstances which at the present time surround the lives of diplomats' wives. Much has changed since I stopped being one nearly eight years ago and I am fully aware of this, having kept in touch with many of our old friends in the Foreign Office. I know, for instance, that the attitude of many of the wives towards their husband's profession has altered; they no longer necessarily feel they themselves owe it a duty; nor are they so willing to live in their husband's shadow. The profession's attitude towards their emerging problems has also changed, for there are today many more young women with professional qualifications married to diplomatic officers. Although, sadly, it is usually impossible for them to continue in these professions, nevertheless the Foreign Office does now make every effort to remove obstacles in the way of their finding some kind of work when serving abroad. It is laid down under the Vienna Convention that countries may refuse to allow foreign women employment; but it is seldom that countries now insist on this. Previously an ambassador might refuse permission for a wife to take a job, but now if he does this he has to justify his refusal to the Foreign Office. Of course the language barrier often makes it really hard for a wife to find anything at all, but sometimes secretarial jobs are possible, or academic or research positions can be found. For after all not only do wives need the occupational therapy of work, but working wives are more in line with today's social trends. (A questionnaire sent out by the DSWA showed that some three-quarters of the women who replied wanted to work.) Furthermore, they quite rightly feel they can more successfully enter the life of the host country and make valuable contacts from the vantage point of a job, contacts impossible to make in the ordinary run of embassy life.

The interests of Foreign Service wives and children are represented by the DSWA. Christopher used to call it the Foreign Office's secret weapon, but in fact it could better be seen as rather a genteel trade union movement trying to improve conditions for the families. Membership is for life and many ex-wives – widows or divorcées – remain in touch with the DSWA. Past triumphs include increases in the number of holiday fares for children to join their parents serving overseas, and the Association is now working towards nursery-school provision for posts abroad. This is at present disallowed to keep in line with entitlements in the UK. But parents abroad feel strongly that sending their nomadic young children to the local nursery school might help them to adapt to the general environment more quickly and effortlessly.

The Foreign Office did a lot to help set up the Association in 1965 (when the Foreign Service Wives Association was amalgamated with the Commonwealth Relations Office Wives Society) and sometimes finds its persuasive voice useful to apply pressure on the Treasury in some quest or other. There is little doubt that the financial cuts imposed on the Foreign Office – with its entire diplomatic staff said to be no bigger than Harrods – are affecting many conditions of service. With branches in most embassies, the DSWA has its headquarters in London with a complement of officers. Jane Reid, the chairman, stressed above all that being married into the service was becoming increasingly a young woman's lifestyle. The process of moving house and pulling up roots – said to create the third biggest crisis in a woman's life – is most easily borne by younger wives. Moreover, in the early stages of marriage they have their small children to keep them busy and often find the whole thing rather exciting and reward-ing. It is later in life that they feel lost and lonely and frustrated at not being able to return to their careers or jobs, when their children have left home.

In the old days the senior wives were kept busy by channelling their energies into their husband's profession, which they regarded as sacrosanct and in some cases treated more seriously than did their husbands themselves. The entertaining was formal and extremely elaborate, and in addition they organized a great deal of activity for the embassy wives in the way of charity work, sewing bees, etc. But now this particular breed of ambassadorial lady – white gloves and a hat, who drove fear into the hearts of all the junior wives – has disappeared, and it is in particular these senior wives – women of around forty-five – who prefer home postings. They may be the mothers of the eighteen to twenty-one age-group, most anxious about the problems affecting their young people in this day and age; problems such as the decrease in university places and rise in unemployment, and all the other perils affecting today's youth. The wife may find herself agonizing – remote in her Far Eastern posting – about how much pot, or worse, her adolescent son 3,000 miles away is getting through. With only one holiday fare a year paid for students, she knows she may become completely cut off from him with all the consequent dangers. It is often these wives who persuade their husbands to retire early from the service, and who can blame them? But if they succeed in this, the problems for an ex-diplomat in his late forties or early fifties seeking work are enormous. Those with contacts in the world of commerce and industry, made through having had economic jobs during their Foreign Office careers, are best placed to find an alternative job, but what are the prospects for the specialists in political analysis who abound in the Foreign Office?

I remember, for my part, being surprised by outsiders asking where, if given the choice, I would most like to be posted. In reality the choice is greatly influenced by family circumstances, such as elderly parents, health problems, the children's education. Freedom of choice is thus proscribed. There used to be a Foreign Office questionnaire asking families, among other things, where they would most like to go. Christopher always put 'Rome' and, in answer to the reason for his choice, put 'Why do you think?'

Today, however, new factors have entered the calculation. Some postings entail danger – diplomats can be the natural target for terrorists and, in turn, the security measures to protect them restrict their private lives. In addition, there are postings to the ever increasing number of countries whose very fabric is falling apart and where the conditions of everyday life are extremely difficult.

Although many wives find the life trying and the occupational problems harsh, the reverse can equally be the case. A diplomatic wife was once quoted as saying, 'You have to be adaptable. You don't know which bit of you is going to be useful.' This seemed to be borne out when I was talking recently to my friend Maria Fairweather and she told me how, from a professional standpoint, she for one had been helped by being married to a diplomat. Maria is a simultaneous interpreter. Aged forty, she is half English, half Greek, attractive, intelligent and articulate. She and her husband Patrick, a Counsellor, are at present on a home posting. The things she told me, besides describing her own case, seemed to throw some light on what is happening among Foreign Office wives in general:

> To be an interpreter is about the most perfect job you can have being married to a diplomat. I got married at nineteen and didn't go to university, although I got in and all that; so my only qualification was the knowledge of languages which I had because of my background. I was very child-orientated as a young mother, and I have always actually liked travelling around and being involved in Patrick's job. After all, you don't have such a close involvement in any other career. And what's more, you do acquire other abilities *en route*, which you wouldn't have a chance to do otherwise. In fact, yes, I do happen to be a good luck story. Our postings were lovely and everything happened at the right time. We just happened to be posted in Brussels when I was the right age to be trained. The children were then eleven and twelve, and had gone to boarding-school, so I had time. After the training I took the freelance test and my languages were Italian, French and English. Greek? It wasn't then an EEC language, and although I had a Greek father I was educated in England and brought up in French, so I only had a very basic knowledge of the language at that time. However the last thing to fall into place was that the English booth in Brussels was still very empty as it was fairly soon after we [UK] joined [the EEC]. One thing just led to another and I really owe it to the Foreign Office that I have my career at all. Because if I hadn't learned Italian *en poste*, I wouldn't have had the third language when I did the test in Brussels, and I wouldn't have had the opportunity of doing that test if we hadn't been posted to Brussels. And then finally I acquired the necessary fourth language – Greek – during our last posting in Athens. So you see, from my point of view, I've definitely got as much out of the Foreign Office as I put into it. Yes, easily – and I've enjoyed it as well.
>
> Mind you, there are problems; one is that just when you get established

– people know you and lots of work is coming your way – you're posted. We've just got back to England now and I'm having to get started all over again. It's a difficult market here – there are a lot of good interpreters and relatively little work and it'll be two years, you know, before I get really dug in again. But at least I accept the fact that I'm very lucky even to have had the opportunity of a profession.

I suppose I'm still of the generation that believes that my job has to come second to that of my husband. I have to admit that. But a lot of young women don't – and they're right not to. I think it's just a matter of age; those who are under thirty – say – seem to think differently from those over. The vast majority of young women marrying into the Foreign Office now simply do so on the understanding that they will also have jobs. Of course there are exceptions, but many of them do take a very militant line. How do they rationalize the position they take? Well, some of them say they will just stay in England when their husbands are posted but others are adamant that they will force their husbands to resign, they say, and I think they will. That's why I think it is so important to emphasize that girls just should not marry into the Foreign Office if they want to carry on a career of their own. I think this has to be taken seriously into consideration because there just is no way round it completely.

There is now a new development. Young women are joining the Foreign Office, already married, on the understanding that they can take their husbands with them on postings. A young friend of ours – she is very bright – is doing that. She and her husband were at Cambridge together and it is she who is planning to join the Foreign Office. He is a very talented teacher but is now doing a computer course on the assumption that it is something he can use in other countries. So the point I am making is that this is a problem which is now starting to affect men as well. Can *he* work in the different countries? Will *he* be happy? etc. Of course less will be expected from a husband accompanying his wife – from the point of view of how they entertain and what part the spouse plays in the life of the embassy.

But to return to the more normal case where the spouse is a woman, I think the idea has now entirely disappeared that the wife actually owes something to the Foreign Office. A young wife won't accept that at all. I mean if an embassy wants her to do something, then she will only do it if she actually wants to. Our generation still believes in the theory of 'service' to the Foreign Office, but young wives see things quite differently; their slogan is: 'She doesn't have to, no one's making her; she's only doing it because she wants to.' Of course, some of them now say they think we should get paid for all the supportive work we do for our husbands and entertaining, etc. 'Two for the price of one' is wearing a bit thin; but I try to convince them that if we were ever to accept public money, not only would we *have* to do all those things but we would also have to submit to a control; to being told how to use the money. Yes, I suppose if a wife is performing some specific service – like accompanying her husband on an official visit – she might get her expenses paid. But on the other hand if you start to pay wives' fares too often there'll be an outcry about wasting public money and papers like the *Sun* up in arms.

But I do think that we should avoid blaming everything that goes wrong on the profession. After all there are things that go wrong in any life – problems between a man and his wife can arise whether they are abroad or at home or wherever. And I think it is very important to try to see things as they really are and not use the poor old Foreign Office as a scapegoat for everything that goes wrong.

7

Brussels – Le High Life

We set off to take up our new post in Brussels on 4 September 1969, in two new cars. Having parted with the Jaguar, Christopher, succumbing to his weakness for elegant, expensive, fast cars, replaced it with a dark green Daimler; and for the children and me there was a hatchback Hillman Imp. Robin, an observant child, made the point that he thought it incongruous that, although there were five of us – including Konrad – and only one of Daddy, it was Daddy who always had a car twice the size of ours.

We already knew our new house in Brussels. It was beautiful and the most comfortable family house we ever had, standing in an attractive crescent called rue Émile Duray which skirted, set below it, pretty formal gardens and the old Abbaye de la Cambre. To the right of the crescent there were two smallish lakes – les Étangs d'Ixelles – and then a huge flower and vegetable market. Behind our house was a long, fenced garden with a small lawn and trees, bushes and flowerbeds. The house was five storeys including the basement. (Kate, aged twenty-one months, learnt to climb like a mountain goat well before she was able to walk.) There was a huge loft at the top which we converted into a playroom for the children. On the floor below were the children's bedrooms, and below that our suite of bedroom, dressing-room and bathroom on one side and guest room with bathroom on the other. On the first floor, to one side, the drawing-room overlooked the old Abbaye, and at the back was the dining-room with a table large enough to sit fourteen people and French windows leading to the garden. Adjoining it there was a kitchenette with a dumb waiter in the corner to bring the food up from the huge kitchen on the ground floor. Finally there was a small entrance hall with black-and-white tiled marble floor, from which rose the handsome staircase.

The furnishings throughout were the Department's best, with a few additions bought locally such as the two huge crystal chandeliers, one in the drawing-room and the other on the landing. Our own possessions fitted in remarkably well. The *faux* Correggio took its place proudly on the wall of the dining-room, and Grandfather Brice's tall, winged candlesticks looked more at ease in their new Belgian capitalist setting than they had in the Algerian revolutionary one. Christopher's enormous collection of books fitted well into the various bookcases. (The packing of the books and their unpacking was Christopher's job. It could be said that this was his only contribution to the process of moving, but he certainly carried it out meticulously.) The house was beautifully decorated – apart from the kitchen area and the back stairs. As new chatelaines of embassy houses are usually allowed to carry out one improvement at least, I decided that the repainting of the back regions of the house should be mine. This was not only necessary but might also serve as a conciliatory move towards Maurice and the formidable Victoria, the Belgian couple who – as cook and butler – had served successive occupants of the house. Maurice, previously a miner who suffered from an occupational chest complaint, had been pensioned off by the State. It was therefore necessary for him to find work outside his own tax area, and the light work required by a butler in an embassy was just right for him. He was reasonably well-disposed towards his fellow men, but his wife Victoria was definitely not. A short, solid, square woman – contrasting with her husband's fragile build – her eyes, set in a porridge-coloured face, were like small blackcurrants and took on their most malevolent look when directed at 'Madame'. I do not wish to digress at too great a length about my relationship with Victoria which, with all the entertaining we did in Brussels, was of necessity very close. But perhaps I should at this stage make it clear that I have never been capable of coping with the moral position presented by the master and servant relationship. I have, in fact, never even managed to call a servant a servant. Whenever we had domestic staff I tried to retrieve my moral position by referring guiltily to 'the people who help us in the house' or 'the lady who very kindly does the cooking for us'. It goes without saying that this unctuous liberality was not lost on the indomitable Victoria, who instantly recognized me as potentially one of her most vulnerable victims and never missed a chance in the next two years to drive her advantage home.

This then was the setting to the new life awaiting us that day in early September. Christopher, however, appeared to get off to a bad start:

> Reached Brussels by road at eight in the evening of 4 September with a sick headache. A single day in the office before the weekend was like biting on rubber. There was a sense of needing urgently to get hold of the job but also of powerlessness about where to start. It is the time of the *rentrée* when political Brussels is beginning to rub its eyes after its summer sleep. The hibernation here takes place in high summer.

The diary then goes on to describe the current political crisis concerning the dual community. Christopher, of course, knew the implications of this, having boned up on Belgium's political, social and cultural background in the preceding months. (But perhaps the preparatory work he enjoyed most was reading Maeterlinck's *Life of the Bee*, a literary masterpiece which, I have noticed, is not always ascribed to Belgium.)

Belgium's history is a dramatic one, and it is now difficult to accept that this orderly country was turned into a battlefield on so many occasions. It belonged to the Roman Empire, France, Spain, Austria, France again and then the Netherlands, before becoming independent in 1831 and proclaimed at the Treaty of London of 1839 to be an independent and perpetually neutral state. Following that, during the reigns of Leopold I and II, the country made great economic progress and the links with the Congo brought it increasing wealth. Because of this history Belgium remained intrinsically divided into two parts – Wallonia and Flanders – and it was not until the very beginnning of the twentieth century that a law was brought in to establish the parity of the Flemish language with the French. This affected the whole of Belgian politics henceforward, and at the same time provided much professional interest for Christopher, and material for his diary.

Although we in Britain are sensitive to the problems of divided communities, because of tragedy of the Northern Ireland conflict, we cannot quite comprehend the division between the Walloons and the Flemings, and why they use their languages as a focus for their dis- agreements. The reasons are complex, for in spite of the fact that the northern part of present-day Belgium, previously part of the Nether- lands, spoke Dutch, the period 1794 to 1815 brought with it a French predominance and the prevalence of the French language, even in the Flemish part of the country. This dominance continued until after the 1914–18 war, prior to which time Parliament, higher education, the administration and judiciary were all carried out in French. It took the unacceptable contrast in the First World War, when the Belgian Army was made up of soldiers who were all Flemish, speaking no French, commanded exclusively by Walloon officers who spoke no Flemish, to bring about the political awakening of Flanders. Even then it was only in the 1930s that the Flemish language was fully acknowledged in government offices.

In the following years the Flemish community fought on every front to make their language recognized as equal with French, but it was a battle fired by the bitterness of social division and the former underdog was fighting for much higher stakes than merely linguistic ones. Since 1945 and continuing during the years we were in Belgium, a changing pattern in demography and prosperity tilted the balance in favour of Flanders and the Flemish people. This brought on a sociological reaction whereby the newly dominant community moved from its previous sense of inferiority to one of superiority, and for the Walloons the same thing happened in reverse. The final twist to the language problem was Brussels, claimed by both sides and not knowing itself exactly where it stood with regard to either of them.

For the foreigner living in Belgium or the tourist this language disagreement has wider connotations. The towns and villages have both Flemish and French names, and although in dual-language Brussels the signposts give the place names in both French and Flemish, this is no longer the case when the traveller reaches Flanders. Here he will vainly look for signs to his destination of, say, Tournai, without realizing that it has now been transformed out of all recogni- tion into Doornik, just as Courtrai will have taken on the pseudonym of Kortrijk.

Many senior members of the Belgian Ministry of Foreign Affairs had been seriously affected by the new law which removed any discrimination between Walloon and Fleming. Previously the Walloons had held the majority of senior positions, but since the qualification of fluency in French/Flemish had been established, many risked losing these to their Flemish colleagues. So we saw quite a few of our friends toppled from grace to ignominious jobs whilst struggling to learn the difficult language. (We called them 'the frustrated Walloons'.)

Although the major part of Christopher's work at the embassy was with his Belgian contacts about the negotiations regarding Britain's accession to the EEC, he was genuinely fascinated by Belgium's internal political scene. The intrinsic interest for him lay in its complexities. At moments of crisis he went to the gallery of the Belgian Parliament to listen to the endless wrangling about the linguistic issue. I remember a Belgian MP telling me that Christopher had become such a well-known expert that many a local politician would go to him for advice. Indeed, his political journal bears this out by dwelling almost lovingly over this subject – a subject which many foreign observers found boring and treated as a twentieth-century anachronism.

National characteristics are attributed to the people of every country – and the Belgians are no exception. For example, the foreign diplomat who said it was wonderful being posted to Belgium because it was so central and within range of everywhere lived to regret it, for Belgians are certainly sensitive about their country's status in Europe. Like the British, the Belgians are ardent royalists; King Baudouin and Queen Fabida are a most attractive couple. The class structure is pretty rigid, with the nobility, the bourgeoisie and the working classes occupying distinct and separate places in society. (The equivalent of our *Who's Who* is called *Le High Life* in Belgium.) Private enterprise dominates and the public sector has a minor role there. Both Walloon and Fleming are at the same time *gourmand* and *gourmet*, and the Germanic and French cuisines are reflected at their best in Belgium. They drive their cars with the minimum of safety, having only introduced driving tests in the 1960s. Another factor which contributes to the driving perils is their unequivocal adherence to the law of '*priorité à droite*': a regulation which requires drivers of cars proceeding along a major thoroughfare to give way to those intending to enter it from any side street, however obscure, provided it is on the right. The impracticability of this rule has been proved time and again by the fact that all damaged cars in Brussels bear the wounds on their off-sides. (Our worry for Christopher was great as he was blind in his right eye. However somehow his lovely dark green car survived those years.)

In spite of being the birthplace of Maurice Béjart and Tin-Tin, the Belgians are not a radical people (perhaps even less so than the British) and they have a down-to-earth quality. This was often brought home to me when, in the beautiful Forêt de Soignes, we would walk past the huge, stagnant, black pool bearing the name Etang des Enfant Noyés. The life-style of the Belgian nobility (which is extensive as all daughters inherit the title as well as all sons) can be on a grand scale. As personal taxes are lower in Belgium than in England, the landed gentry often do not follow a profession (at a party soon after our arrival in Brussels Christopher asked his neighbour, an attractive young Belgian lady, what her husband did. She looked at him in astonishment and said, '*Do*? He has his estates'). Some of them own several houses: one in Brussels occupied for the court season; another in the country where they take large parties for the shooting season. Christopher caused consternation when we first arrived by his negative response to the constant question, '*Vous chassez?*' It seemed inconceivable that an Englishman should depart from the hunting, shooting and fishing prototype. Many of them went skiing, and in the summer a few weeks were usually fitted in at the seaside. If not heading for warmer climes, they most favoured the resorts of Nieuport, Knokke and Le Zoute on the windy coastline between the French and Dutch frontiers.

Christopher described one of our country weekends staying with a hospitable, well-to-do family who were great friends of ours:

Have spent All Saints weekend with the Liederkerkes at Paihle. The atmosphere is feudal. When they need servants, the Curé asks for recruits from the pulpit. They live in what was the orangery of their seventeenth-century family château, which was itself burnt down when occupied by American officers in 1944. The Americans, who were drunk, watched it burn happily. With it went a priceless library of the Bishop Princes of Liège.

On reflection I suppose the life-style of the well-to-do British is not much different from that of the rich Belgians, but I happen to know much less about it. Of one thing there can be no doubt and that is the warmth of the welcome Belgians extend to foreigners. I have known no other country whose people so genuinely appreciate the presence of a foreign community.

Our new life in Brussels was virtually trouble free: certainly when compared to Algiers, the facts of domestic life in Brussels were almost exactly the opposite. Not only was running a household as easy in Brussels as it had been difficult in Algiers, but our lives were further improved by the popularity of the British embassy among the Belgians. Although Christopher and I had made many personal friends among the Algerians, the British embassy there nevertheless represented a capitalist society and was not high in the popularity or influence stakes. Cuba, a comrade revolutionary state, took the first place and its young ambassador was often publicly singled out for recognition. However, in Brussels there was no doubt that the British embassy was highly favoured for a variety of reasons. Historically Britain had come to the rescue of the embattled country on various occasions, though not necessarily from altruistic motives. Her historical record was therefore clean; which was more than could be said for the French, Dutch and German. Additionally, not only was our language popular but the Belgians sometimes used it for neutrality purposes. For example, when visiting the Flemish part of the country it was pointless to speak French (this being seen as a reflection of the superiority of the hated Walloon), whereas English was happily accepted and usually understood. I can even remember certain Walloon friends speaking French with a slightly English accent, proving not only that they had had an English nanny but also that they wished to occupy a neutral position outside the linguistic strife.

So, all in all, this meant that our Embassy had the advantage of respect, admiration and friendship. Belgians were delighted to accept invitations to our parties without all the wooing which had been necessary to attract the more recalcitrant Algerians to our dinner table. This made the whole process of entertaining straightforward, which was fortunate, as giving parties became a central part of my life in Brussels.

I suspect that it is generally imagined that diplomats entertain purely for their own pleasure, but nothing could be further from the truth. The parties take a great deal of hard work to organize and then can prove both tedious and exhausting for the host and hostess. What is more, the attitude of guests is often to take diplomatic parties for granted and think that a diplomat's major function is to give them. There are many stories – some of them undoubtedly apocryphal – about how the locals, of any country, can treat their diplomatic hosts, stories which show that the diplomatic host, far from being in receipt of gratitude, is instead in line for criticism. I like the one about the ambassador who is receiving the local British community to the Queen's Birthday Party which he is holding in his garden. The ambassador receives the long line of guests, dutifully shaking each one by the hand. The guests start mingling and whooping away at each other immediately after they have completed what they see as a chore. The ambassador continues with the handshaking: 'Oh, *hullo*, good to see you again. How *are* you? [In many cases meaning '*Who* are you?'] Yes, we *are* lucky with the weather. Certainly a great deal better than last year. Not at all, it's very good of *you* to come.' The ambassador then becomes exhausted and, realizing that it will all start again quite soon when the guests are ready to leave, thinks he will go and have a few minutes' rest in his bedroom. However, even his sanguinity (and most ambassadors are well endowed with it) is ruffled by the sight of two of his guests actively employed on his bed. He remonstrates, only to be met by two indignant looks and, 'But what's the fuss – it *is* a government bed, isn't it?'

I think diplomatic entertaining should be seen as contributing something to the promotion of better international relations. Not only does the diplomatic couple create bonds with the local community, but through inviting his professional contacts to his home the diplomat strengthens his own personal relationship with them. This in turn adds to the mutual trust without which countries cannot successfully co-operate. More and more embassy entertaining is concentrated on establishing an agreeable forum for visiting firemen to carry out part of their mission. With communications as they now are, fewer and fewer decisions are made by ambassadors and more and more by visiting politicians, senior civil servants, etc., but the embassy staff are required to create the setting for them to do this successfully.

I have the details still of a diplomatic party we gave for the Parlia
mentary Under-Secretary of State for Education and the Vice-Chan-
cellor of Essex University. I have forgotten the purpose of the visit,
but can well remember my own involvement. It started with Christopher saying, 'Darling, we'll have to give a dinner party for a junior
minister on 8 June as the ambassador will be away.' My first thought
on most occasions was how to break it to Victoria, who was particularly averse to all the work involved in these big formal events. (She
had proved this on a previous occasion when, recognizing the warning signs of impeding rage, I had implored her to stay calm – foolishly
adding that otherwise I might cry. '*Eh bien, Madame, pleurez alors.*'
Game, set and match to Victoria.) 'Do you know him?' I then asked
Christopher. 'No.' 'Can he speak French?' 'I shouldn't think so.' 'Is he
bringing his wife?' 'No.' 'Is he a vegetarian?' 'I'll ask.'

We then wrote out the guest list, choosing mainly people whose
function in life related to education. In this case the final list was as
follows: the British Council representative, Alethea Hayter; the
director of the Beaux Arts Museum; the headmaster of the British
School in Brussels; a Belgian socialist MP; the director-general of the
Youth and Sport section in the Ministry for Education – all with their
wives – and finally an attractive young Belgian girl to make up the
numbers. Arrangements were then made to send out the cards, work
out the seating plan, decide on the menu, etc.

Entertainment in Brussels was formal and the Belgians were
sticklers for protocol. It was the kind of place where we could do with
that time-honoured guidebook written not long after the war by the
late Sir Marcus Cheke entitled *Guidance to Diplomatic Service and
Other Officers and Wives posted to Diplomatic Service Missions
Overseas* or *Some Do's and Don'ts of Diplomatic Etiquette and
Other Relevant Matters*. This was designed as a guide to the basic
rules of social behaviour for members of the diplomatic service and
their wives and is still relevant in parts. For instance, it stresses the
importance of seating people correctly at formal dinner parties, and,
using an old-fashioned but rather charming style, the author makes
the following suggestions:

The order of precedence at table – called in French *placement* – is a serious

My brother and me on Scraps and Titbits

Me (*at back*) with two friends at
Grenoble University

Christopher aged five

Middle East Centre for Arab Studies, 1950: Christopher is in the middle row, fourth from right

The diplomatic staff of the British Embassy in Algiers accompany the ambassador to present his letters of credential to Ben Bella: ambassador Trefor Evans centre, Christopher second from left

Henrietta in her very own pool with her admiring mother, Club des Pins, Algeria

Christopher with Henrietta and Robin at
Ellis Green, 1966

A court reception, Brussels, 1971: King Baudouin (*centre*) and Queen Fabiola (*left*) receiving guests

Henrietta and Robin at Dunmow fête

Kate aged about eighteen months

The Biggs family including Konrad at Villereau in 1974

Signing the visitors book at Château Barton, Bordeaux

At a Paris cocktail party with Françoise Giroud (*left*) and Alex Grall (*right*)

Christopher at Cavalaire

Our last day at Villereau

Kate wearing her father's top hat on his return from presenting his credentials to the Irish President in July 1976

Edward Heath, Roy Jenkins and me launching the Christopher Ewart-Biggs Memorial Fund at the Foreign Office in October 1976

My introduction to the House of Lords on 3 June 1981: Lord Goronwy-Roberts (*left*) and Lord Greenhill of Harrow were my sponsors

Working on my book in the Renwicks' house during a holiday in Washington during the summer of 1983

subject and should never be trifled with, however tiresome and foolish it may sometimes appear. You have to remember that however modest and easy going a fellow Mr X may be, if he is from another Mission he is, at whatever level, also representing his country in your house. If in the interests of a harmonious table you have to downgrade someone, always warn them beforehand and have a complimentary explanation ready: 'Mme X speaks nothing but Ruritanian and yours is so wonderfully fluent I hoped you would forgive me.' If you place official guests wrongly, they may protest officially next day, or even leave your house after the soup.

It goes on to point out that it is wiser to work out the seating plan for your party *before* sending out the invitations, 'for fear of striking an unexpected snag too late'.

If you have a knotty problem which your own colleagues cannot solve, ask the Protocol Department of the Ministry of Foreign Affairs for the right answer and let the onus rest on them. But don't get caught with the acceptances already in before you go to them: 'How should I seat these people, please?' one hostess asked a certain Chief of Protocol; 'Madam,' he answered, 'I can only advise you not to give that particular dinner.' If that should happen, nothing but a galloping attack of appendicitis can save you.

The day of the party arrived, to be recorded by Christopher in a rather cynical way:

Dinner for our Parl. Under Sec. for Education at Emile Duray. He is here for the European Ministers of Education Conference. A soft, round, rather mediocre person who is no match at all for Simonet, the Socialist politician. S. more affable and less conceited than usual. About his position on the community question (he will abstain on agglomeration, rational autonomy, etc., which he thinks will get through) he says, 'A politician's first duty is to get elected.' Our Minister on museum charges says, 'I'm very interest in the idea of season tickets. They'd make very good presents, wouldn't they?'

The day's activity preceding our big parties usually passed off in more or less the same way. 'Anything I can do?' Christopher might ask, confident the answer would probably be 'No'. 'Not really – thank you – except remind Archimède that we need him.' (Archimède was the Embassy messenger who sometimes became an extra *maître d'hôtel* in his spare time.) 'Yes, of course I will. What are we eating?' My records show that for that particular evening I had negotiated with Victoria to have vichyssoise soup, followed by prawn cocktail served in half grapefruits, roast veal accompanied by innumerable vegetables, and finishing with profiteroles. (I always kept a record of menus to avoid giving guests the same dish on a future occasion.) Christopher had looked quite happy until I got to the pudding, and then he became less so. Although this was a great Belgian delicacy he never took to it, remaining loyal to his schoolboy passion for bananas and cream. I can still see his single eye fixed balefully on the great pyramid of chocolate-drenched éclairs as they made their way into the dining-room and inexorably towards his plate. 'What about the seating plan?' he said, hoping to do better for himself out of that. 'Do you need any help with it?' Mindful of Sir Marcus Cheke's injunction, we made every effort to place our guests correctly according to precedence. And, although perhaps unknown by those outside protocol-dominated circles, every single place round the table has a significance; by which I mean that, whilst the most important gentleman takes his place on the right hand of his hostess and the second in line on her left, the place allocated to the third gentleman in seniority is on the right of the most senior lady, and so on. The same allocation applies starting from the other end of the table occupied by the host, and this leaves the least important guests occupying the centre of the long table. This system, however absurd and obsessional it may seem to outsiders, is nevertheless adhered to by all within the professional circle, and it only takes any of them a second's view of the table plan to see if there is a flaw in the *placement*.

However, after looking at my proposed seating plan Christopher, lamenting, often tried to juggle a few of the guests around to position a more glamorous lady at his side. For it seems usual – although there are, of course, many exceptions – that the brilliance which has propelled men to the top of the heap (thereby, among other things, earning them the place of honour at formal occasions) is rarely reflected in their wives. Nor have these ladies been compensated with glamour. Perhaps the only conclusion to be drawn is that very able men need a complementary force rather than a competitive one, whilst the insecure man pursues the outstanding, glamorous woman to bolster his ego. Whatever the reason, it meant Christopher had to resign himself on many occasions to being flanked on both right and left by solid matrons. On such occasions he indulged in his favourite pastime of telling anecdotes – translated into French – thereby flaunting Sir Marcus Cheke's warning, which went like this:

> Until you know people well beware the temptation of wit and the dangers of humour. It is exceedingly hard for a foreigner to understand the sort of humour which comes naturally to us, and almost equally hard for us to indulge naturally in the humour which appeals to foreigners. Failures in this line can lead to sad misunderstandings.

If not misunderstandings, Christopher's stories, certainly those from his 'sheikh collection', left some rather puzzled faces.

Christopher would then depart to the embassy. He recognized that it was better not to interfere with my arrangements and had never much liked administration anyway.

My next job was one I loved: arranging the flowers. I went to the flower market, bought a huge variety of different flowers and then, with the help of branches from the trees and shrubs in our garden, filled the vases, producing the pluralist effect which I like so much. A vase in the hall to welcome the guests and then several in the drawing-room and another on the dining-room table with flowers carefully manipulated to reach out on each side close to its surface and not obscure the vision of the guests.

Dinner party days were overshadowed by the fear that someone – perhaps even the guest of honour – might cancel (or 'chuck', as our ambassador called it). This one remained unscathed, but a few months later Christopher recorded the following in his journal: 'Gave dinner party. Senator Hougardy was meant to be the main item. But he had flu, he said, and was represented by a pot of flowers.'

I kept clear of the kitchen, having done my level best to remember every single necessary ingredient in my previous day's shopping: anything to avoid a collision with 'button-eyes'. When Christopher got home everything was ready, with the name cards in front of the places round the table and the seating plan outside the dining-room to help the guests find their seats. 'Remind me who's coming,' Christopher used to say, getting into his bath. I did – at the same time rehearsing him in the pronunciation of complicated Flemish names, at which I was more adept. (We eventually gave the first prize for unpronounceability to Baron Regnier de Wykerslooth de Rooyesteyn and the Comte de Crombrugghe de Picquendaele.)

Suitably reminded and reflecting his most British diplomat look in his dinner jacket, he joined me in the drawing-room to await the guests. With the great fireplace blazing it was a bit warm, but the Belgians liked the look of it and thought it very British. Moreover, it provided a vehicle for comment – '*Quelle belle cheminée*' – to fill any of those initial gaps in the conversation, forbidden in diplomatic circles.

Christopher left the introductions to me. He knew his weaknesses: as I have mentioned before his memory for names and faces was certainly one of them. (His confidence had been seriously undermined once in Algiers when the Indian ambassador said to him, 'Christopher, I just cannot tell you how much my driver likes you.' Christopher, sensing this hinted at some immense gaffe, said nervously, 'But I'm afraid that can't be so because I don't know your chauffeur. I've never even met him.' 'But he tells me that whenever he is waiting at the entrance to a reception to take me home you invariably come up to him, shake him warmly by the hand and start up a long conversation – mainly about politics. I can't tell you how much he appreciates this.' Christopher, with that well-known sinking feeling brought on by such revelations, then realized that the young Algerian whom he had always taken to be a somewhat reticent junior minister in the Algerian Government was in fact the Indian ambassador's driver.)

However, my short-term memory usually stood me in good stead, and I succeeded in making all the introductions correctly, although I may not have set eyes on more than half of our guests prior to that evening. Archimède then announced dinner and we went into the dining-room preceded by Konrad. His role had already been defined in an article in one of the society magazines. This recorded that the monocled Counsellor at the British embassy was so 'snob' that he even had a cocker spaniel especially trained to precede the guests into the dining-room and show them their places *à table*. Konrad never had a finer hour.

Although, of course, I have forgotten most of what was said that

evening, an exchange between Christopher and one of his neighbours, and a few other remarks, have for some inexplicable reason
stuck in my memory. The woman seated next to Christopher was
talking about her sister, who with her husband had been posted to a
South American capital. Christopher, obviously bored out of his
mind but wishing to be helpful, told her a story about a friend of his
also serving in South America, but in a city where the security position was not all that it might be and where members of the diplomatic
corps were advised to go around armed. And some, he added, even
wore *banderillos* to ensure they always carried enough ammunition.
'What, even when wearing their dinner jackets?' she intervened, outraged. Lawlessness was one thing, but the betrayal of social convention was much more serious.

The conversation at my end of the table went quite well. Our junior
minister, as anticipated, did not speak French, but Simonet's English
was more than adequate. The two men did not have a great deal in
common, but in an amiable fashion discussed the Education Conference which the British politician was attending. And then Simonet,
talking about one of his own political heroes, told a charming story.
Monsieur Van Acker, one of the great veterans of Belgian politics,
then president of the Chambre des Deputés, came from a working-
class family and had left school at ten-and-a-half to sell shrimps. The
anecdote described how one of the flowers of Belgian aristocracy, on
being elected to Parliament, called on Van Acker, the president. Van
Acker, at his desk, without looking up said, 'Take a chair.' The visitor,
aggrieved, said, 'I am the Baron Snoy et d'Oppuers.' Still without
looking up the old Socialist said, 'Then take two chairs.'

The meal at last over – although Maurice and Archimède served
with speed and dexterity it was prolonged as each dish had to be
offered a second time – we moved back to the drawing-room where
coffee, liqueurs and cigars were passed round. This gave Christopher
an opportunity to carry out some official business and, liberated from
the matrons, he talked at length with Simonet about the position of
his party in the current political movement over the Community
problem (later to be used in a despatch or telegram to the Foreign
Office). I tried to give our two guests of honour the opportunity to
talk to all present by manoeuvring those guests who had been unable to

speak to each other during dinner into little groups. Some hostesses took this task over-seriously and, instead of leaving guests happily chattering, might reshuffle them several times, obliging them to start all over again. Diplomatic hostesses can, unfortunately, become so blinded by organizational demands that they forget that the prime function of entertaining is for people to enjoy themselves. I have known many a large diplomatic function end up as an organizational triumph – and nothing more.

The party was now drawing to an end, and after Archimède had made his last round with whisky and fruit juices the senior lady stood up and she and her husband said their goodbyes. Other guests followed suit, leaving a hard core of friends who stayed behind for one last drink and to hear a final anecdote from Christopher. Then – after paying off Archimède – with a sigh of relief Christopher and I settled down to the best bit of the evening – the post-mortem – with our feet up.

I loved that bit. Sometimes from my vantage place between the two leading guests I might have gleaned some political titbit for Christopher. Sometimes Christopher might even have set me the task of extracting certain information, basing his hopes on Belgian politicians or civil servants being less guarded when talking to their hostess than to their host. If successful, I laid those trophies before him like a dog with a bone. Not having scored that evening, I told him instead how Simonet, soon wearying of our visiting politician with whom he had little in common, had talked with me and his other neighbour, Jacqueline Boël, a highly intelligent and very radical member of the great banking family. To amuse us he told us the story of how at the Commission Office that day he had been talking to the head interpreter, whose simultaneous translation he much admired. Curious, he had asked him how far behind he was when translating 'simultaneously' – a sentence, a few words, two sentences? The chief interpreter answered incredulously: 'Behind? Not at all, I'm usually in front.'

Christopher made yet another plea for the abolition of the profiteroles – holding out little hope as his neighbours had demolished about six each – and I asked him what had brought on such paroxysms of mirth at his end of the table. He told me that the conversation had become so fraught with his stodgy ladies that he had been obliged to resort to stories from his 'sheikh collection'. There were a number of these, mainly based on the visit to the Queen's coronation of the sheikh of Qatar, for whom Christopher had been responsible. They were very funny (usually told against himself), reflecting as they did the image of the tall figure in full diplomatic uniform with sword trying to control the wayward sheikh while the interminable ceremony went on with efforts at conversation from Christopher such as, 'This, oh sheikh, is a very old mosque,' (about the abbey) – 'Well, why don't you build another one?' Soon after that, there followed an unforgettable moment. At a particularly hallowed part in the ceremony, Christopher was suddenly aware of inaudible muttering from the high-ranking officers among whom they were sitting. Looking desperately at his sheikh, he saw with horror that his charge had taken his shoes off and, with his feet up on the rail in front of him, was carefully examining the spaces between each toe. Christopher summoned his final resources of the Arabic language and said, 'Oh sheikh, in our mosques we keep our shoes on.'

These stories lost nothing in translation and, delivered to the accompaniment of Christopher's own whole-hearted appreciation, never failed to make people laugh.

Christopher's journal of our time in Brussels, although in the main recording his professional activity, also reflects how he was adversely affected by the accompanying social life. On 18 December 1970 he wrote:

> British businessmen's lunch at the Cercle Gaulois [a club]. Rather dreadful. Some nauseating talk about the fiscal advantages of living abroad – and they could not understand why at the same time they were not allowed a proxy vote against Mr Wilson. This sort of thing, and the attempt to delay the abolition of capital punishment, and the talking out of the Private Members' Bill against stag hunting and coursing, strengthens my feeling against the Tories.

And again at dinner with a member of one of the great banking families:

> At dinner with the Eric Janssens, in a sweeping park of well-kept immensities of lawn and great lavish banks of rhododendrons, on a terrace

of an expensive mansion, drinking and dining *en grande luxe*, the First
Secretary of the Indian Embassy and I discuss Bengal. Four million
refugees have come into India; another six million could follow them. 'We
are finished,' he keeps saying, 'We have had it.' The scene of the conversation and the subject of it make an appalling contrast.

But his worst suffering came from cocktail parties. After one 'in the
hellish din and heat of a cocktail party' entry on 8 February 1971, he
recorded:

Ludicrous ordeal at the Château St Anne [the international club] where
the Chief of Staff of the Belgian Air Force has invited a head-splitting
superfluity of people, packed tight. It is not a cocktail party but a demo-
graphic experiment. What unspeakable pretention to inflict such a thing
on people under the guise of entertaining them. And where is a society that
sees its pleasures thus?

And even after one of our own:

J. returns in time for large cocktail party at Emile Duray. It is said to go
well but I find it fearful. I am much less than at ease. In a frenzied attempt
to break out of silence and banality I ask a Latin American blonde what
her priorities are. After a moment of astonishment and a few syncopated
wriggles she replies that her life is *'un tout'*. Mine at that moment felt far
from being that.

On 11 June 1971 – less reverently – he wrote: 'The Queen's Birthday
Party again. Very wearing on the feet. I whisper that I would forgive
the Queen her massive evasion of Income Tax if she would let me off
celebrating her beastly birthday.' And at our very last party in
Brussels – the one given in our honour by the ambassador – he
recorded:

Perhaps because I am going, I find it easy, or easier than usual, to make the
right noises. Shout for a bit with Anxiaux [until recently Governor of the
National Bank] about the monetary crisis. He fears a serious recession in
Europe when the dollars start flowing the other way. Then I am over-
powered by a man who proves to be the Belgian Sainsbury and insists on
waving his noxiously fuming cigarette under my nose until I am ready to
strike him. In the end I wriggle away impolitely. It is a filthy and anti-
social habit as well as a suicidal one.

On reflection, it is amazing that I held out against giving up smoking for the first seven years of our marriage.

One of the reasons for Christopher being positively allergic to cocktail parties was that they used to bring on migraines. Although he never drank anything alcoholic, the effect of the noise and cigarette smoke, combined with his effort to have a serious conversation – the purpose, he maintained, of cocktail parties – brought on these sick headaches. His diary showed how painful they were: 'Migraine, if that is the word for it. For an hour perhaps I feel very like dying.' I didn't have the same problem, being quite happy to chatter briefly on a great number of subjects with a large number of different people having successfully – unlike him – worked out how to liberate myself from a clinging guest without giving offence (or at least I hoped so). 'Well, as I'm afraid I won't be able to stay long at this party I suppose I had better rotate a bit. Lovely to have seen you.' Or, 'I'm so sorry but I must move on now as my husband asked me to look out for so-and-so. But see you again very soon and it's been so nice talking to you.'

So although the implications of the social side of our lives weighed less heavily on me than on him, I did suffer one consequence: a gastronomic one. Never since my adolescent years have I been able to take in more than small quantities of food at any one time. Concern for the original eleven stone may have triggered this off – together with a disposition towards nervousness. Anyhow, time and again I found myself unhappily faced with a huge helping and the feeling of a trapdoor coming across my gullet. 'Is there something wrong, Madam?' from a succession of aggrieved head waiters and, feeling themselves personally insulted, hostesses watched my plate, still bearing three quarters of its helping of 'waterzóy' or rable de lièvre (a particular torment), being removed by the maître d'hôtel. I learned the trick of keeping my hands folded just above the discarded plateful until he came to take it away, but the eagle-eyed maîtresse de maison usually spotted this and remonstrated with shrill cries: 'Madame, voyons – mais j'insiste.' Christopher, entirely sympathetic and also appreciative of my 34-24-34 physical result, then tried to distract the indignant hostess with some relevant anecdote.

In parallel to all this ran the life of the children. Henrietta and Robin were fairly happily settled in two small neighbouring Belgian schools, where they had been accepted without knowing a single word of French. However, aged eight and six, they were well placed to learn the language by ear. On their first few days they were extremely bored: they just sat there in a vacuum of incomprehension, but gradually they related certain sounds to objects. The first day 'Prenez vos cahiers' meant nothing, but the second day, rather than becoming 'an exercise book', it straight away became the book they all did their lessons in, which meant that from the start they actually *thought* in French and were able to reproduce the words in perfect accents. Robin's nice teacher fell into a quandary of indecision about whether to penalize him for reading with a stress on the wrong words, as a result of not understanding the meaning of the text – no fault of his – or to judge him purely on the articulation. She generously decided to take the latter course, so only a month or so after starting on this new language Robin was getting ten out of ten for reading! Henrietta, on the other hand, had a less acute ear but a more probing, retentive mind and tended to absorb the language mentally rather than purely orally; a process which took more time but also made the language stick longer. Naturally, they learned the Belgian accent or, more precisely, the Bruxellois. This consisted of a slower and more measured articulation. I have myself always welcomed the few adjustments the Belgians have made to the French vocabulary, especially in their logical interpretation of 'seventy' and 'ninety': *septente* and *nonente* give me a feeling of security which France's *soixante-dix* and *quatre-vingt-dix* do not. However, I have noticed that the French never miss an opportunity to pour scorn on this sensible innovation as they tend to ridicule, in general terms, the Belgian accent. The Belgian is often used by the French – as the British use the Irishman – as a focus for humour and to provide the buffoon figure in anecdotes. This must be one of the reasons for the strong sense of inferiority felt by the Belgians towards the French and the Irish towards the British.

Meanwhile Kate, just over two, was ready to enter formal education. An obvious setting was provided by the huge attic which, with the help of white paint and a few bits of furniture, was idyllic for a playgroup. Kate and four other embassy children attended 'school' there about three mornings a week. Their teacher was Anne Frederick, a lovely girl who came with us from England. Although she had no training, her imagination and love of small children helped her to think up the most innovative educational activities for them. At the end of each session the children would be led away by their mothers proudly bearing some incredible confection made out of coloured paper, cardboard, egg boxes, empty tins, etc. I remember thinking even then that Kate might never again be so contentedly schooled.

Life in Brussels contributed many of the advantages of a country existence to all the children, and the big rambling house and garden even made it possible for them to have a series of pets. First there were the white mice kept in the upstairs bathroom – but they outlived their interest value. In fact we happened to discover that whilst a Russian experiment had succeeded in keeping white mice alive for a record length of time, our own mice had of their own accord and without the help of modern science already broken the Russian record.

We decided to include hamsters in the menagerie as well, and Annie took Henrietta and Robin off one day to buy two male hamsters at the market. Very excited, they came back on the tram with the two ratlike animals in a travelling box. When decanted into the smart cage they had also bought, it was discovered there had been a battle and one had an enormous gash along the side of its small body. Christopher and I realized it must go to a vet and took it off to the surgery, where there was quite a queue. Now, although patients tend not to discuss their ailments when waiting to see the doctor, it is quite different with the owners of animal patients. There was one lady with a poodle peering gloomily out from its fringe of black curls. 'La grippe,' she explained when we asked what was wrong. Then there was a lady with a cat crouching in its travelling basket. Her answer, in resigned tones, was more alarming. 'Le typhus,' she said. We began to wonder if our devotion to rat life (hamsters are reputed to be Syrian rats) was not rather exaggerated and any unwelcome repercussions from it hard to rationalize to the Treasury doctor. When our turn came Christopher, holding the tiny creature between his long fingers, asked the vet, busy stitching up the wound, if he was used to working on such small animals. 'No,' said the vet rather sniffily, 'horses are my speciality.'

We thought this medical intervention should bring an end to the

127

affair. But this was not to be, for ten days later our hamster, having had his stitches safely taken out, gave birth to a splendid little family of three. It then became clear that our two 'male' hamsters on their journey back in the tram that day had made both love and war.

During our time in Brussels I had one important outlet from my routine of arranging parties, going to them, looking after the children, etc., and that was a return to learning. Indeed it is important for women such as myself, who not only lack a profession of their own but also put most of their time into the service of their husband's, to do something purely for themselves. So I decided to take Flemish lessons. I was highly proficient in French, but after all Flemish was the country's dual language. A venerable old professor, filled with old-world courtesy, was found and soon I was driving off every Thursday morning to 27 rue de l'Oiseau Bleu, on the outskirts of Brussels, where Professor Christians lived. His house and its contents charac-terized genuine Dutch taste and culture and he seemed truly delighted to have me as a student. He worked out a special course to suit me and with infinite patience tried to instil some of the difficult language into my head. Flemish resembles Dutch closely and differs only through having retained some of the original grammatical complexity which modern Dutch has shed. (I think the purpose of this was deliberately to make Flemish independent from Dutch.)

There can be no doubt that the guttural sounds are difficult for an Anglo-Saxon throat. However, on the other hand, knowing German and English does help in understanding the written language since so many of the words stem from one or other of them. I did not do well because the German words I had learned from all the Fräuleins of my early childhood kept reintroducing themselves in the place of the difficult Flemish vocabulary. I made desperate efforts to pronounce correctly and to get my homework done, but the end result of the two years' visits to rue de l'Oiseau Bleu was no more than the ability to ask the way when lost on a visit to Flanders and a shaky comprehension of – say – a passage in a Flemish newspaper. But therein lay my greatest triumph and reward for all the swotting. For Christopher, who had made no attempt with the language, turned postively green with envy when I told him how interesting was the leading article in *Der Standaard* (the major Flemish daily newspaper) and how its analysis probably gave the clue to the resolution of the current communal squabbling.

However, apart from the pleasure my effort gave to our Flemish friends, the whole experience was of great general benefit to me, because the time thus devoted was entirely in my own interests and not – as was usual – in the interests of the embassy and the family. It was, I think, then that I started to recognize that for those to whom selflessness is not a virtue but a characteristic there is a fundamental need to do something for themselves in order to restore some necessary balance within them.

I went in for some social work too. It is fairly normal – or used to be – for embassy wives to do charitable work to help with a local social concern. Such activity would be organized by the embassy branch of the DSWA. Naturally the need for this work is a great deal more pressing in countries of the developing world than among the affluence of Western European industrialized countries, and although Belgium has never been a welfare state or had a National Health Service such as ours, the level of social security and welfare benefits is high. So without the spur of social deprivation and human destitution staring us in the face, it was difficult for me to find a focus for embassy wives' benevolence. However, suddenly – tucked away among that affluent society – I found exactly what I had been looking for. This was a children's home called Claire Matin run by the Salvation Army in Drogenbos just outside Brussels, and it was in great need of help. Children whose parents, for whatever reason, were unable to care for them were taken in there, for which the home received some funding from the commune but not nearly enough. Moreover, an institution run by an organization such as the Salvation Army did not attract a great deal of philanthropy in a country where only one per cent of the population profess the Protestant faith.

I can so well remember my first visit. I was received by the officer of the Salvation Army in charge; she was in uniform and held the rank of major. Puritanical in her attitude, as might be expected, she ran the home under strict disciplinarian rules. Although the children were well cared for, she was pitifully short of funding and staff. I asked the major how we could best help her. She said with money, but if we had a little time available then helping with the children's mending would be invaluable. I went back to report to my ambassadress, Diana Beith, and the other wives. We agreed that, as a start, we would meet every fortnight at the house in Emile Duray and take on the mending.

And so it went. One of the wives collected the battered suitcase from Drogenbos before each session and then we emptied the shabby contents out under the beautiful Waterford glass chandelier and settled down to patching the tattered shorts and jeans, sewing buttons on the buttonless shirts and darning the socks. Soon the project took on a wider dimension and some of the more nimble needlewomen started to make rag dolls, knit small garments, cut out dresses and nightdresses, etc., with the aim of raising funds to increase the home's income.

Although there was a certain amount of grumbling about those afternoons, I remember them as being happy and cheerful. All the embassy children came too – up to nineteen of them eating a gigantic tea and running their rival show in the attic and the garden.

However, the reward for all the hard work came later – and in a most unexpected way. This was several years on when, returning to Brussels from our Paris posting for a visit, I was having lunch with Mary Soames – Christopher Soames was at that time a Commissioner at the EEC. After we had finished, she apologized for rushing me but said she had an appointment. I asked if it was anything interesting. 'No,' she said, 'it's a meeting to plan the fund-raising ball for some children's home out at Drogenbos. It's being organized by all the richest and grandest Belgian ladies and they've roped me in. They hope to raise x Belgian francs.' I couldn't believe my ears. It was too much even to imagine that the modest beginning – the shabby little garments spilling out over the drawing-room floor – had actually developed into a major drive by the top Brussels ladies with all the financial benefit that entailed. This was, I think, the only time in my life I received tangible proof of having given help. But I did not dare admit to the departing, grumbling figure that it was I who had been the pioneer.

Christopher's political diary during these two years reflected the inner and outer framework of his professional preoccupations: a commentary on internal Belgian political life, mainly concerning the linguistic question, and his work with the Belgian Ministry of Foreign Affairs about their government's attitude towards the negotiations for Britain's entry into the EEC. But the diary also reflected critical events both in world affairs and his own personal life. Thus for 10 November 1970 there is an entry which reads:

> De Gaulle is dead. I say to Risopoulos [Belgian MP] whom I meet at the theatre that we can now draw a line under the eighteenth century. The Memoirs, which I have just finished, are extraordinary. What grandiloquence. What megalomania. Some passages are almost unbelievable: *'Du coup, se dissipent les nuages .... Puisque, à la barre du navire de l'Etat, il y a maintenant le capitaine.'* Or, *'J'ai pu conduire le pays jusqu'à son salut.'* Even if true he might have let someone else say it! This volume is a voluntary for the world's biggest bassoon.

But previously, on 7 July, a more ominous entry, giving an example of how the Foreign Office sometimes stoops to bribing members of the service to take up unattractive postings in return for promotion:

> On leave in Ellis Green. I have just turned down the post of Deputy High Commissioner in Calcutta, on medical grounds that I cannot take H. there. But anyway it would be an exorbitant price to pay for promotion. By all accounts Calcutta is the lowest circle of the earthly inferno. But could no doubt have an agonizing fascination; it is the point at which Indian society is breaking up; it is a nexus of horror and squalor. But the job itself does not look much good. Derek Day [Head of Personnel Dept] says that I am offered it because they want to promote me and think I have a cool head. But it is a backhanded compliment. The jump into the next grade is crucial and I have been anxious not to be left behind. Now I have voluntarily foregone the opportunity. This feels odd; a moment of trauma. But I comfort myself with the thought – not my own – that the quality of life matters much more than the framework of it.

Indeed the quality of our lives at that time had all the advantages of being surrounded by such rich local culture. We visited Ghent and Bruges to admire the marvels of Flemish art. Ghent with its splendid cathedral, containing within it the Van Eyck masterpiece *The Adoration of the Lamb*. Surrounded as it is by nurseries devoted largely to azaleas, rohdodendrons and begonias, Ghent also claims the title of 'City of Flowers', and every five years it stages the internationally-known 'Floralies' pageant, one of which coincided with our time in Belgium. And Bruges, the ravishing medieval city almost surrounded by water, with its fifty bridges and its wealth of architectural and art treasures. Even now I only have to half close my eyes to imagine myself in the Memling Museum looking at the haunting face of the girl depicted again and again by the artist, the face that held Christopher enthralled on so many visits, although one occasion was also the scene of a family disturbance:

> To Bruges with children. My dismal performance as *père de famille* causes misery. While we are lunching in a third-rate *estaminet* I sulk over the gastronomic glories of Bruges that have been passed up. But in a better restaurant I should have been agitated about the children misbehaving! Happiness and unhappiness are not rational. At all events, I manage to see the marvels of the Communal and Memling museums. How wonderful is Memling's symmetrically beautiful girl who comes in all guises, as St Ursula, as the Madonna, and, on the back of one panel, with her hair falling round her bare breasts. Bruges needs visiting again.

Our exploration of the country gave us a great deal of pleasure and taught us many things about it. For instance, it made us aware of one element which so strongly characterizes modern Belgium and that is the paramount importance of the 'communes', headed by towns like Ghent, Bruges, Antwerp, Liège, etc. When we went to Antwerp, the capital of Flemish Belgium, famous among other things for its amazing Rubens collection, its Napoleonic quays and its wool trade, we recognized that its people tend to think of themselves, before anything else, as 'Antwerpenaars', proud of the close links of their town with ports in Britain and Germany – as well as Strasbourg. From my present place in the House of Lords I am often reminded that the contents of 'the Woolsack' originated in Antwerp.

But if the choice of where to go for a Sunday outing was left to the children, we always went to Waterloo. The battlefield, about three kilometres outside the little town, is so small that I found it impossible to believe that about 140,000 men took part in that battle in June 1815. No changes or buildings have been permitted on the terrain since the Duke of Wellington and his successors were given all rights over it. The battle headquarters of the Hougoumont farm and La Belle Alliance stand out so unexpectedly from the surrounding open farmland. The children with Konrad never tired of running up and down the steps of the pyramid built at the Butte du Lion on the spot where the Prince of Orange was wounded. Then, too, they loved visiting the panorama of the battle, the souvenir shops and the cafés. The discrepancy between the overwhelming evidence of the name of the vanquished general with the small Wellington Museum – the only memorial to the victor – showed an illogical contrast. On one visit we entered the little museum and looked around before signing the rather neglected visitors' book for the curator, who proudly showed us one entry which read as follows: '*Bernadette Servan Schreiber – sœur du futur Napoléon*'. Many a French eyebrow might have been raised by such a reference to one of France's most controversial contemporary sons.

We knew it could not be long before news of the next posting arrived. In the end it came unexpectedly when we were on leave in Essex. Christopher recorded it on 14 July:

> A curious interruption. My name was put to Soames [then British Ambassador in France] as Minister to Paris. He said he wanted to meet me. It was implicit but not quite explicit that his acceptance of me was conditional on this. So, after telephoning, Jane and I flew yesterday to Paris to dine with him and stay the night. We dined *en famille* in the garden. He and his wife were very friendly but I still felt rather like an *au pair* girl being interviewed for the job. He explained that he would expect me to 'do everything' as Michael Palliser had been doing, and particularly deal with the Quai. He is rumbustious, even I fear 'robust' . . . . But I suppose it is a good job although I have some misgivings.

The reason for his misgivings was that he had expected a return to his Middle Eastern circuit and was therefore surprised to be retained in the EEC one.

A week later his journal noted the final decision: 'Soames has written to the Chief Clerk to say that he "took to" me. So all is settled. I am to be succeeded in Brussels by Richard Hanbury-Tenison at the end of September or beginning of October.'

When Christopher told me that Soames wanted a meeting with him, my instinct warned me it might not go well. I had never met Christopher Soames, but I instinctively knew that my Christopher with his shyness and misleading old-fashioned look, might not immediately impress the kind of person I understood Soames to be. On the other hand, I knew that my own more outgoing style might impress him, whilst at the same time I felt my supportive presence would be a confidence booster to Christopher. So I made complicated arrangements for the children to be looked after, bought a new dress, as I only had gardening clothes with me, and took the plane with him, the result being that Christopher's journal *should* have read: 'He took to *us*.'

8

Never Had It So Good

Some people's lives run relatively smoothly, whilst those of others have ups and downs; but there are people, I think, who at a certain time feel they have reached such a pinnacle of satisfaction that the years leading up to that moment take on the proportions of mere foothills. I know that, for me, the time we spent in Paris reflects such a high point. Everything conspired to make it so. The family unit was intact. We were all together; alive and well. Christopher's job, Minister and No 2 in the Embassy (equivalent in rank to an ambassador in a smaller mission) was not only one of the most coveted in the service, bringing with it a wide range of political interest, but also one of prestige and privilege, a job which made us feel we were doing something worthwhile. And then there was France and the French. I must admit to a strong tendency towards Gallomania, which the dictionary describes as meaning an unreasoning attachment to France and French customs. I've always been like that. It is not only the physical ingredient of France and the enveloping beauty of Paris I love, but also the French capacity for communication and their ability to share joy and sorrow. I have since been lucky enough to benefit from the steadfast quality of their friendship, which includes loyalty to old friends fallen out of luck. But I do recognize that there are deep and fundamental differences between the French and the English. Many of these are based on past and present rivalries, and we tend to be critical one of the other. For instance, we are critical of the French because sometimes their practical considerations overshadow moral ones. And they criticize us for not working hard enough and being so hopelessly inhibited. So, as a people they do present a challenge which a British diplomat is well advised to recognize and stand up to as well as he may. For instance, initially — and if he has any sense – the diplomat posted to Paris might as well accept the unique quality of France and all things French (I found that easy), and it would be sensible of him to speak pretty good French himself (I was lucky enough to do so already). But I remember Christopher wistfully reflecting that, should a diplomat fall short of these requirements, then the waters might fold over his head and Paris would never hear of him again. Bonaparte made an important statement to a group of Englishmen after the signing of the Peace of Amiens in 1802, when he said: 'The two most powerful and civilized nations on the earth; we mutually deserve each other's esteem; and we ought to unite in cultivating peace, literature and the fine arts and by so doing form the happiness of mankind'. That was the sort of thing Christopher and I had in mind during those four and a half happy and fulfilling years.

We arrived in Paris on 13 October 1971. (It must be more than a coincidence that diplomatic families so often switch postings on the thirteenth of the month. It is as if airlines were forced to lower their fares on that superstitious day and a grateful government grabbed them.) As far as we were concerned, the day did bring bad luck: Christopher described our arrival at our new post:

Reach Paris in the evening from Brussels where we have driven in convoy to retrieve the dog and two hamsters. It was strange to be there without as it were belonging. We pass our house in the dark and see the curtains drawn and the new occupants' car outside. Not a good feeling. Last night we spent with Patricia Calmeyn at the Château de Drogenbos, a setting for *The Forsyte Saga*. I scrape my silencer off on her gateway. This delays our entry into Paris, which is in itself a nightmare. The strike of the metro drivers has turned the city into one enormous traffic jam. It takes us an hour and a half from the Gare du Nord to the rue François 1er. The cars are killing the life of Paris. They are anarchy and strangulation. Go to bed tired and apprehensive. It is a new bed brought at the last minute from London, since the Pallisers [our predecessors] carry their nuptial couch around with them. Rather surprising and endearing.

The bad luck was not confined to that day. Next morning I asked a pallid Robin what was wrong: 'My tooth aches,' he said. 'Oh, darling, are you absolutely sure?' I pleaded, forced to think more of my day ahead, already filled to capacity, than his tooth. He nodded painfully.

The administration department at the embassy gave me the name and address of the dentist most favoured by the other mothers. (Embassies everywhere have lists of approved doctors and dentists whose fees are met by Government funds, permitting embassy staff to enjoy the same advantage as do people at home under the National Health Service.) Robin and I set off down the huge staircase followed by Annie and Kate to see us off. I was just wondering how to fit Robin into the still unloaded car, which had the look of a down-market Oxfam shop, when there was a piercing shriek. Kate had somehow caught her small, three-year-old thumb in the hinge of the massive entrance door leading into the apartment building. Keeping hold of my insides, I looked at the minuscule limb which had entirely lost its rounded appearance and taken on the form of a flat wodge of papier mâché. We returned upstairs and I flew to the telephone to find out the name – this time – of the *doctor* most favoured by embassy mothers.

Christopher, usually successful in avoiding domestic dramas, found himself diverted from his planned flight to the embassy to drive poor Kate to *le docteur Dax* – an immensely smooth general practitioner, often wearing a January suntan, whom we were to get to know well in the coming years. Meanwhile Robin, by that time cross at losing the limelight to his sister, was taken by me to the dentist.

The official habitat of Her Majesty's Minister Plenipotentiary to the French Republic was a large and elegant first-floor apartment in the dignified eighteenth-century setting of the 8th arrondissement. Some of its windows overlooked the beautiful little circular Place François 1er at one end, and others the street itself. (There was one point – too close by far to our bedroom – at which cars during the night and the day changed gear when passing from the street into the little square.) It was structured, as in a Feydeau play, with all the rooms leading off the immense central hall and then communicating with each other round it. This meant there were three doors to each room – except for our bathroom and lavatory which had a mere two each. On coming in through the solid front door, one found on the right an exquisitely elegant drawing-room, its beautiful white marble fireplace flanked by panelled walls painted in a soft eau-de-nil with matching silk curtains draping the line of windows overlooking the street. The vast parquet floor bore a marvellous Persian rug originating, apparently, from Carlton House Terrace, the foreign secretary's house in London. And this spacious, perfectly proportioned, rectangular room was furnished with a mixture of French period furniture and elegant English upholstered sofas and armchairs in harmonizing pastels of pink, blue and lilac.

Leading from this extreme formality and through folding doors was a smaller square reception room, also with a great fireplace but a homelier atmosphere and more work-a-day furnishings. This became the family den. The next room was within the angle of the house, giving it an attractive lack of symmetry; again with a fireplace and its window overlooking the fountain of the little Place François 1er. This became the main guest room. Still moving round the central hall came the bedrooms: the master room, to be occupied by Christopher and I, followed by three others more simply decorated; and finally the tour ended at the dining-room, which was to the left of the front door and opposite the drawing-room. Behind all this grandeur lurked the kitchen area, entirely out of proportion to the rest. But the eighteenth-century French cared not enough for the comfort of *les domestiques*, for whom each apartment was allocated two or three *chambres de bonnes* on the top floor.

'We must start moving the furniture now,' Christopher said at the end of that accident-prone day. 'That'll make it feel more like home.' A few hours later nearly every bit of furniture had changed places, and we collapsed into bed feeling very much like the dog that had been turning round and round in its basket trying to make some imprint on it.

'You'll be all right, won't you?' Christopher said next morning – the morning the luggage was due to arrive. He noticed a particularly traumatized look spreading over my face, already disfigured by a heavy cold that morning; 'If anything goes wrong, just ring and I'll come back, but I must try and get stuck in at the office.' (His own anxieties were reflected by the entry in his diary: 'The first days are unsteady, rubbery, provisional, both in the office and among the packing-cases of the new abode. I hold my first office meeting. Better than I had expected. There is the eternal problem of where to start, a mass of small decisions to be taken on insufficient premises.')

The enormous packing-cases then made their appearance. At that time wood shavings were still used for padding purposes and the expertise – or lack of it – of the removal firm came to light. The children were the first to discover that we had made the wrong choice from the three estimates offered us in Brussels. When they opened one of the toy cases they found that an insufficient amount of wood shavings had allowed Lego to intermingle with chemistry sets, pieces of jigsaw puzzles, dominoes, Monopoly and so on. Pluralism was all very well – but this was too much. Lamenting loudly, they started the mammoth task of sorting it all out. However, the emergence of their bicycles soon diverted them and they happily started to thread their way through the packing cases strewn round the hall. (The fact that the hall was big enough for a cycling track was the one thing which, in the following years, made them excuse and accept the aloof formality of their house.)

Between blowing my nose and wiping my streaming eyes, I went doggedly on plunging my hands into the wood shavings and extracting objects. I came to one of our prized possessions: the lovely old barometer which had hung on walls in so many countries, often perplexed by the rapid change of atmospherics it was asked to digest. I drew it out carefully – it had just undergone expensive surgery – and walked with it over to the wall by the front door. That was the place for it, there was no doubt: it would then be the first thing you saw on coming into the flat. The telephone rang, and I propped it carefully up against the wall while I went to answer it. The caller was an entirely unknown French lady, and as I was trying to take in what she was saying my eye was caught and my whole being frozen by the sight of the precious heirloom, unhappy at having been balanced on its pointed end, slowly but inexorably crashing to the ground. Still holding the receiver, I cried out in pain – this must have startled the French lady, who up till then had probably thought the British impassive. Powerless and rooted to the spot, I gazed at the wreckage of broken glass, twisted arms and escaping mercury chasing itself round the floor at the other end of the hall.

There was nothing for it. Christopher was forced to leave his office sanctuary and return to the real world of the home scene to calm his hysterical wife.

We had looked at some schools on our earlier reconnoitring visit to Paris from Brussels, and as a result all was arranged for the two older children to start school next day. Henrietta had been inscribed at Sainte Marie Auxiliatrice, a convent, with lay teachers, run on rigid lines by a Spanish order but conveniently placed close by in the shadow of the Eiffel Tower. Robin was filling the place vacated by Marie and Michael Palliser's son at St Jean-de-Passy, which was a school run by the parish Jesuits and, although not in the same area as Henrietta's school, not too far down river from us. Henrietta had to be at school at 8.30 a.m. and Robin at 8.45, with the lunch hour of both schools stretching from twelve noon to two o'clock and collection time at four o'clock.

We set off the first day surrounded with the maximum amount of panic. Henrietta – then as now – was unconcerned about time, and it did not take Robin, who was to be dropped second, long to work out that the more she dawdled the more likely he was to be late. 'Henrietta, hurry up,' he yelled, standing by the front door clutching his satchel, hoping and praying that his clothes would be as appropriate for St Jean-de-Passy as they had been for the Belgian St Philippe. 'Co-o-o-o-oming,' came Henrietta's voice from beyond the hall full of wood shavings and half-opened packing cases. Finally she arrived, threading her way neatly through the chaos, looking her usual inscrutable self.

They survived their first morning with the fortitude diplomatic children are obliged to summon up, especially when their Belgian accents were mocked. On the way back for lunch along the Right Bank we started to play the game which became a daily diversion. 'Quick, let's catch the train while it's going over the bridge,' said Robin. This took place at the point just below the Trocadéro where the road passes under the metro line, and the aim was to drive under the bridge at the precise moment a train was hurtling over it (I well remember the comforting rumble over our heads). This game entailed either driving ferociously to catch an approaching train or holding back to wait for one. Both measures drew retribution upon us from the bewildered Parisian driver, who at the best of times is not the most tolerant of beings. At first, our Belgian numberplates attracted the contempt the French reserve for 'ces idiots Belges'. However, when we

became equipped with our CD numberplates their reaction turned
to one of maddened rage which such proof of diplomatic immunity
undoubtedly provokes in drivers all over the world. I believe the
reason the ordinary law-abiding citizen is so incensed by CD
plates is that he ignores the fact that in early times a diplomat
could not always carry out his functions unless protected from the
laws of his host country, but sees such immunity purely as a
protective mechanism against paying any parking fines. Harold
Nicolson admirably described the origin of diplomatic immunity in
the lectures he gave at Oxford in 1953 entitled 'Evolution of
Diplomatic Method':

> The origins of diplomacy lie buried in the darkness preceding what we
> call 'the dawn of history'! They came at a stage when the anthropoid
> apes inhabiting one group of caves realized that it might be profitable
> to reach some understanding with neighbouring groups ·regarding the
> limits of their respective hunting territories .... It must have soon
> been realized that no negotiation could reach a satisfactory conclusion
> if the emissaries of either party were murdered on arrival. Thus the
> first principle to become firmly established was that of diplomatic im-
> munity ...

There seemed little sense, however, in explaining this origin to the
Parisian drivers we had so thoroughly confused along the Quais.

'The ambassador has invited us to dinner on the eighteenth. It's
in our honour,' Christopher told me at the end of that traumatic
day. 'Here is a list of the other guests – perhaps you had better do
a bit of boning up.' I looked at the piece of paper with the names,
including brief biographical notes beside each one, knowing I must
learn it sufficiently to avoid mixing them all up; but, secretly, I was
wondering what I should wear on that important evening. When
the day came I had decided on a dress of black silk jersey, made by
Tzaritza, with a wide sweeping skirt, long full sleeves and the back
of the tight bodice slit to the waist but held by the high neck.
(Originally the front of the bodice was also slit from the high neck
down but, nervously, I had stitched it up, leaving only the top half
open; Christopher had called me a coward.) The very tight sash
was a mixture of vivid green and black.

Although we had to return home for Christopher's monocle,

without which his entire self-confidence collapsed, we arrived in good time at the beautiful house in the rue du Faubourg St-Honoré, which has been the British Ambassador's residence since the Duke of Wellington originally bought it from Napoleon's sister Pauline. It still contains all her treasures. The ambassador immediately gave his blessing to my dress by running his fingers up and down the slit at the back; this gave me a little confidence. Many of the guests featured prominently in the life of the country and I still remember the whole evening clearly. It was the origin of our friendship with the good-looking and talented couple Robert and Elizabeth Badinter. A brilliant lawyer, Robert became Mitterrand's Minister of Justice and has been responsible for abolishing the death penalty in France. At dinner, at one of the five round tables set for eight, I sat between André Fontaine, chief editor of *Le Monde* newspaper, and Denis Baudouin, the press attaché at the Elysée. Much as I enjoyed the conversation with my neighbours during dinner, I was rather shocked at one exchange. Christopher Soames – who decided on the menus and interviewed the chef himself every morning – was showing considerable satisfaction that his instructions to serve the grouse very rare had been observed. I wasn't so sure, from the looks on their faces, that the French guests entirely agreed with him as they watched the blood seeping out of the small birds on the plates before them. Impervious to this, he was pressing the bread sauce on his guests. Now we all know the critical attitude the French have towards our cooking; they make it even more obvious by labelling their most banal dishes with an English tag. Boiled potatoes are *Pommes de terre à l'anglaise* and cold collation is *Assiette anglaise*. But in spite of that I was rather shocked when I heard M.Baudouin, my neighbour, rejecting the bread sauce in a peremptory way by saying, '*Non merci, M.l'ambassadeur, je me méfie des sauces anglaises.*' The ambassador looked distinctly hurt.

'How did you get on?' I asked Christopher as we drove home, having stayed for a last drink and a post-mortem with Mary and Christopher after the guests had left. 'Well, anyhow I feel we've made a start with meeting the French. But what individualists they are – and intolerant too. There were two of them at dinner actually talking across the English lady between them because her French wasn't quite good enough, they reckoned. What about you?' 'Well, I managed to hold my own. André Fontaine even congratulated me on my French; but sounded surprised. However, I did come a cropper once when I turned a couple of deputy under-secretaries from being Foreign Office "mandarins" into French "*mandarines*" [as eaten at Christmas]. They nearly fell off their chairs laughing.' 'But how are we going to remember them all?' said Christopher despairingly. (He feared he might forget all of them whilst his distinctive black eyeglass would be remembered.) 'Well, I'm going to write a comment beside the names of the people I talked with, to help remind me,' I said, producing the list. 'Beside M. and Mme Racine I shall put 'both very small', and beside Denis Baudouin "he likes bullfighting", and for Mme Fontaine "very cosy lady", then when we next meet them it might help me remember who they are.' Christopher looked relieved.

Since our arrival we had tried to make some domestic arrangements and had engaged a Spanish couple and installed them on the fifth floor. Although they had the recommendation of an agency and good references, it immediately became clear that they were inefficient, aggressive and each had a *very* loud voice. Moreover, they immediately demanded higher allowances than those originally agreed, and within a week their two children arrived, unannounced, to be housed and fed by us. However, we were told that Spanish domestics in Paris – a real mafia – were so highly organized that resistance to their demands might bring on a visit from their trade union representative, and the idea of a Spanish version of Arthur Scargill knocking on our door was too dreadful to contemplate. (Christopher solved the dilemma in the end, as described in his journal on 29 December, when the children and I were away skiing: 'Have arranged the departure of the Mafia, our fearful Spanish couple, at enormous financial outlay, but feel much relieved. They were very oppressive.')

We gave our first party on 4 November – only three weeks after arrival. This was a big cocktail party in honour of the British consuls from Bordeaux, Marseilles, Lyons, etc., who gathered together each year for their conference in Paris, and it was the custom for the minister to receive them. We had decided, in addition to guests connected with the conference, to take the opportunity of including most of the embassy staff, whom we did not yet know, and Parisians to whom we had been given introductions before arriving. The result was that the party consisted of over a hundred people of whom Christopher and I knew practically no one. He obviously didn't enjoy it much: 'Our first C.P. – for the Consuls. Have a terrible time trying to identify people and also to remember who recommended whom. ... I never get the trick of it. And social obligation draws a curtain over my mind.' As my own whole preoccupation had centred on the administration of the party I was less perturbed than he at knowing so few of my own guests. From the organizational and visual point of view it seemed all right; with the children looking quite nice and, spurred on by the promise of heavy financial gain, handing round cocktail eats, fires burning in both fireplaces, and masses of flowers everywhere. (However, I learned that evening not to trifle with the Parisian *maître d'hôtel*; for, when I went to pay those we had engaged, I noticed they had not done the washing up and remonstrated. Serge, the leader of the group, gazed at me contemptuously and said, '*Madame, nous sommes maîtres d'hôtel, pas "plongeurs"*.')

Soon Christopher's journal reflected signs of strain. On 19 November: 'The pressure of work is horrible. Too much on my desk; too much to do. It will be better when I am more *au fait*. I can see that in this job one can do everything or very little. There doesn't seem to be anything in between.'

The reason he found his job so intensely busy was partly because a great deal was going on in the world requiring Anglo-French consultations, together with the work Britain's entry into the EEC involved, and partly because at first he was feeling his way in finding the best method of working with his new ambassador. His journal of 12 December reflected the diplomatic preoccupations:

Have to start thinking of a year which I have not seen here – for the Annual Review. It has been a pivotal year, a year in which France took a turning in her history. And in ours, because the change in her view of Europe centres upon our entry into it. The door to the change was opened by the departure of de Gaulle but history is not so personal. The perspectives were already changing. The General died in this year of change but his European policy was dead before he was. The crucial event was the acceptance that we would join the Community, the moment at which a positive will to see the negotiations concluded was injected into it. That moment came in May. The turning-point was when Heath was able to reassure Pompidou of our European intentions – it was a matter of personal confidence, of a sense of rapport. But the series of successful events in the negotiations started at the time of a monetary crisis in the Community in which the Germans prevailed over the French. Before that the Soviet-German Treaty had shocked the French with the realization that Germany was assuming a political as well as an economic prominence . . . . While France had the undisputed political leadership of the Community, whatever the real economic balance, she had no motive to see us come to share or steal it. As soon as she saw that she was losing that predominance to the Germans, the need to have us to weight the balance became overriding.

The triangular relationship will remain the problem . . . . There will be a problem of balance – to develop our new *entente* without appearing to be ganging up with one against the other. We shall have to tread carefully . . . .

The question is what remains of Gaullism. A large residue of principle and sentiment – much less of practice . . . . The desire remains, and to some extent the delusion, that France should have an independent power of decision and a primacy in Europe. This produced the concept of what the press here are fond of calling France's position of 'originality', that is to say the right to be eccentric within the Western Alliance. But all this is now qualified by a practical sense of the limitations on France's capacity to act independently, of the need for holding Western Europe together and developing the Community, and for counterbalancing and containing the emergent power of Germany.

We shall not be walking hand in hand into the sunset with the French. There will be strains upon our new relationship. They derive both from character and doctrine. French policy differs in basic attitude from that of ourselves and of the Germans about how Europe should conduct its relations on one side with the United States and on the other side with the Soviet Union . . .

Although I cannot imagine two men more different than Christopher and his new ambassador, they developed an excellent working relationship as well as a genuine affection for each other. Christopher, as the No 2, ran the embassy generally, presiding over the 10.15 morning meetings, and did all those things which need to be done at a responsible level. (The embassy staff at that time was made up of 50 diplomats, 59 other UK-based staff, such as PAs, secretaries, etc., and 120 locally engaged staff. In all 229, which is a sizeable embassy.)

Soames, in his capacity of political appointee, was able to maintain close contact with the leaders of Britain and France, whilst concentrating his interest primarily on those elements of Anglo-French relations that might have a lasting beneficial effect. Christopher, following the lifelong habit he shared with Denis Greenhill of giving people names, gave Soames the nickname of 'the elephant'. He was alluding not only to his size but to some extent to his style. 'The elephant shows that he can put his feet down gently,' he wrote in his journal when Soames had been successful in an effort of persuasion or reconciliation. And towards the end of their association he elaborated on the metaphor, describing 'the Great Pachyderm' as 'winning support and affection everywhere with tremendous trumpetings, brushing aside opposition with a genial swing of the trunk or an occasional savage prod of the tusk'.

'I'm really not sure that it's wise for you to borrow Diana's diamond tiara for the royal visit. It'd be just our luck if something happened to it. I've always been a great believer in sod's law.' Christopher's voice sounded genuinely concerned. Diana Beith – still in Brussels – had made this generous offer to help me look my very best for the state visit the Queen and Prince Philip made to France in May 1972.

The visit, designed as a suitable endorsement of the renewed political amity between Britain and France, was well timed and imaginatively organized. Not only was it an exercise in Franco-British public relations at the highest level, but it also attracted a great deal of interest from the French themselves. For after all they are at heart committed Royalists – although they had a funny way of showing this to their own royalty – and we at the embassy found ourselves suddenly fêted by Parisians who, up till then, had paid us little attention. Many of them remembered the Queen's previous visit in 1957 and were determined to be included on the guest-list for her present one. They inundated us with proof of their Anglomania: accounts of childhood holidays at Frinton; personal experience of English nannies; devotion to rice pudding and bread sauce; and undying loyalty to our language. But one elderly lady exceeded the bounds of credibility. On hearing that Prince Philip was keen on wildlife she – getting it a bit wrong – declared that she wouldn't have a word said against British royalty. We defended ourselves against this onslaught as well as we could and, rather than telling them they were not on the list, took refuge by saying that the lists had not yet been drawn up.

Arrangements for the visit started with the embassy being responsible for advising the Palace, liaising between them and the Elysée, and drafting the Queen's speeches for her consideration. Meanwhile the embassy wives were busy practising their curtseys and worrying about what to wear for the royal occasions. Over this I must admit to having been very lucky. First Diana's lovely tiara duly made its appearance, and then, to my amazement, one evening at dinner, Marie-Thérèse Clermont de Tonnerre, publicity director at the famous couture house of Chanel, said to me, 'You look pretty slim, Jane, would you like to borrow a couple of our dresses for the state visit? We sometimes lend the ones which are modelled each afternoon to people like you.' I couldn't believe my ears. 'But Marie-Thérèse, what do you mean? If this is a way of enticing us to buy something from you, it's really no good as a diplomat's salary wouldn't even rise to a Chanel T-shirt.' She assured me nothing was further from her mind and urged me to come round and try some dresses on. This I did; grateful for my continued small appetite which made it possible to squeeze into the beautiful dresses.

'My God – what *are* they going to say about this at the office when they see it?' Christopher was reading the papers in bed with his breakfast, as he always did. (The English papers arrived in Paris at the crack of dawn and a heavy package containing them and the French nationals was plonked on the Minister's bed at about 7.30 each morning. It wasn't that he absolutely *had* to read them, but he liked to arrive at the morning meeting well informed and able to score the odd point off the Press Counsellor.) That morning he had noticed an article in *Le Figaro* entitled, '*La visite d'Elizabeth II – sommet franco-anglais de l'élégance*', with sketches of the dresses to be worn by Mme Pompidou, Lady Soames and many more of the leading ladies. But what bothered Christopher was the drawing in the bottom right-hand corner with the caption: '*Pour Mrs Biggs, femme du ministre plénipotentiaire de Grande Bretagne, mousseline bleue et jaune* (Chanel).'

'If only they'd said you'd borrowed it. Now everyone 'll think I'm a bloody millionaire,' he said gloomily.

The first evening of the visit I wore one of the two dresses, delivered by taxi at our house after Chanel's afternoon showing and to be collected the next morning in the same manner. Christopher described the evening thus:

> We go to the President's dinner, theatre and reception for the Queen. Versailles is like a dream of its vanished royal splendours. It is evident that the French have spared nothing to make the aesthetics of the visit quite exquisite, and, being the French, they have succeeded. First the dinner at the Palais du Grand Trianon, followed by a performance of the second act of *Giselle* in the Théâtre Louis xv, skilfully restored fifteen years ago, and ending with the Reception in the Galerie des Glaces.

I still have the menu and programme for those gala occasions. They are in themselves works of art.

The next day, 16 May, the Queen received the President and Mme Pompidou for dinner at the embassy. The tableware had been brought over from Buckingham Palace for the occasion and the great state dining-room had never looked more sumptuous. The Queen made a speech in her good French – the original text had been lovingly composed by Christopher and he suffered intolerable pain at the changes imposed on it – and the President's reply was gratifyingly warm in European sentiment. After dinner, in all our finery we set off to the Champs de Mars to watch the equestrian performance: 'After the dinner the Cadre Noir and the Garde Republicaine perform on the Champs de Mars. It is a noble spectacle; spoilt yet made more courageous by the relentless rain. A few thousand Parisians nevertheless find it worth getting drenched to see it. The clouds over this visit are real not metaphorical ones.' I can remember seeing the Queen shivering during the spectacular performance. Wearing an elegant evening cloak which was hardly designed to protect her from such unusually cold, wet May weather, she did not have the comfort of rugs which the small fry, such as us, were enjoying at the back of the pavilion.

After a one-day visit to the warm weather of Provence, the Queen and the Duke of Edinburgh – now joined by the Prince of Wales whose ship was at Toulon – continued their programme in Paris. A reception given by the Commonwealth ambassadors which the Queen visibly enjoyed and where she seemed at her most relaxed. Then the races at Longchamps and in the evening the ball at the embassy. An elaborate marquee had been erected for the dancing at the back of the house between the two wings of the state dining-room and ballroom. There were huge banks of flowers everywhere and the beautiful house, so transformed by the famous Paris interior decorator M. Frank, became the most stately of pleasure domes. Whilst the Royal Family, the President and most honoured guests dined upstairs, the remainder of the guests – about 1,200 – waited downstairs for the dancing to start. During this interlude Christopher and I, with other embassy staff, were responsible for looking after them and, according to instructions, attempted to keep them spread evenly throughout the various drawing-rooms in preparation for the introductions which were to be made on the arrival of the royal group. But the French don't like being penned up, and having first become restless they then became hot, and when finally some of the ladies started to faint Christopher and I felt things were getting seriously out of hand. But all was forgotten when the Queen made her appearance looking the very image of royalty in a shimmering white dress. The ambassador led her off to introduce some of the guests, ranged round the edges of the rooms, Mary Soames did the same for Prince Philip, and it fell to Christopher to follow suit with the Prince of Wales. Knowing his weakness for remembering names, I anxiously watched the tall figure, looking more than ever the proto-type diplomat in evening dress, leading off the young heir to the British throne. I saw him making a series of introductions and when, his responsibility over, he returned, I said, highly relieved, '*Well done* – but why did you always choose people from the back row? The ones at the front looked furious.' 'Well, I could only be absolutely certain of remembering my friends from the Quai d'Orsay and, of course, they were modestly standing behind all the dukes and duchesses. But it was really amazing how much the Prince knew about foreign affairs – he absolutely stunned them.'

And finally there was the Queen's reception for the Embassy staff in the garden, and the presentation of decorations and gifts to those members who had been most closely responsible for the arrangements. The sun had finally come out and all the families were waiting their turn, ranged in a huge horseshoe round the lawn. This was the moment for Henrietta and Kate to perform their much rehearsed curtsey and Robin the courtly bow. But although Henrietta and Robin did well enough, at the last moment four-year-old Kate took fright, glued herself behind my legs and started throwing her current toy, a duck called 'Chickey', up and down in the air. And then it was too late – the Queen had passed on and Kate had missed her opportunity.

The next day the royal party departed: suddenly it was all over. The occasion made up of so much pageantry and splendour was behind us. Christopher in his despatch to the Foreign Office said:

> If success is the fulfilment of expectation and intention this visit more than succeeded. Though it conformed to the traditional pattern of protocol it was far more than just another of those state visits at which the Parisians shrug their shoulders and grumble about the traffic. It was an event in French life. It seized the imagination of the French people and enhanced their view of Britain. The Queen was for them exactly what they wanted and expected of her, a figure of magic and fascination, of royal mystique that is at the same time miraculously human. It was this that enabled the visit to accomplish as nothing else could have done its essential political purpose. For it was also more than merely a glittering and successful piece of international ritual. It was an act of state. It made its particular mark on the history of our two countries, and was intended to do so ...

But for Christopher – the ambassador having gone away for a few days – there came a sad postscript to the visit:

> 26 May – the Duke of Windsor is dying. We have to make elaborate plans for what will happen when he does. J. and I have to put off our planned weekend in Brussels to which for some nostalgic reason (or perhaps as an escape from a world of larger difficulty into one of petty success) I had been looking forward.

And then on 28 May, Sunday:

> The Duke of Windsor dies in the small hours of the morning. It is difficult to see this death in any way different to all other anonymous deaths. The early hours are much devoted to the telephone and little to sleep. The announcement is made at 6 a.m. At 3 p.m. I have to go to see the Duchess and take her through the arrangements. She and the body will fly together

to London on Wednesday. Now that he is dead he is respectable again. My painful interview is less awful than it might be. She is in command of herself, reasonable and dignified. She agrees to everything. The only difficulty is that she cannot remember for more than a few minutes at a time. We have a macabre conversation about what 'he will wear'. She is undecided whether it should be full military regalia or not. I have to find words to say that it will not matter as the coffin will not be opened (though I suppose there is the Tutankhamun case). Churchill was buried (says the Palace whom I consulted on the point) in his pyjamas. All the time I am talking to her in the drawing-room jammed tight with furniture a pug dog, under my chair, makes the most disgusting noises.

And then, despairingly, on 29 May: 'Still undertaking. The Duchess has now collapsed and will not go with the coffin. Everything has to be altered.'

By the summer of 1972 we felt as if we had been in Paris most of our lives. The beautiful flat had become almost like a home, the more so after we had injected some of our own taste by redecorating the dining-room and hall. Our domestic problems were solved. We had taken advantage of the modern-day cooks, who are girls – *jeunes filles de bonnes familles* – who wish to travel and become expert through courses such as the Cordon Bleu, and then hire themselves out to families living abroad. First they practise their expertise cooking lunches for businessmen in the City of London, but after that they search for diplomatic employers whose lifestyle they know will give their talents full scope. The prospect of big dinner parties filled them with satisfaction, and when I announced the date – far from grumbling like Victoria – they let out a stream of ideas as to the menu. But I always did the shopping, first because none of them spoke much French, and second because that was a way of keeping the huge food bills down a little. I went to the market on the way back from taking the children to school early in the morning. Sometimes I witnessed contests of wit between the vendors and housewives and the notes of shrill Latin voices flew around. But one morning I even took part in the contest and scored a remarkable victory. The vendor of oranges, always taking me for an American, addressed me with an exaggerated American accent every time I went to his stall. Finally, exasperated, I said I was English, not American. '*C'est la même chose,*' he said, but nearly went through the roof when I said, 'Right, well that means you must be Belgian.'

As the turnover of these girls was high (they always had another capital to see), we very much relied on the continuity of Amelia. She was Spanish and meticulous in her work; a shirt, she maintained, could not possibly be decently ironed in less than fifteen minutes. Being a superb needlewoman she often made alterations to my evening dresses to give them a new look. We all both depended on Amelia and loved her, and among the many, many letters I received after Christopher's death, hers stood out: 'As you did me the honour of allowing me to share in your happy days, I would now like to share in your sorrow.'

The final member of the staff was Percy, our driver. (The Foreign Office had settled on one of their well-known compromises by paying for him out of public funds whilst we provided and maintained a car.) Percy was very thin with piercing blue eyes and a gammy leg. He had two shortcomings: he drove the car on the clutch (we were obliged to replace it annually) and he had a weakness for the bottle. 'Yours is the wrong profession for drinking,' Christopher implored him, 'You'll kill us both.' But Kate loved him and would tickle the back of his neck when it was his turn to drive her to school. And there was his special language. Married to a French wife and having lived away from England for the last twenty years, he could no longer speak either language perfectly. Instead he combined the two with astonishing results. Here is an example of a typical one-sided conversation he might have had with Christopher whilst driving him to some destination: Don't worry, sir, I know the 'route' – first we go to the 'roundpoint' where the 'impair' numbers on this side of the street take over from the 'pair' ones. What's that, sir, my cough? Well, yes, I've got a bit of a 'bronchite'. The wife tells me not to 'fume' so much and to go to see the 'chirurgien' at the American Hospital. Mind you, I like going there because the 'infirmières' are so 'joly'. Soon the whole Embassy found their own language heavily influenced by 'Percy talk'. He took a particular pride in the task of collecting VIPs from the airport, and passed on to us any gem overheard in the back seat. One of the best was from Angela Greenhill. She was very impressed by the motorcycle outriders provided by the French to escort the Permanent

Under-Secretary at the Foreign Office and his wife into Paris: 'I wish we could have these at home, Denis,' she said enviously. 'I think we should try and get a cleaning lady first, dear,' came the sage reply.

Our dinner parties in Paris, compared to those in Brussels, presented an additional challenge: namely to counter the unreasoning bias against English cooking held by the French. Our cooking girls rose to this challenge and positively dazzled the guests with dishes unknown to France, such as smoked haddock mousse, steak and kidney pie, and all the English puddings which the French have to concede are better than theirs. Indeed, even the humble nursery apple crumble was greeted with delight and I was often asked for its recipe. The decision about the wines was made not by Christopher – who was at that time teetotal because of his migraines – and certainly not by me, with my weakness for '*un petit rouge*', but by Stephen Spurrier. Stephen was a young English wine merchant who had recently set up the Cave de la Madeleine near the Faubourg St-Honoré and subsequently became accepted by the French themselves as an authority on wine. I used to ring him up and tell him our menu for the evening, and he sent the wines to go with each course.

My records show what a great number of official visitors flocked to Paris, and the consequent parties we gave for them; such as for the visit of the Royal Philharmonic Orchestra, or for Department of the Environment officials in Paris to study older housing policy in France; another for the whole cast of Peter Brook's *Midsummer Night's Dream* and French guests from the theatre world to celebrate the first night; another for the visit of the British Delegation to the Anglo-French Parliamentary Group, and many, many others. But one party which has stood out in my memory was for Goronwy Roberts – at that time Minister of State at the Foreign Office – described by Christopher in his journal as 'very Welsh and philosophical'. We invited all the diplomatic staff to a buffet lunch to meet their Minister. How could I have foreseen then that only five years later Goronwy, with Denis Greenhill, would be a sponsor for my introduction to the House of Lords.

The guest-lists for these parties were largely made up of people who through their occupations were connected with the occasion, but we always added a few extra people from two permanent lists we kept;

one was a list of beautiful people and the other of single, glamorous girls. (It is a fallacy that diplomats just entertain other diplomats — apart from our own opposite numbers in other embassies, we saw little of the diplomatic corps.)

'Mummy, you know there's a fire on in the little drawing-room,' said four-year-old Kate following me into the kitchen one evening where the last frenzied preparations were going on for the dinner party. 'Yes, of course I know, darling. Serge has just lit one in each drawing-room.' Kate opened her mouth to say something else, but obviously deciding that grown-ups were a lost cause she turned on her heel and left the kitchen muttering something to herself. It was only a fluke that she was overheard by her sister. 'But Kate says she's never seen a fire lit in the *middle* of the drawing-room before.' This had the instant result of four grown-ups hurtling to the scene of action where, sure enough, an overturned electric fire was burning a huge hole in the carpet. 'Mummy, take care,' said a much mollified Kate as she watched me in my flimsy little evening shoes, holding up the skirt of my long evening dress, jumping up and down on the burning carpet trying to quench the flames. With a sofa pulled over the blackened hole and windows opened to clear the smoke, we went back to our preparations.

The three round tables looked elegant enough. Laid for eight people, each one had different-coloured long tablecloths with matching candles in the candelabras to help guests identify their places. The *placements* had been carefully worked out and Christopher was satisfied with his neighbours, who for once were sufficiently decorative. ('But don't you think so and so is a bit intellectually pretentious?' I asked, hopefully, of one of them. 'Doesn't matter — it's better to be pretentious than not to try at all,' he said contentedly.)

The guests started to arrive. Christopher and I together welcomed them and then I took over to carry out the formal introductions because I was better at it. (We were considered good diplomatic partners, each possessing characteristics which complemented those of the other. My contribution was to create the well-organized, relaxed background which gave Christopher the confidence to project his original intellect and individualistic humour so appreciated by the

French.) However, the appearance of our tenth guest set alarm signals ringing madly inside my head. 'Who on earth is that man?' I whispered to Christopher. 'Oh, my God, don't *you* know who he is?' In our panic we overdid our welcome and then, giving Christopher despairing looks, I took him off on the round of introductions. In the trade, introducing two people whilst knowing the name of only one is a well-known trick. Fixing the nameless face with a steely look and using a confident tone: 'Monsieur, may I introduce you to Madame Verney', and so on round the whole circle. Meanwhile the awful truth was dawning on me. As we sometimes, for convenience, made the arrangement for two consecutive dinners simultaneously, this gentleman had obviously come to the wrong one. 'My wife was *desolée* she was not able to be here,' he said. Thanking God for small mercies, I raced out of the drawing-room to unearth the list of guests for the following occasion from my desk, and through a process of elimination I identified the mystery character as being M. Jean Schwoebel of *Le Monde*. An extra place was hastily squeezed in round the table and namecard written out. We then went in to dinner. But M. Schwoebel must have pondered long and hard at the overdone welcome and the cramped seating arrangements. (I know of a worse experience when another diplomatic hostess was forced, at the last minute, to replace an absent *maître d'hôtel* with a visiting nephew. The startled young man, thrust into a white coat and hastily drilled, performed his task superbly. But when offering the dish to the hostess herself she entirely lost her head – probably out of relief – and instead of saying '*Merci*' in clipped tones she looked up at him and said, 'Darling, you *are* an angel'. Her guests thought her highly democratic.)

Finally the party was over; the three *maîtres d'hôtel* had been paid their fees and the two English girls had finished the massive clearing away. 'Well, apart from the Schwoebel drama, was it all right?' Christopher asked.

'Yes, I think so – more or less. But the Meringue Vacherin nearly ended up on the floor a few times. The meringue was a bit glutinous and some people were having a dreadful tussle serving themselves. But there was a hilarious moment. I noticed our guest of honour kept peering anxiously at the Admiral's wife on his other side. I couldn't think what was wrong. Then eventually Konrad made his appearance from under the long tablecloth, and he burst out laughing. What he had taken as an advance from the formidable-looking lady had in fact been Konrad brushing up against his leg.'

'What about the *chef de protocole* on your left – did you get on all right with him?'

'I did my best, but I'm afraid I became a bit fed up because he is such a dreadful snob. Having dropped names all through dinner (I asked him what the French for name-dropping was and he said "le name-droppin'"', he thought), he then went on and on about some duke he knew who had fallen off and hurt himself on the hunting field, until I couldn't bear it another second and said, "Well, it's very dangerous for the fox too, you know." I'm afraid he didn't look pleased. Sorry about that.'

'Oh well, it could have been worse. Do you remember how badly you behaved at that enormous dinner at Versailles. You were cross because one of your neighbours had completely ignored you until the very end of dinner when, with a haughty look, he said, "*Eh bien, Madame, et qu'est-ce que vous faites?*" and you said, "*Je suis dans la restauration.*" He then fell into a complete panic, thinking by sitting next to a restaurant owner he had demeaned himself, and nervously asked, "Where?" You then finally put him out of his agony by telling him you really meant you ran rather an elegant little hotel/restaurant in the rue François 1er for your husband, the Minister at the British Embassy; and that made him feel better.'

'Yes, I do remember,' I said rather guiltily, 'but anyhow I did have this nice, non-contentious conversation about the English and French languages this evening. I was saying how much I liked "*le rush*" for rush-hour traffic, and then tried my theory that each language only lacks words for which national characteristics have no need. Thus in English there is nothing for "*débrouillard*" and "*bricoleur*"; in French no words for "self-conscious" or "considerate". But I persuaded them that English was the language of sensuality by pointing out that, whilst an uneven roadside verge is an "*accotement non stabilisé*" in French, we call it a "soft shoulder". But what about you?'

'Well, I had a very nice time, for once, with my neighbours at dinner, but afterwards I became quite infuriated by one of our

Westminster MP guests.' 'What happened?' 'It was right at the end and I noticed him out in the hall so, thinking he was looking for you or me to say goodbye I went up to him and all he said, looking at me, was, "Where's my coat?". God, what manners.'

I should admit that whilst Christopher's major occupational drawback was absent-mindedness, mine undoubtedly was a lack of discretion. First, I like telling people things and I can still see his haunted eye fixed on me across a crowded room, praying I was not divulging some state secret he had been foolish enough to confide to me. Second, I *have* been known to over-react to the type of person – not unknown in diplomatic circles – who combines being arrogant, opinionated, dogmatic and reactionary. However, we devised a way of stopping me in my tracks. The codeword was 'Kippers', and Christopher whispered it when he saw the danger signs and this made me laugh instead. Robin caught on, and sometimes in the middle of a discussion, not intended to be heated, I heard the small, fair-haired boy urgently muttering, 'Kippers, Mummy, kippers.' But I think it is fair to say that perhaps too much is asked of diplomatic wives. They are always expected to be there; to look nice; to say the right thing; to have no definite news of their own; to remember everyone's names; not to complain; and so on. Sometimes they rebel.

But there *were* the occasions when Christopher was particularly pleased with me. Searching for some intellectual outlet, I had applied to be an *auditrice libre* at the Sciences-Po just off the boulevard St-Germain, and had earmarked as interesting a course on the history of the French Socialist Party and another on the setting up of the EEC. These were the lectures I tried to attend regularly. On the morning of a large lunch party for one of our Labour Party parliamentarians – John Silkin, as I remember – I managed, between shopping and flower arranging, to go to my lecture on *politique comparé*. I arrived back just in time to greet everyone and during lunch succeeded in positively flabbergasting our guest of honour with my expertise and detailed knowledge of the birth of the French Socialist Party. I felt him make the mental adjustment that diplomatic wives were perhaps less the creatures of the salon and more radical in their attitude than he had imagined.

However, it was occasionally Christopher who refused to dance the minuet, as witnessed by his journal: 'Memorial service at Versailles for Nancy Mitford. In the condolence line I walk past [Sir Oswald] Mosley without shaking his hand. Not pleased with myself, but might have been still less pleased if I had shaken his hand after saying I never would. My defence is that I am not religious, but I am superstitious: I could not shake hands in a church with someone who had sold his soul to the devil.' On another occasion he was equally frank, this time about the newly elected leader of the Tory party, whom he nicknamed 'the madonna of the menopause'.

I cannot claim that the children entered into either the spirit or the actuality of our parties. Henrietta gave them a wide birth, but was obliged to protect herself from straying guests by putting up a graphically illustrated notice on her bedroom door saying, 'The loo is not in here – but straight on and to the left.' Robin considered the whole performance fake (and indeed who, when viewing a room full of people standing at close proximity shouting at each other, could blame him), so he only took part if paid to hand things round. But Kate took another line. In order to prove to herself that she was leading a normal life, she pretended that the party just was not happening. For instance, when she needed help with her homework or tucking up in bed, etc., she marched straight towards me in the drawing-room through the throng of guests, as if they didn't exist, to remind me of a maternal responsibility. At dinner parties she sometimes came to the table and sat on my knee, sucking her thumb, looking straight through any guest who had the temerity to address her. One evening there was a contest among the guests to make her smile. Luc de Nanteuil, now French Ambassador at the UN, won. 'What did you say to her, Luc?' – as Kate positively beamed at him. 'Easy,' he said. 'I didn't say anything – I just slipped twenty francs into her slipper.' Enslavement to the diplomatic pit of perpetual politeness could not have been applied to our children.

To balance our Parisian life with excitement, enjoyment, hard work and artificiality all mixed up together, there was Villereau. Soon after our arrival in 1971 we rented a little house in the Essonne valley, close to Fontainebleau, about sixty miles from Paris. Villereau was a tiny village and there was an even smaller one next door called Dimancheville. (We earned admiration from the French for having discovered a village so appropriately named for weekends.) The lawn – or grassy slope – reached down to the river bank, and we taught our French guests cricket (they never took to it because of the many ways of losing), and from the little bridge we introduced then to Pooh-sticks. The flocks of children who were always there played badminton, football and paddled for miles along the river in their boat. Sunday walks along the river banks provided the most relaxed settings for political discussion, and when our dear friend Roger Massip, diplomatic correspondent for *Le Figaro*, had been a guest the newspaper's Monday leader often reflected the ideas exchanged. (His Anglophile wife Renée, coming out of our bathroom one day, made the immortal remark about the TCP. '*Vous ne pouvez pas imaginer*', she said, '*l'émotion que j'ai éprouvé en voyant la bouteille de TCP dans votre salle de bain.*') And one of those walks was long remembered for what Henrietta said. The topic was Peter Brook's Paris production of *Timon of Athens* and the rather shy little girl suddenly remarked, 'What was Shakespeare's last word?' We all admitted defeat. '*J'expire,*' she said triumphantly. (I am ashamed to say that soon this was absorbed into Christopher's personal repertoire!)

For Konrad, too, the weekends were heaven on earth, but sometimes when hurtling along the river-banks he ended up in fights with neighbours' dogs, and on one occasion Christopher's hand was bitten when separating the contestants. In his usual mild and polite manner Christopher asked if the dog was injected against rabies. '*Non,*' came the immediate reply, 'but it doesn't matter as I'm fully insured.'

Entries in Christopher's journal showed how much he loved the place and needed its calm as an escape from the pressure of Paris: 'At Villereau having a very good day. Indulging my masochistic and new-found obsession with chess. It is not as if I had that kind of mind. Such as I have is deductive and slow where chess needs one fast and inductive.' And again: 'At Villereau in the snow. Daunts staying. Colvins and Françoise Jockey to lunch. Content.' But the Sunday evening returns to Paris were dreadful. Mile upon mile of bumper-to-bumper, ill-tempered, impatient French drivers. Sometimes to avoid this we set off in the early hours of the morning, having moved the sleeping children from their beds to the back seats of the two cars and then moved them back to their beds in Paris. This, from their point of view, was an excellent system but disastrous for us as we failed to get much sleep at either end. So all in all, although those weekends stand out in my mind for all the warmth, friendship and fun they inspired, it was tiring for me. 'What help do you have down here?' a guest once asked. I showed him my two hands.

Towards the end of 1972 Christopher Soames was appointed a commissioner to the EEC. The whole family had been liked and respected in Paris. Not only had Christopher succeeded in his mission of propelling his country into the European Community, but Mary with her warmth and intelligence – not to mention her Churchill connections – attracted a great deal of affection. Furthermore, the French liked the way all five Soames children were part of the team and played such an active part in the life of the Embassy. And their parties, with dear Jane Morton as social secretary, were run on well-oiled wheels.

Christopher started writing drafts for the farewell speeches. On 31 October he noted: 'C.S. gets a good press this morning. It is funny to read my phrases in all the newspapers. The one about the need for a second European Renaissance got two headlines in the French press.' And on 2 November: 'More speech writing. At one time am working on a farewell speech to Pompidou by one Amb. and a credentials speech to him by his successor. I am becoming a platitude factory.'

The farewell parties in their honour started up and on 6 November the President himself entertained the departing ambassador.

> Pompidou's lunch for the Soames. To our surprise, Jane is next to the President and I next to Mme P. When she sees the table plan Jane turns in desperation to Peter Ustinov and says, 'For God's sake tell me something funny to tell him.' He cannot ...

However, all went well – I need not have feared. The President was charming and immediately put me at my ease. Afterwards Mme Pompidou showed us round the Elysée – including the rooms she had been criticized for modernizing: 'As if Paris did not contain enough of the *dix-huitième* without these two or three rooms,' she said.

The Soameses were leaving on 8 November. On the morning before, the whole Embassy staff came together to say goodbye to them in the front hall of the chancery. Christopher on their behalf made the presentation of a silver box and a speech – it was a mixture of humour and sentiment – and here are the notes he made for it:

This is the Ambassador's last day in the office, so we are here to say goodbye to him and to Lady Soames. He has said all his official farewells, he has made all the speeches. He has shaken the hands of all the many people who are called Monsieur le Président, including the real one along the road, who said some very nice things about him and Lady Soames. The President said one very striking thing that has not appeared in the press. He said, 'You have won.' That I think really sums it up. You have wound up your very successful mission here and are moving on to another no less important for the future of Europe. But this is a different kind of moment. This is the scene in the courtyard at Fontainebleau. This is where the Emperor takes leave of his Old Guard. And we, like the Old Guard, remain behind dutiful but bereft. The Paris Conference [EEC summit meeting] was a very fitting end to your mission here. We have been up to the Summit. Our man Mr Heath stuck his ice axe in up there with the best of them. It was a considerable achievement. But one doesn't reach the Summit without a base camp. The base camp was this Embassy. And under your leadership, Sir, it was a very good base camp indeed. We shall remember other things. Your extraordinary habit of never seeming to have time to read the telegrams yet always having read the only one we have not. Your equally extraordinary habit of swooping instinctively on the essential point while the rest of us are still labouring towards it by the time-honoured processes of logic or trial and error. And those wonderful office meetings – the cloud of cigar smoke, the sparks of wit, the rumblings of menace for those who had not done their homework – something rather like communing with a volcano. We shall miss all that now that you are leaving us.

The ambassador, visibly moved, wiped his eyes. 'You were too good, Christopher,' he said. 'You quite bowled me out.'

The next day, 8 November, the journal records: 'The Soameses depart with two doves in a cage on the back seat of the Bentley and Churchillian tears. Today there is a deafening silence in the Embassy.'

Christopher was then chargé d'affaires for one week before the arrival of the new ambassador. On 11 November he noted:

The annual diplomatic deep-freeze at the Arc de Triomphe while M. Pompidou sets light to the unknown soldier or whatever. Then in the afternoon to Notre Dame for the British Legion's commemoration service. I have to lay a wreath. . . . We should forget war, not commemorate it. The Anglican priest at least avoided the usual metaphysical compromise and did not try to reconcile Prince of Peace with God of War. He dwelt on the uselessness of war, while the British legionaries looked disapproving.

And again on 13 November:

Soeharto is here. At the reception at the Quai he talks for quite a long time with Abrasimov, whose hair I notice is tinted mauve. The Russians are good at forgetting. In the evening there is the usual gala at the wonderful little theatre at Versailles. Béjart followed incongruously by Les Sylphides. When I point out the extraordinary contrast to the Chef du Protocol he says they just order it by the yard – an hour and fifteen minutes.

On 15 November Edward Tomkins and his wife Jill arrived from their previous Embassy in The Hague. They were given the traditional welcome for newly arrived ambassadors to Paris, whereby real candles are lit in all the great chandeliers throughout the house. Edward, with his beautiful French – from his French mother – and his real gift for conversation did so much for Anglo-French friendship, and he and Jill – who in addition worked hard to conserve the house in its pristine beauty – were very popular in Paris (as will be shown in Christopher's journal on their departure).

By this time I had managed to assemble all the children together in one school – the École Alsacienne near the Jardin de Luxembourg. Neither of the previous schools had been very satisfactory, and Kate had put her small foot down when I tried to coax her into the Jardin d'Enfants of the École Bilingue (an excellent school which taught French children English and English children French). With an unlaudable degree of chauvinism she said that English was quite good enough for her and threw more tantrums than I could have believed possible when taken to school. But they all loved their new school. Established by the Alsatians a century ago, it had a special *esprit* of its own and the children (boys and girls) were treated and taught in a more relaxed fashion than in a typical French school. Soon Kate was chattering away in French. 'So you *have* learned French after all,' we said to her. 'Certainly not,' she said, 'I've just copied the other children.' She usually got the last word – as is so often the case with the youngest of a family.

Percy and I shared the school runs. I took the three children in the morning and collected them at the end of the day: he covered the lunch-time runs. 'Madam, I wish you'd stop that 'enrietta from lying on the floor-boards at the back of the car when I take her to school,' he said rather plaintively one day. 'Why on earth do you do that, Henrietta?' I asked her. It transpired that at this school, priding itself for an anti-snobbish stance, another girl had accused Henrietta of coming to school in a Rolls-Royce. 'No, no,' said poor Henrietta, 'it's certainly not a Rolls but a *very very* old Daimler. And anyhow it doesn't belong to us', she threw in for good measure. Unconvinced, her inquisitor then darkly suggested it had been a chauffeur at the wheel. In desperation Henrietta said, 'Oh no – certainly not. That's just a very good friend of ours.' After that how could she be blamed for making herself invisible on the floorboards.

However, the transport system brought on an unexpected romance. Annie, trying to learn French, joined the school run to go to her language course close by the children's school. But as her morning lesson stopped half an hour before theirs she filled in the time at a nearby café. Each day a good-looking young waiter called François brought her her cup of coffee. This came to a conclusion about three years later with their marriage. (I will not go into the shock this was to the 10th Baronet, Annie's father.)

The three children were by this time bilingual and, on looking back, they all now agree that the École Alsacienne was the school they liked best of all; but, in spite of this, we came to the agonizing decision to send Robin to an English boarding-school in September 1973. It had been difficult to meet the energies of a fairly rumbustious ten-year-old boy within the formality of our lives and home; moreover, we recognized that the longer we left it the harder it would be for him to catch up in the English educational system. He himself liked the idea of going to the Dragon School in Oxford; but it was I who found myself entirely unprepared and unable to cope with the trauma brought on by his departure. Christopher's journal bore this out: 'Jane to Oxford to see Robin; in a state of depression. Is this system right – or should we break with it?' And again: 'Robin returns to school. Jane is in despair.' I could not bear the thought of not being able to continue to participate closely in his life any more; see him when he was ill; talk to the teacher if something was wrong, be there for a special match in which he was playing, and so on. Each time I saw him off at the airport it was like suffering a physical and mental amputation. (Mothers further afield often had to make decisions between temporarily deserting a husband to be with a child.) But although the first terms were extraordinarily painful, I think in the long run the security provided by the permanence of the Dragon School was of benefit to Robin.

Christopher, besides missing his son, was most affected by my despair and in an effort to comfort me he bought me a new car and I picked up the lovely, shiny red Triumph Stag on my next visit over to see Robin.

As in Brussels, again in Paris I cajoled the wives into doing some social work, but this time with the additional objective that the work should create a forum in which to meet each other. It is an unexpected truth that big, glamorous cities such as Paris can prove inevitable deserts of loneliness for junior wives and secretaries, whereas small, difficult postings may provide the intimacy and common bonds which prevent loneliness. I soon discovered that a Cheshire Home was planned in southern France and decided we at the embassy might work towards raising funds to furnish, say, one or two of its rooms. With considerable courage (for it had not been done in the Paris embassy before) I announced that with this aim we might start fortnightly sewing afternoons at rue François 1er. I can't claim that the idea went down with a swing, and when the wives arrived on that first Wednesday I sensed a heavy air of disapproval. However, the hard core of needlewomen came from the chancery guards' wives (chancery guards concern themselves with the security and certain administrative arrangements in a mission and tend to serve only two-year postings), and soon furry animals, patchwork, baby clothes, crochet and knitted garments, etc., were piling up. The sale was to take place at a reception in the residence on 13 November 1973 for which, of course, tickets were sold. The French guests were astounded by 'le tombola' and 'le raffle' (phenomena little known in France), and even more so by the homemade marmalade, fudge, biscuits, cakes, etc., which even the French think we are better at than they are. The profit made was enormous and we were all delighted with ourselves, and also, having spent those afternoons together, we all knew each other a little better – and for that I was deeply grateful.

I never again embarked on a venture as ambitious, but did establish the idea of building an 'emergency or crisis fund' which could be used if a need arose. This was quickly and successfully set up in ingenious ways. One wife organized a get-fit session in return for payment; another gave embroidery lessons; a group started writing a cookery book, etc. But the first award we made was an unexpected one. After a match at the Parc des Princes the disappointed supporters of Leeds Football Club ran amok and caused considerable damage to property. An elderly gentleman, in their way, had his specs knocked off and smashed. Our crisis fund provided him with a new pair. We hoped it would be helpful to him and in a small way repair Britain's image.

On 1 January 1974, Christopher began his new diary with a *tour d'horizon*:

The New Year starts very doubtfully. Our own situation in England is awful. The three-day working week which begins today is like saying I need to eat less, therefore I am pulling out my teeth. Here in France there is an undoubted malaise, a doubt about the President, what may be a failing fount of decision, a government that has not met the demands of public feeling. Europe cannot tell what will be the effects of the rise in oil prices, that has changed the whole basis of its economy. Some good things could come of it: the end of the cult of growth as the basis of society, the narrowing of the gap between developed and under-developed countries, the impulsion to European unity. But the outlook is uncertain; the prognosis doubtful; the economists caught with their trousers down. One can hope but one cannot affirm.

Then, in March 1974, the Embassy was unexpectedly involved in a most tragic affair. At Senlis, about thirty miles outside Paris, there was an air crash. I wrote an account for the DSWA magazine:

On the afternoon of Sunday 3 March, a huge DC10 of Turkish Airlines took off from Orly with 346 people on board. 185 of them were British, mainly British Airways passengers from Paris to London who had transferred to this flight because of a strike at Heathrow. When the aeroplane reached 13,000 feet above the countryside north of Paris, the door of the baggage compartment at the back flew out. The sudden depressurization caused the floor of the passenger compartment above to cave in. ... The controls running through the floor were jammed. In consequence, one minute later, the aeroplane flew more or less level and at about 1,000 kilometres an hour into the forest of Ermenonville, near Senlis. It cut a swathe over 500 metres long. It, and everything and everybody inside, were reduced to small pieces. . . .

The most tragic difficulty, and that which concerned the Embassy most directly, was that of identification. Very few of the bodies were immediately identifiable, none was complete. Moreover it very soon became clear that the passenger list of this aircraft did not give exact information about who was actually on it. The names of the British passengers were hastily added, often wrongly spelt, some of them had exchanged tickets and were travelling with tickets issued in someone else's name. This all made it impossible for the authorities to know exactly who was on board.

There were two ways in which the French authorities set about the task of identifying the dead. . . . First, the French forensic authorities worked painstakingly for two months and succeeded in identifying 83 British passengers – many more than seemed likely at first. But, in preparing death certificates for the rest, the French had to rely on circumstantial and documentary evidence – such as jewellery, clothing, passports, driving licences, etc., found on the scene of the crash. It was to help in this that large numbers of British relatives were flown over to France. They were taken in bus loads to the little town of Senlis, to the small police station which I imagine, in normal times, is a quiet, undramatic place, but was then filled with the intimate belongings of 346 people – twisted and mangled rings, brooches, spectacles, watches. In one of the little churches long lines of trestle tables had been put up and onto them had been piled, in damp and tattered profusion, the clothes that had been found. Also books, photographs, handbags, children's toys and letters. But pitifully few when matched against the number of owners.

The Consulate-General was overwhelmed with work – a lot of it of a very technical nature, but it was obvious that here was a situation where the wives could make an important and valuable contribution. We organized ourselves into teams to be at Senlis police station to meet the groups of relatives being brought out by British Airways and other travel agencies for purposes of identification. We met them there at the place where this awful, and to many of them still incomprehensible, thing had happened, to try to make it more bearable for them. We were there also to help in a more practical sense to interpret between them and the less than Anglophone, but more than sympathetic and compassionate, Senlis police. We were there to guide them round the harsh contents of the little church and to feel with and for an elderly mother when she recognized the lacerated remains of the coat in which she had last seen her daughter. We were there to talk to them and – even more important, perhaps – listen to them: to discuss the enormity of the tragedy and to explain the appalling problems faced by the authorities. Once the search was over and the formalities completed, we took them to small cafés in the town and ordered their meals and shared in their relief that some of the ordeal was over. . . .

As far as the relatives were concerned, there is no doubt that our presence was of use. Without us the difficulties of filling in the complicated police forms might have been even greater and without us the feeling of shock even stronger. We saw them all again at the funeral which was held on 9 May. They made us feel as if we were their friends and that we truly had helped them to endure the grotesque act of violence which had so brutally struck at their lives.

The final tragic irony came just over two years later when some of the wives bereaved in the crash wrote me letters of sympathy after yet another 'grotesque act of violence'; the one which destroyed Christopher.

'*Le Président de la Republique est mort.*' We were all in the bar of the little hotel at Courchevel on a family skiing holiday in April 1974 when the newscaster's voice told us this. There was a stunned silence. Although it had been a well-known fact that he was ill and his bloated and highly coloured face gave proof of a heavy intake of cortisone, the real nature of it, a malignant and lethal deterioration of the bone marrow, had never been disclosed. The President showed a wonderful, indeed heroic, courage in choosing to go on to the very end of his strength. The physical and mental struggle, the strain of this enormous act of deception, must have been horrible. (Later his staff admitted in the final stages to hearing him crying with pain in his office.) But as Christopher put in his journal:

It is a frightful thought that a man could be secretly and mortally ill behind closed doors and yet have so much power. The Fifth Republic, as it has evolved under its only two Presidents, makes the Elysée the centre

167

of decision and President P. clung to the steering-wheel right to the end
and died at it. But now there is a political vacuum.

We returned to Paris the following day and Kate, who from afar
had been attracted to the President, went straight to her record-player
and stood gravely listening to the song she had put on – it only had
one line: 'I love *you* Mr Pompid*ou*.' She was paying her respects to the
man who, in her words, 'was sort of fat and nice'.

The leaders of Britain's three political parties came to the memorial
service at Notre Dame. Afterwards there was a small lunch party for
them at the embassy; a few people from the embassy, including
Christopher and I, were invited. The mood was sombre for more
reasons than the central one. Mr Edward Heath's electoral defeat on
28 February was reflected in his tense look, and Harold Wilson,
viewing the future without an overall majority, looked little better.
Since Jeremy Thorpe appeared the most cheerful, I took my plate (it
was a buffet lunch) and sat down beside him. 'Why have they both
brought their doctors with them? Do you know? After all, they're
only in Paris for the one day, and French medicine is not exactly
backward.' 'Good question,' said Jeremy, who seemed in excellent
spirits. 'In fact I asked the PM the very same question myself.' 'What
did he say?' 'Well, he said he only decided to bring Dr Stone when he
heard Ted was bringing his, because, as he put it, "I don't want Ted's
doctor going and stuffing a hypodermic needle into *me* if something
goes wrong."' And then, to the accompaniment of a great deal of his
own enthusiasm, Mr Thorpe added, 'So I said, "Of course, Prime
Minister. Quite understand. 'Fraid I can't bring mine because I think
he's too busy – but I could bring my dentist."'

Anyone who has ever spent August in Paris knows of the phenomenon
which overtakes the city. As Parisians take their holidays *en bloc* – the
majority in August – this leaves the city with a special ethereal quality. The frenzied pace slows down. The reduced flow of traffic runs
smoothly. Many of the restaurants and small shops close down for
the month. There is a lull; bringing with it a greater intimacy between
those who remain there. With the ambassador taking his holidays in
August, the skeleton embassy was run by Christopher as chargé
d'affaires. '*La saison des chargés d'affaires* is upon us', he would say

with relish. (The No. 2 automatically takes charge when his Head of Mission is out of the country and is even accorded a percentage of his superior's higher allowances to help him with the extra entertaining.)

'Who'll be here in August this year ?' I asked. 'Humphrey Maud and Robin Renwick in chancery, David Miers for the economic section, Andrew Palmer for the press section, and I'm not yet sure who from the commercial, consular and defence departments.' The relationship between the members of the August group became so close that I remember Nick Spreckley (first secretary in chancery) coming back after his August holiday saying everyone had even developed a secret language while he had been away and he couldn't understand what anyone was saying any more. Some remarkably talented colleagues served in the embassy during the four and a half years we were there. And the undeniable proof of this lies in the fact that so many of them hold positions of responsibility and influence in today's Foreign Office. And what is more, in spite of all the new people I have met since my connection with the Foreign Office was severed, the inner circle of my friends still comes from those august brethren, and when today I give a party my first thoughts instinctively turn to the 'Paris mafia'.

This left us to take our holiday in either July or September. For our first two years in Paris we returned faithfully to Ellis Green, but then, with the children grown a little older, we made wonderful journeys of exploration in France. Some of these are described in Christopher's journal:

6 September 1975 : In the morning leave for Tours, with complete team of children packed into the small fast red car, to stay the night with Henri and Nicole Clermont de Tonnerre in a 19C château bought by her grand-father Sciaffino. . . . We take photographs in the beautiful light of the Loire and visit the Renaissance garden at Villandry – with its ornamental vegetables.

And then, next day:

Drive to Autun, stopping at Bourges to see the cathedral (a sister to Notre Dame de Paris but more solid, with 13C glass of great beauty). Stay at Le Vieux Moulin which excites the children. See the cathedral's romanesque interior with vivacious 12C carvings, the famous portal and the pillars. Le

Musée Rolin [in Autun], which has the marvellous 12C 'Temptation of Eve' and the painted 15C Virgin of Autun.

And then to Bonnieux in the Vaucluse to stay with Alix Rohan Chabot, and here he wrote:

Visit La Fontaine de Vaucluse, a disappointment. A hole in the ground surrounded by horrible attributes of the tourist trade. Then the Abbaye at Sénanque, alone in its valley and its Roman severity, a place of sinister beauty in the rain. The Cistercians are gone but one gets the chill flavour of their life. In the sun they would have gathered the lavender, but it must always have been a place of shadow.

And then after a few days staying at Cavalaire with the Palmers, he wrote:

Return to Paris. It is exactly nine hundred kilometres of which it must have been raining for six hundred. A rather dangerous drive because I am trying to tell the children a science fiction story at the same time. It was about a man who discovered how to make the cells of his body lighter than air.

Sadly, on a visit the previous year to Cavalaire – the pretty little tourist town not far from St Tropez – we lost our beloved Konrad. Christopher and I went there alone for a few days' holiday with our friends the Palmers, and just as we were leaving the François 1er flat Robin said, 'Oh, do take Konrad with you – he's always so sad when you're away.' So he went with us – proud to take his place in the smart wagon-lit. But immediately on arrival at the Palmers' house he wandered off in the garden and as it was raining he couldn't find his way back by scent; his sight and hearing were already bad. We searched for him in the little town until midnight. Then, after a storm during the night, Christopher went down to the town again in the morning, obsessively. Flood water was pouring across the street. We searched on. The beach, the port, the town, the hillside. We asked everywhere. We put an advertisement in the press. The next day, 20 September, Christopher made the following entry in his journal: 'Konrad is found dead in the sea. We collect him at the port in Cavalaire and bury him under a cork tree.' And then he went on, as if writing an obituary for an old friend:

His life was devoted to gaining the sympathy of humans and giving his to them. He was less successful with his fellow dogs; he never attacked them but seemed to pass remarks that caused them to attack him, *par bêtise* no doubt. He had only one amorous adventure, with an unknown lover in the Club des Pins in Algeria. It seemed to exhaust him. He had no cano-sexual tendencies. He seemed to prefer human beings and gave himself to pleasing them. He began as he meant to go on, appealing from the shop window in Baker Street where Gavrelle saw him and could not resist him. When she died five months later, I put him into [youngest stepdaughter] Brigid's bed that morning and the puppy comforted the child. Now this last connection with that part of my life is broken.

As Kate had developed asthma – with an allergy to most animals – we did not get another dog. Konrad was replaced only after Christopher's death, when an anonymous Irish well-wisher gave my children a spaniel puppy who, in turn, brought comfort to three grief-stricken children.

9

Diplomatic Manoeuvres

We were in our fourth year in Paris and preoccupied with where and when the next posting might be. I had no wish to leave Paris, but Christopher understandably had had enough of being the No. 2 and wanted an embassy of his own, allowing him finally to take the decisions and to send telegrams and despatches out under his own name. At last there was news in April 1975: 'A telegram comes to say that I am going to be the Deputy Under-Secretary at the Foreign Office dealing with the Middle East, Africa and United Nations. It ends by sending me warmest congratulations.' So he had made it – he had been given one of the four jobs coming immediately under the Permanent Under-Secretary, head of the Foreign Office. His sense of achievement was enormous and, for someone as filled with self-doubt as he, the public aknowledgement of his ability was what mattered most.

However, for a complexity of reasons, the appointment was cancelled, and this reversal had the most fundamentally demoralizing effect on him. Fortunately a case such as this is rare in the Foreign Office, but nevertheless the occupational hazard does exist whereby a diplomat and his family prepare themselves both mentally and organizationally to take up a particular posting, and through no possible fault of his own the appointment is reversed at the last minute. Diplomatic transfers are worked out through a chain system; if one link is broken then naturally several others are affected. But I remember it was worse for our friends in the Quai d'Orsay, where there was a more flexible central organization. They never took a posting for granted until they actually occupied it. They never forgot the tragic example of a French ambassador appointed to Madrid. His luggage had even arrived there and he was *en route* by sea from his previous post in a South American capital when he received the news that his new embassy had been transferred to a political appointee.

Christopher was despondent and I did my best to persuade him that if his career was to suffer a delay then what better place to endure it than Paris. We agreed that it was the quality of life that matters more than anything else.

Sometimes, when he was feeling lower than usual, he would linger at home to tell me of his anxieties. Then, suddenly realizing he was late for the morning meeting at the embassy, he would dash for the car, his red-lined dark blue overcoat – which he called his *manteau electoral* whenever there was a possible change of government in the offing – flying out on each side of him. Downcast by absorbing his worries, I might ring one of the young men at the embassy. 'Is Christopher all right? He seemed so desperately low when he left home.' 'Well, he's fine now. His jokes were better than ever at the morning meeting,' came the reply. Then I would realize once again that, in our case, an anxiety shared was not so much an anxiety halved but rather an anxiety off-loaded.

So we started on what seemed like a postscript to our time in Paris. Even more than before we availed ourselves of all the advantages of life in France and of all the friendships it afforded. Christopher's journal on 5 August reflected this:

> The '*canicule*' persists. Paris is as the Persian Gulf. It is my birthday. Jane organizes a surprise party at lunch, so I come in rather late as usual from the office to find the house full of friends. Very warming to the heart. Resolve to squeeze happiness out of the rest of my active years.

Then once again we made preparations to say goodbye to our ambassador and welcome a new one, and the journal reflects Christopher's ideas for the farewell speeches on the one hand and credentials for the incoming ambassador on the other. The following extract shows his view of how the Community should evolve (years later I used extracts from it for my own maiden speech in the House of Lords):

> 27 October 1975: While I have been here a great deal has happened. Not just the surge and flow of diplomatic manoeuvre, the ups and downs of our

relationship which over the years is like that of a marriage between two people who know one another both too well and not well enough, but a fundamental change in the whole framework in which we have to operate together. The power relationship in the world has changed. The premises of Western European economics have changed – the economists have had to go back to their drawing-boards and economics has become a game in which the amateur has as much chance as the professional. And, nearer home, there has been a change in the pattern of Europe. And despite the difficulties and hesitations of transition, this is I believe a change that will shape the history of the future. It offers (I suggest) not only a prospect, but the only prospect, for us all. For my country it has involved two vital and intricate processes of negotiation and decision: the first to establish the basis on which we belong to Europe, the second to obtain the unequivocal consent of the British people to this. I know that viewed from the outside, viewed from here, this second process looked like a disheartening sideshow in the affairs of the Community. But viewed from a wider angle, from the historical perspective, it was more than that. It was necessary as a foundation for the future. It turned a contested option into a final and unequivocal one; it removed the commitment from the area of political controversy.

We should not confound the difficulties of the process of making Europe with the historical option we have all taken to pursue it. The process is bound to be gradual and difficult. What is important is that the need to continue with it is accepted as a constant of policy and as a factor in taking national decisions. Europe will be built by becoming a habit.

There are three areas of subject matter. First that of the interests which we plainly have in common, and over which common action is therefore possible. Secondly, the area in which an effort, and some measure of sacrifice, is needed to reconcile different interests – this is perhaps the main area of activity in the Community. Thirdly the area in which our interests or institutions are so different that there is for the present no possibility of reaching common positions over them, so that they are susceptible only to national action. By the habitual and repeated process of seeking compromise and the highest common denominator in the Community machinery – and I include in this the machinery of political cooperation – by this long and laborious and habitual process, building a little more case-law and habit and precedent each time one can hope to extend the first of these areas, that of common interests, into the second, that of reconcilable interests, and the second can slowly encroach upon the third, that of diverse interests.

It is in this organic fashion that I believe the system will grow, not according to pre-ordained blue-prints or existing patterns. The process must be pragmatic, but there must also be a constant will to move forward, a sense of dynamic. Pragmatism must not mean a preoccupation with the present at the expense of the future. We must be practical but we must also dream a little. It sometimes helps to turn what is into what ought to be if one acts as if what ought to be is what is . . . .

An Ambassador is above all a Liaison Officer. And one of the most important functions of a Liaison Officer is constantly to remind his principals that whatever their differences of view about how the battle should be fought, they are fighting the war on the same side.

A few days before the ambassador was due to leave, Princess Margaret came on an unofficial visit to Paris to see the remarkable exhibition of Scythian gold showing at the Grand Palais. Afterwards the ambassador and Jill Tomkins gave a dinner party (their last) for the royal guest. It was a Saturday evening and I remember it had not been easy, at short notice, to assemble a sufficiently glittering throng for our royal visitor. (In France, as in Britain, the glittering throng tend to go away to their smart weekend houses.) Moreover, being Saturday, the guests hoped to get to bed in fairly good time but, knowing the Royal Princess's reputation for staying up until the small hours, feared they might not. The evening was very successful and the Princess showed great appreciation of the exhibition and enjoyed herself at dinner, sitting between the ambassador and the young Aga Khan. Afterwards she was anxious to speak to as many of the guests as possible. She preferred to do this standing up, smoking cigarettes through long holders, whilst certain guests were brought up to her. The time went on. At about midnight Geoffroy de Courcel (previously French ambassador to London and at that time secretary-general of the Quai d'Orsay), said to me rather anxiously, 'I really am hoping to get home soon. I have to go to Vietnam tomorrow morning with an early start. Do you think the Princess will be retiring soon?' 'I'm not at all sure, as she's obviously enjoying herself. But as you must know her well from your time in London, why don't you go and explain about your Vietnam visit. She will then of course urge you to go home.' Gratefully he followed my advice. I moved across the room with him and watched him bow over her dimunitive form and heard him repeat the rehearsed piece. But then it didn't continue according to plan; the Princess got her lines wrong. 'I think you're very, very brave,' she said, looking up at him admiringly. The Baron de Courcel did not get home until very late that night.

The Tomkins' farewell party was on 13 November. Once again Christopher made a speech, notes for which he included in his journal:

The moment has come – a sad moment for us – to say goodbye to our Ambassador and Lady Tomkins and to give them all our good wishes to take away with them.

This is the second time in this Embassy I have had to do this. Three years ago I was standing up like this trying to find words to say farewell to Sir Christopher Soames. I am not the Knight on the battlefield who has had two horses killed under him. I'm the horse that has lost two Knights – both KCMGs. It gives one the feeling that for Ministers, as for First Mates, seconds-in-command, plumbers' mates, the survival of this species of No. 2s depends upon a certain capacity for adaptation.

With Sir Christopher Soames, for example, I was a kind of mahout, perched on a large and unpredictable pachyderm. The mahout has one serious disadvantage – he has a goad; but he has no brakes. To stop the elephant he has to dismount and push from the front. This involves the grave risk of getting trampled underfoot.

With Sir Edward Tomkins it is not like that at all. Where his predecessor was a politician he is a professional in the best sense of the term. With him, the image I have is that of standing on a footplate beside the driver, watching dials, shovelling coal, while the locomotive runs smoothly along the diplomatic rails through the varied and hazardous countryside of French foreign policy. Occasionally we give a polite whistle as we take on water at the Quai d'Orsay. Sometimes we have to stop when there is an obstruction on the line. Sometimes instructions from our owners get us shunted into a siding . . .. Sometimes we are whizzing happily down the main line to the terminus at the Elysée . . . .

More seriously; one of the most effective of those time-honoured weapons of diplomacy is something very simple. But you can't use it if you haven't got it. And that is friendship. To be able to use it you need one essential quality that some people find extremely elusive – you have to be liked. That is the quality that Edward and Jill Tomkins certainly have. I cannot tell you how often people in Paris have come up to Jane and me and said how *sympathiques* are our Ambassador and his wife, and how much they have enjoyed meeting them.

And these qualities – the generosity, the conversational gifts, the warmth towards people, the ability to get on with them – are what have earned them the affection of the French, and have also earned them the affection of us all in the Embassy.

And let there be no mistake about it: Her Majesty's Embassy in Paris is no ordinary post. Her Majesty's Ambassador is no ordinary person. It is a post of maximum interest and maximum prestige in the Service. It means dealing with all those fascinating, gifted, argumentative Frenchmen. I once said in words that must be written on the heart of the Foreign Office that this is not only a nation of individualists but an individualist nation . . . .

And now that you are retiring, Sir, from the Service, it must be a great satisfaction and comfort to know that you reached such a very distinguished place at the wicket. And the rest of your team – all of us here – your Embassy here – will be sorry to see you go – not bowled out by a googly from Monsieur Sauvagnargues [French Foreign Minister]. Not run out by Mr Callaghan [then British Secretary of State for Foreign Affairs]. But going back to the pavilion after a very creditable innings – of sixty not out [age of retirement in FO].

Afterwards Christopher was the first to admit that his speech contained a rich blend of mixed metaphors. But it was well received and I remember Jill asking for a copy of the notes for her scrapbook.

Ten days after their departure the new ambassador, Sir Nicholas Henderson, and his wife Mary arrived. His former post had been Bonn. Again the candles were lit in Pauline Borghese's beautiful salons to honour the new envoy.

On 14 November, between the departure and arrival, Christopher recorded:

It is Dublin. It has been cleared with the Secretary of State. It sounds interesting at least; possibly dangerous. Something I could, I think, do. One can at least perform in the best medium, English. There will be a lot to learn though, I have never followed the Irish affair. My resolution will be to avoid agitation, internal and external.

And my own reaction? I found it impossible even to imagine leaving Paris, so our precise destination was immaterial. But there was no doubt at all that Christopher was pleased with the appointment. I remember a Paris friend, with a greater than usual degree of chauvinism, saying: 'But Christopher, may this Dublin job not seem narrow after the vast scope and range your present position has provided?' Christopher's answer – serious – was as follows: 'No, it won't be like that, because you see it can only be through the governments of London and Dublin developing a mutual understanding and trust that the Northern Ireland problem will ever be solved. So through my work there I will be in a position to contribute constructively towards a peaceful solution. After all that is an ambassador's highest motive – to negotiate peace and prevent conflict.'

Our departure date was fixed for three months later, so everything we did was for the last time. Our last Christmas. Once again we put up the tall Christmas tree in the hall; and as on previous years we gave a party round it for the embassy children and in the evening a supper and dancing party for the staff. This was the party I liked giving most of all. We usually wore some kind of fancy dress or head-dresses – and played the silly party games which the inhibited English only permit themselves at Christmas. The new ambassador came wearing the head of a bull, and Henrietta, with her intimate knowledge of French slang and gift for hitting on the right word, said that he was '*vachement bien*', and I was so pleased that Christopher wrote in his diary: 'Jane does it all miraculously well and they all seem happy.'

Christopher's first entry for 1976 – as in previous years – reflected worry about the annual review. But it also revealed the important professional justification for keeping the journal at all:

> At home struggling fragilely with the annual review. It is difficult in itself to synthesize the story of this journal for a year into a few pages .... The essence is that Giscard has changed less than he says at home and more than he admits in foreign and defence policy; that he has weathered the recession well; that he has created a new diplomacy; that we have made our choice but not made it look valid.

Although our last months in Paris gave us ample proof of the place we had achieved there, the artificiality of those great social events began to tell on us. And the environment, made up of exaggerated civilities – even banalities – was sometimes oppressive. (Many years later I remember congratulating Alix Fontana Giusti, whose husband

Luigi was minister at the Italian embassy, on her contented look amidst London's diplomatic life. 'Not for much longer,' she said. 'After twenty years, *le petit sourire* is beginning to wane.') Christopher's journal reflected this scepticism. After a party at the house of one of the defence attachés: 'An expensive flat, an expensive dinner and the very distillation of banality. It raises questions in the mind about waste of public money.' And on 9 March:

> Diplomatic dinner at the Hôtel de Ville. An annual grand occasion and an anachronism, in the ridiculous carapace of the boiled shirt. The food carried in by a procession of waiters with contemptuous or bored faces. Lemoine, curator of the Château de Versailles, says he is sitting where Louis VII sat; his neighbour says this is a doubtful precedent ...

Then again: 'A formidable evening. Cocktail party at the embassy, concert (Beethoven Mass), and supper chez Mme Prate. It's all becoming too much. Jane fits in cocktails at the Dutch embassy as well.' It was true that I bore a heavier social burden than he did, for on many evenings while he was still busy at the embassy I went alone to one or more cocktail parties. I really quite enjoyed them – Percy drove me there, and after I had skated over a few subjects with one or two guests he picked me up and dropped me at another one to repeat the same process. The cocktail-party round as an institution is certainly open to attack, but even such superficial occasions create another framework for people in different countries to make contacts, so I was probably right to slog on behalf of both Christopher and myself. After I had finished my stint, very often Percy and I collected Christopher and went on to a dinner. (There were not many quiet evenings in front of the telly.) Not liking to keep him waiting, we then sent Percy home in the car, putting up a prayer for the clutch.

'The ambassador keeps calling things codswallop,' Christopher said to me soon after the arrival of Nicko Henderson.

'But what *is* codswallop?' I asked.

'Well,' said Christopher wryly, 'by a process of elimination the only things that are *not* codswallop seem to be what he himself thinks and does. Of course, he is charming and has an enquiring mind, but I wish he wouldn't interrupt so much. I know I speak slowly, but sometimes at the morning meeting – which I take because that's what he wants – I can hardly get a word out. It is as if he were psychologically disinclined to listen.'

'Do you get cross?'

'No, for someone like me who never shows anger, to do so would only make me look preposterous, I'd be so bad at it, and it wouldn't help. But this morning, after about five interruptions before I had even got to my point, I really was fed up.'

'So what did you say?'

'I didn't say anything, but very slowly I picked up my pen off the table, very slowly screwed the top on, carefully put it into my inside coat pocket, folded my hands in front of me and just waited.'

I wondered whether anyone had even noticed this stupendous act of rebellion.

But if annoyance, frustration and anxiety are permitted no outlet they must find other means of expression. Christopher's migraines became more and more debilitating during our last months in Paris and his journal, an escape hatch, reflected signs of strain. It must be said that the morale of an entire embassy depends much on the ambassador and furthermore that the working relationship between him and his deputy is very close and sometimes undergoes tension; perhaps even more so than in other professions which lack its particular circumstances. Christopher, whilst climbing up the promotion ladder had by that time been No. 2 in the Manila, Algiers and Brussels embassies. It was high time for him to be his own master.

Our farewell parties started as early as 1 March. We felt quite overwhelmed by the number of friends who asked for a slot and there were hardly enough dinner, lunch or drink times to avail ourselves of the invitations.

On 16 March we heard that the Irish Government had given *agrément* to our appointment (the official agreement for which ambassador designates have to wait before disclosing their destinations). It was the final end to uncertainty.

'Darling, when are you going to start getting things ready for the packers. There's only another few weeks before they're due and by this stage you're usually busy clearing out drawers, getting rid of clothes the children have grown out of, spring cleaning for the successors and so on. But every evening when I get home, everything still looks exactly the same.' Of course, he was right; those preparations made all the difference to the eventual move. Furthermore it was vital for all diplomatic families who lived in houses or flats containing both personal and government property to see that the removal firm could distinguish between the two. The trick was to empty one room altogether and isolate all personal possessions in it for packing and removal. 'But, I *am* planning it all in my head – really,' I said. But, of course, clearing out my desk drawers could only point to one thing: leaving my beloved Paris, and I still couldn't admit that was really going to happen.

However, I was still happy enough giving parties. One of the last ones, just before Robin went back to school, was a ping-pong tournament, not only for all the children but also for the embassy enthusiasts who included some brilliant players. We put up two extra borrowed tables and the children worked out a complicated chart whereby everybody played everybody else (there was a strong possibility that the tournament would stretch on into the not so early hours of the following day). We ate hamburgers, hot dogs, baked potatoes and ice cream. Robin was a well-practised and stylish player, and Christopher, in spite of his single eye, was highly competent. With his sleeves rolled up, beaming face and impassioned play he could not have looked less like the stereotype image of HM Minister Plenipotentiary to the French Republic.

Then we gave our own party to say goodbye to Paris. We rolled up the carpet in the small drawing-room (the one little Kate had discovered on fire, a drama which seemed so many years ago) and turned it into a dance floor. Angela, the last in our sequence of cooking girls, laid on an elaborate buffet supper. It was a glamorous event. Christopher reported it briefly, but obviously with satisfaction: 'They are all there, the friends from the Quai, and the journalists, the beautiful girls, the literary world and 3 Government Ministers. It leaves us with the thought that we have at least made some sort of mark here.'

Then – inevitably – the end came. Christopher's journal for 23 April declares: 'The packers. They are upon us early in the morning. They are swift and efficient. They put our personality into cardboard boxes and leave the flat no longer ours.' He records his final diplomatic task:

In the middle of it all, we go to lunch with Gabriel Robin (the President's private office) in the Elysée and eat from Giscard's kitchen. I ask him the last question about Direct Elections to the European Parliament and the Tindemans Report and after lunch go back to the office to write the last minute to record his answers . . . . Take away my personal things from the office and disappear from it. That evening the last of the despedidas. We go to Castels [nightclub]. But Jane has no voice. It is perhaps her way of refusing to say goodbye to France . . . . We leave the flat with nothing more of us in it, for Villereau in the afternoon. The sun is shining and I am not too unhappy. Mow the grass for the last time. Everything is now for the last time.

10

Packing and Preoccupations

'Whew, makes you think of a banana republic,' was Christopher's irreverent reaction to the untidy early morning look of London's suburbs as we drove in from the night ferry.

Nor was 31 Radnor Walk much better. For the past six years we had had four young men as our tenants and, although they regularly paid the rent, they had been a bit hard on the furniture. Several broken chairs propped up round the walls were visible proof of this.

'Darling one,' – the careful note in Christopher's voice warned me he was about to bring out the mildest of criticisms – 'do you think that sofa cover might have been a mistake?' I could only agree that it was a disaster. The material had looked all right when chosen on a flying visit to Peter Jones from Paris – at the same time as deciding on the wallpaper for two bedrooms, a carpet for the drawing-room and paint for the kitchen walls. 'Oh, well, we'll never have to live with it and perhaps the new tenants won't mind,' I said. The little house had moved a long way from its pre-Mr Oga pristine white and gold look.

We had been allowed two months between Paris and Dublin to prepare ourselves for the move and take some leave. The element which has since dominated my memory of that time was the heat: 1976 will be remembered as the year of the heatwave, and those soaring temperatures and Christopher's death will remain inexorably linked in my mind.

First his journal records that on 4 May, the day after we got back, we were sensible enough to take advantage of being back in London by going to the theatre:

Otherwise Engaged by Simon Gray, directed by Pinter whose influence on it is evident ... the whole thing very well done; an examination of indifference, restraint, adultery and the brittleness of life. On the way out a man says, 'A pity so much talent should be wasted on such a subject.'

His major preoccupation during those two months was to absorb as much Irish history as possible and inform himself about the current state of Anglo-Irish relations. In a paradoxical way he was well placed to do this, having never previously been involved with the Irish question. 'It's so vast,' he used to say when the papers were full of the agony of Northern Ireland in the early 1970s, 'it's better to keep right outside it than just to dabble in it.' So his mind was uncluttered by superficial knowledge or any trace of bias, and this enabled him more easily to look at it all from the ethical as well as political viewpoint. To complete our ignorance we had neither of us ever in our lives been to Ireland.

His enthusiasm to get his mind round an entirely different political situation was obvious. Previously a new phase of Anglo-French relations within the European Community had faced him on arrival in Paris. His new assignment was to work towards building greater trust and understanding between Dublin and London. It was a very real example of the intellectual and political flexibility needed by diplomats to make adjustments from one complex political situation to another.

On 7 May – only six days after leaving Paris – there was an entry in his journal describing a meeting with the head of the Republic of Ireland department. He had previously been with us in the Paris embassy:

See Bill Harding in the office and lunch with him. He is much occupied by a small but fairly serious drama on the Irish frontier the night before last. Eight SAS men with eleven weapons between them and only two of them in uniform were arrested by the Garda four hundred yards inside Ireland apparently as a result of an error in map-readings.... Finally the men are released on bail.

On 10 May we went to see our future house. I was temporarily freed of maternal obligations as the children were all away: Robin at the Dragon School and Henrietta and Kate still at school in Paris, staying with schoolfriends. Christopher's reaction was positive:

In Dublin yesterday and today. Stay in our future house with the Galsworthys [Arthur Galsworthy was our predecessor]. It is better than I expected, not beautiful but pleasant enough and in an almost idyllic setting, despite the Garda prowling in the park. There are more people looking after the Ambassador's creature comforts in the house than there are looking after his policy in the Chancery. The Embassy is run on a shoestring . . . . All the time I was there the Embassy was taken up with the question of the SAS men . . .

My own first impression of that unusual house was equivocal. It is now hard to distinguish how much of the reaction came from a genuine indifference to the house, the inability to wrench my preoccupation away from Paris or even the vague premonition of doom which seemed to affect me. I suspect I did not make a good initial impression on the members of the embassy. I looked over-casual on arrival, in my favourite jeans and dark blue velvet jacket, and then went the other way, looking defiantly sophisticated in a Paris dress for dinner. Nevertheless I remember finding myself interested in their discussion about Irish politics and, also, I dutifully noted what was needed for the house. Unfortunately for us, it had all been recently decorated leaving only the library to be redone to our own taste.

Some of the Department of the Environment's furniture seemed incongruous against a rural Irish setting. The drawing-room was bursting with spindly, French-style gold furniture set on a very golden-coloured carpet. The dining-room, however, was thoroughly British and the numerous bedrooms were extremely comfortable. The room I liked best was a tiny circular turret room high above the rest of the house. I planned to turn it into a warm and cosy retreat.

The large white Palladian-style house was surrounded by an enormous garden. In front, as you drove up, a rose garden, and behind a vast lawn with a hard tennis-court usefully – but unaesthetically – cutting into it. To one side, beyond the numerous glasshouses and conservatory with plumbago growing in it, there was an immense vegetable garden filled with every kind of vegetable and fruit tree and bush. 'What happens to it all?' we asked Arthur Galsworthy. (He had only recently remarried – so one mouth had just increased to two.)

But Christopher guessed the answer and muttered to me jokingly under his breath: 'Somewhere near by there will soon exist a small village calling itself "Biggsville", full of people living off our produce!' (The proof that he might have been right came later when, on our tour of the house, I spotted a vast deep freeze. Opening the lid revealed only one thing – the instruction booklet.)

There were too many magpies around, either flying overhead or scattered around among the rosebeds.

The history of Glencairn is a strange one. Its original owner, Boss Croker, a Tammany Hall boss, married to a Cherokee princess, came over to England from New York and owned a remarkable horse which won the Derby. The story goes that Edward VII, taking him for a bounder, refused to shake the winner's hand when presenting him with the prize at Buckingham Palace, and Boss Croker was so angry that he left the country to live in Ireland, taking his horse with him. He bought the house at Glencairn and expensively fitted it out with solid mahogany panelling and doors, etc. When his horse – who in the meantime had also won the Irish Derby – died, he buried it in the garden: the gravestone is still there.

Before returning to London, and while Christopher was at the chancery that afternoon, I went to inspect some schools for Kate. The Dublin posting had seriously upset our original plan of keeping Henrietta and Kate in the French system, as Ireland is one of the relatively few countries lacking a French lycée. After a great deal of agonizing thought, even including the possibility of Henrietta continuing to work towards her *baccalauréat* by correspondence, we had registered her at a boys' school called St Christopher's near Glencairn, where she could transfer to the English educational system. (This school had the advantage of teaching the A-level curriculum rather than the Irish school-leaving certificate.) Also as a result of my afternoon's investigation we decided to send Kate to a small nearby French school in the hope that an extra year of that language might cement it in her mind.

Our next task – a pleasant one – was to go over to Paris to collect Kate. 'Did it feel dreadful saying goodbye to all your friends?' I asked her with a lump in my own throat as I went for the last time along the well-known route to the École Alsacienne to pick her up. 'They all took my address,' she said. 'Do you think you might start wearing dresses when you get to your new school?' I asked her. 'Yes, I suppose I might.' She had – obsessively – turned herself into a boy while we were in Paris. She only played with boys and invited them exclusively to her birthday parties, and she not only wore boys' clothes but succeeded in emulating the way boys stood, walked and ran, etc. (Her major triumph was one day at a fair when she was shown to the gents.) She had firmly and logically maintained that she could only make the change back to being a girl when starting afresh at a new school, to avoid confusing her present schoolmates.

Even on this visit Christopher continued his Irish education: '17 May: Reading *Ulysses*. The stream of consciousness involves a lot of dross but there are nuggets in it: "I believe it was a nun that invented barbed wire." Back to London by air in the evening.'

On 18 May we went to Buckingham Palace for the traditional audience the Queen gives to her Ambassadors before they depart to their new posts. We had received instructions about what to wear and the form the occasion would take. I was to be in an afternoon dress with hat and gloves and Christopher in morning dress. The audience was at midday. Although I owned a vast selection of clothes from the fashion-conscious years in Paris, I was not convinced that any of them corresponded to the definition of an afternoon dress. Christopher was no help. I went to Jaeger, the one close to us in the King's Road where I was still a well-known customer, and asked for an afternoon dress and hat. The attendant looked doubtful and finally showed me a very pretty, rather flimsy cotton flowery dress and a hat made of the same material with a floppy brim. Although I knew immediately that it would be a triumph in St Tropez, I suspected it might not measure up to an 'afternoon dress'. Christopher agreed; so in the end I wore a Bruce Oldfield dress of darkish red silk jersey and a very wide-brimmed, fine straw hat of the same colour. This had been my outfit for our last Queen's Birthday Party in Paris and it reminded me of those wonderful annual events which were held in the embassy gardens on the same day as the Queen's birthday parade in London, and were viewed by Paris's smart set as the most important social event in the calendar.

An official car came for us on the morning of 18 May to take us to the Palace. On arrival we were welcomed by the Comptroller of the Royal Household and taken through a trial run of the audience. We were told that, after being ushered into the drawing-room where the Queen was to receive us, we must stop just inside the door and bow or curtsey to her; then advance a few steps into the room and towards her and bow or curtsey again. Her Majesty would then invite us to sit down. At the appointed hour this all took place. We talked mainly of France and Ireland; both countries were at that time topics of current interest. The French President was expected on a state visit the following week, and Ireland, never far from being a central pre-occupation for Britain, was made even more so by the affair of the arrested SAS officers. However, when we were talking about the imminent visit of the French president and Madame Giscard d'Estaing, I suddenly found myself the target of Christopher's piercing, but anxious, single eye. (A sort of unspoken 'Kippers'.) Her Majesty was describing the presidential programme and how Madame Giscard had asked to be shown round some gardens and flower centres. Having so far contributed nothing to the conversation, I joined in, helpfully I thought, by saying, 'It is of course a well-known fact, Ma'am, that Madame Giscard is a great flower lover. That could indeed be the reason she calls herself "Anemone".' Although I smiled brightly at this remark, I don't think the Queen quite understood what I meant.

Christopher recorded the momentous occasion:

Jane and I go to see the Queen. We have about twenty minutes with her alone. She knew about the SAS affair, used the word 'ransom' instead of 'bail'. I tried to explain how the Irish seemed to have got themselves into this without Ministers really wanting it .... When Jane said that Paris was beautiful, she said was it; on her visit she had only seen the Elysée and the Embassy. About Giscard's visit she said, strangely, 'We don't have very much to do with it.' The French had been difficult about the arrangements. Giscard had not wanted to go to Scotland after suggesting it in the first place and he had wanted to arrive at six o'clock in the evening, which would be impossible unless he came to London in a helicopter and she was not going to have that. She brightened when we told her about Boss Croker and Edward VII refusing to shake his hand after he had won the Derby, and she said that her father had nearly done the same with another

Derby winner. Once the audience was over, we backed out and left the palace.

We both continued with our preparations. Christopher's journal recorded the briefing sessions he was given by different government departments, industrialists whose firms had Irish connections, church leaders, the Ministry of Defence and parliamentarians. There is a special department in the Foreign Office who make all the arrangements, a department which acts as a nanny to them. One day Christopher was there to find out the details of his visits and, on the way through the adjoining sitting-room, he brushed against a man sitting in one of the chairs with his back to him; a rather fragile, almost elderly-looking figure. However, when Christopher saw his face he recognized with joy his old friend Peter Wakefield of the Shemlan days. But what a transformation: his former companion was showing signs of intolerable strain. He was home on a visit from Beirut, where he was ambassador, and the anguish of the place showed on his face. He had returned home to see his doctor. He and Felicity, his wife (noted, among other things, for being the best-looking couple in the service) had been through anxious and difficult times at the height of the fighting. Their only recreation was gardening within the embassy walls, and they wore bullet-proof vests to do so.

The two old friends, overjoyed to see each other again, talked for a while and then, wishing each other luck, went their separate ways: Christopher to have his official photograph taken. 'For my obituary,' he said to Peter, laughing.

His journal records the results of many of the briefing sessions. On 12 May: 'In the evening see Roy Jenkins, for about half an hour. Did not think of Northern Ireland in terms of a solution, rather of "distancing", i.e. direct rule continuing but becoming less direct, like the Indian Vice-Royalty, though there were no longer the same slow communications to decentralise authority. Violence might ebb. He favoured reunification in the end. The problem about having a smaller Protestant North was Belfast . . . .'

And on May 13:

Go for a briefing at the Ministry of Defence. The following is discussed: There has been a lack of knowledge about Northern Ireland in both the

British and Irish Governments. The most important development of the past few years has been that there is now greater understanding with the Irish about the problem, and about what can and cannot be done. For our part we have not fully understood the historical constraints to which the Irish are subject. The signs are that support for the PIRA [Provisional IRA] is ebbing. The object of talks with them was to learn more of what they are up to, to educate them, and to disrupt them. They had changed their attitude on withdrawal. They now talked of a declaration of intent, and a time-scale of three or five years. The military want co-operation with the Irish Army but this is impossible for the Irish for historical reasons and because they do not want their Army to appear to have a public security role. Border adjustment would not be a solution; Belfast. The African analogy; it was remarkable that the African states had kept the colonial frontiers.

The briefings continued on 19 May:

Board of Trade. What struck me was we export nearly as much to Ireland as to France, and the commercial section in Dublin [embassy] is something like a tenth of the size of the Paris one. The Department of Trade would like to know more about what is the basis on which trade is done; is it treated as a home market and how have we managed to keep our prominent position when we have the same circumstances as the Germans.

Lunch with British Airways. See the CBI.

The words 'low profile' keep coming up; over trade promotion, tourism information, work and so on. But there is a distinction between recognizing the political and historical constraints on action and using this as a reason for sitting back and doing nothing. The Pakenhams to dinner. Like them. I am reading his [Thomas's] book about the 1798 rebellion. It is very detailed and conscientiously done.

Then, during the afternoon of 20 May, after visiting the Chief of General Staff and attending a meeting at Lloyd's in the morning, he wrote:

In the afternoon go to see the Archbishop of Canterbury at Lambeth Palace. Homely tea and biscuits. He says he has telephoned Cardinal Hume out of a desperate sense of the need to 'do something' about Northern Ireland. Pray together there perhaps. I say that the phrase 'the Reverend Paisley' is a contradiction in terms. He says that Paisley is un-Christian.

In the evening see Merlyn Rees at the House of Commons. He is an attractive personality, with an air of honesty and a pleasant habit of throwing doubt on what he has just said . . . . He said that if you fed into a computer all the assertions one could make about Anglo-Irish affairs, it would scream. There was no coherence in the situation . . . . The Northern Irish would not accept a pace at a time; they wanted everything at once. In the Republic both the parties were conservative. In the North, the SDLP liked Heath and Whitelaw better than Callaghan and Rees, because of Sunningdale, even though it had not worked.

Among the last briefing sessions, he recorded a discussion on 25 May at the Cabinet Office:

Gloom about our European policy. The opponents in the Cabinet still work against Europe as hard as they can. There are two possible ways ahead for Europe. It could develop slowly out of growing habit and the working of the CAP [Common Agriculture Policy] and customs union making for monetary cohesion. Otherwise, there is the 'plughole' theory. The Community cannot afford to let the Italians or ourselves go down the plughole; and, if the Community has to intervene to pull us out, they would undoubtedly stipulate conditions about the management of our economy and this could lead towards a European economic policy.

In May, too, we went on one last visit to France. Kate was given leave of absence from the nearby Christchurch Primary School, which had accepted her for the last few weeks of that summer term. The little eight-year-old girl was proud to be the only one of the three children to come with us on the week's holiday. We went in my new red Triumph Stag (just bought for me by Christopher to replace the one I had loved so much in Paris, but which we had been forced to recognize as 'a Friday car'. Christopher had gloomily referred to it in his journal the previous Christmas: 'Christmas shopping arrangements become complicated as Jane's car wakes up with a mortal noise – in its third engine in two years: oh, British Leyland.') First a night in Paris, then, yet again, down the *autoroute du soleil*, first to Lyons to see our friends the Sargeants (he was consul-general) and then to Séguret and our beloved Vaucluse. We all three stayed in the little house we knew so well belonging to our friend Paul Marc Henry (later French ambassador to Beirut). The mistral was blowing and I can still so easily conjure up the image of Christopher sitting by the little pool in the garden, buffeted by the strong, warm wind, reading Beckett whilst Kate and I picked cherries in the orchard. Then, waving goodbye to Paul Marc, we set off back up the familiar autoroute to Paris to see our friends there. It really was as if Christopher had been right when he said that I just couldn't bear to say a *last* goodbye to France.

On our return, Christopher noted in his journal for 15 June: 'Lunch with Mary Kenny in Chelsea to enable her to do a piece about me in the *Sunday Independent*. A perhaps dangerous venture, reflecting the opposite attitude to the press from that of my predecessor, who treated them as the enemy. Hope it works.'

Christopher's next entry was about the visit he and I made to Belfast:

21/22 June: We visit Northern Ireland. Belfast a sad and derelict place, reminding me of Oran in 1962. At Stormont Castle, no solution in sight. Lunch with Merlyn Rees. The second day is with the Army in a helicopter. They are impressive and get more sensible the nearer one gets to the action. Conclusions: that popular support for terrorism may be declining but this is not reflected in the death roll; that economic/social decay is a factor in security and a disgrace to successive British Governments; that protestant terrorism is complementary to catholic terrorism and must be seen to be an equal target for the security forces.

We were staying with friends previously in the Paris embassy, John and Anne Leahy. John was then on loan to the Northern Ireland Office. They gave us a little dinner party that evening. (For some inexplicable reason the table was set with one place too few, and I remember allowing even this to feed my sense of foreboding.) The other guests were John Hume, leader of the SDLP, and his wife, and John Taylor, a Unionist leader, with his wife. I was struck that evening by the characteristics which make up the Northern Irish personality: a combination of southern charm with some Anglo-Saxon sense of the practical. The evening was a happy one – almost hilarious. I realized that Hume and Taylor recognized Christopher's talent for political analysis and they were visibly impressed that he matched their own passion for story-telling. The evening augured well.

We returned to London to learn of a very unexpected development. Christopher's first novel, *Trial by Fire*, was on the banned list in Ireland. The book – by no stretch of the imagination could it have been described as lewd – had fallen foul of the Irish censor over a couple of love scenes. Although astounded, Christopher was soon mollified by the thought that he now shared this distinction with many great Irish writers. The Irish newspapers reported it gleefully.

Meanwhile we had found tenants for the little Essex cottage and the house at Radnor Walk and finished the packing (although, of course, the bulk of our luggage went straight from Paris to Dublin). This is among the last entries to the journal, on 30 June:

> With the BBC to learn about appearing on television. They seemed to think of interviews in terms of contest. The trick seems to be to keep your head up, to sit still, not to hesitate, to remember that the interviewer is often talking out of ignorance, and not to let yourself be interrupted.

(Christopher asked me if I wanted to go with him; wives were included in the invitation. But I said I could see no possibility of ever having to appear on television, so there was no point. What an irony that turned out to be.)

On 1 July:

> We give cocktail party, mainly for Jean-René Bernard [a good friend from Paris], but there are lots of the old Paris Embassy there – the 'Embassy in exile'. Anyhow it all works. Jane has a miraculous touch for parties. Then we go to a restaurant with J-R, Mauds, and Derek Thomas. A good evening.

There were very few references to the children or me in this journal (it was not that kind of a record) and that is why it has given me pleasure to include the few there were. But I have another reason, for when I look back on those two intervening months, I recognize it as the only period in all those years in which I deserted Christopher as a professional partner. It was not that I actually abdicated my role. Indeed, while he was sitting at the little desk reading Irish history – Thomas Pakenham's book on the 1798 Rebellion; Conor Cruise O'Brien's *States of Ireland*, even *Some Experiences of an Irish RM.* – I busily went off to the Department of the Environment's warehouse to choose the wallpaper and curtain material for the library at Glencairn; ordered invitation cards; prepared our house for letting; bought a few clothes for the children and myself to tide us over until we knew what we would need; and so on. I did all the necessary chores, but for the first time, from a psychological point of view, I ceased to move forward in tandem with him. Sir Richard Burton, when replaced as consul at Damascus, left a message for his wife Isabel: 'Don't be frightened. I am recalled. Pay, pack and follow at convenience.' It was as if I was able to cope with the first two injunctions but was reluctant about the third. I was still looking over my shoulder at our previous life in Paris.

For instance, I spent a lot of time on the telephone to our friends in France; a lot of time seeking out colleagues who had been with us in the Paris embassy. A high point was when we went to the great party at the French embassy for the state visit of the French president. This was the last of the long stream of diplomatic functions that Christopher and I attended together. He was in white tie and tails – they suited his tall, thin, angular frame – and I was wearing a very *décolleté* coral-coloured dress from Bruce Oldfield. It went well with my suntan. Although I have never had any illusions about the way I look, I suppose I did look all right that evening. It was hot and steamy and I can remember how the heat brought out the overpowering perfume of the gardenias which Marie-Alice de Beaumarchais, our hostess, used extensively for decoration. To me it was like being back in France and I was happy.

Next morning Christopher was setting off for one of his appointments – to the Apostolic Delegate, as I remember – and I went to the front door to see him off. Looking at me he said, 'You're so pretty and I love you so much but I sometimes wonder if you're really mine.' 'But no one can or should entirely possess anybody else,' I said, and I still remember how, without a word, he trudged sadly off down Radnor Walk. And yet I could so easily have called him back to assure him that anything about me which was of value belonged to him; for it was only through a belief and trust in what he stood for that I had become what I was. But I was not to recognize this fact until too late, so I didn't call him back that morning – but just watched him going despondently down the street.

On 2 July Christopher and I went to Oxford for the British Irish Association conference on Northern Ireland. He wrote:

Meet FitzGerald, impressive and friendly. Baird is there, sinister and looking the part – reminds me of the OAS. The Northern Ireland politicians play their game of low level, high language polemics. When I arrive, I am taken into a conclave of the committee and asked to make a speech at the dinner. I manage all right after a rush to think of something to say. I tell them that Ireland is not so much a closed book to me as a large number of opened books none of which say the same thing.

Finally, on 5 July, departure:

Drive to Liverpool. The children go by train and we meet them there. It all goes more easily than I had feared. The Captain of the boat had not been told (presumably because the Company were chary about security) that we were travelling on it and when he discovers he throws himself out in a welter of apology and consideration. We are put in the owner's cabin and taken onto the bridge, to Katie's delight.

The boat was like a furnace, and although Christopher and I were comfortable enough, Henrietta, her friend Virginie who was coming to stay with us, and Kate were not. Next morning there was a panic. Whilst Christopher, Kate and I were ready to disembark, there was no sign whatsoever of Henrietta and Virginie. Someone then went to hammer on their cabin door, but there was no response. The ambassador's daughter was missing. Finally two very sleepy looking, slightly shame-faced children made their appearance. They had not only overslept but even continued to do so throughout the banging on their door.

11

Ambassador

The word 'ambassador' must rate high when you consider how often it is used throughout the world as a name for hotels, restaurants, nightclubs, different types of cars, brands of cigarettes, etc. Who, after all, feels tempted to boast, 'I am staying at the Stockbroker', whilst 'You'll find me at the Ambassador' is entirely in order. But what does it actually mean to be one, what is his function and how is he seen from outside? If one asked a Londoner his views, he might say something like this: 'An ambassador is a man who, fortified by a large tax-free drink, is driven to his destination in a very big shiny car, parks it awkwardly in a forbidden zone and is escorted by an anxious official through waiting crowds to a privileged position at whatever ceremony or event he is attending.'

But what it is like for the person occupying the position? It must be said, for a start, that he is treated with considerable deference. He is – after all – a bit of the Queen. He is addressed as Excellency, or now more commonly as Mr Ambassador or Ambassador, except in his embassy where he is called Sir (whilst everyone else within the mission calls each other by their Christian names). The Embassy staff do everything possible to promote him, in his capacity of being Her Majesty's representative, in the eyes of the local community. They arrive ten minutes early for his parties to provide any support he may need; they never leave any other function before he does, having made a special point of going up to him and speaking to him during it, and they will treat his wife with the same politeness. (Indeed there is a whole section in Sir Marcus Cheke's book on the procedure embassy staff should follow concerning their ambassador.) An ambassador is also allowed to use the Royal Arms on his personal invitation cards.

His entertainment allowances – called *'frais de representation'* – are predetermined, based on the amount of entertainment his position should entail. (Some ambassadors – both those near to retirement and those on the close side – save a bit on their *'frais'*, whilst others overspend.) All despatches and telegrams are sent out under the name of the ambassador, making him entirely responsible – either taking credit for that which was good or blame for that which was not. All this, of course, tends to isolate him as a figurehead and cut him off from the sense of fraternity which runs through most diplomatic missions.

Furthermore, an ambassador is the vehicle for breaking off diplomatic relations between two countries, as witnessed by this anecdote which was told us by a French Government Minister concerning relations between Mauretania and the United States:

> Arab-Israeli war. Mauretanian cabinet called together. But this is easier said than done as it is the camel-milk season. By the time they are summoned from their tents the war is over. But must do something. What better means of showing solidarity with the Arabs than breaking off relations with the United States? American Ambassador summoned and told brusquely to leave in twenty-four hours. He starts packing. Head of Mauretanian Protocol arrives. 'What are you doing, Monsieur l'Ambassadeur?' – 'Packing.' – After ten minutes: 'Why are you packing, Monsieur l'Ambassadeur?' – 'Because I'm leaving.' – 'Ah, yes, I see, Monsieur l'Ambassadeur.' Another ten minutes. 'Monsieur l'Ambassadeur, if I may be permitted to ask, why are you leaving?' – 'Because you have broken off diplomatic relations.' – 'Ah, Monsieur l'Ambassadeur, there has been a great misunderstanding. We have broken off diplomatic relations with you, yes. But you have not broken off diplomatic relations with us.'

As to an ambassador's function, Harold Nicolson described it in his 1953 Oxford lectures:

> An Ambassador in a foreign capital must always be the main source of information, above all the interpreter, regarding political conditions, trends and opinions in the country in which he resides .... It must always be on his reports that the Government base their decisions upon what policy is at the moment practicable and what is not. That in itself is a most important function and responsibility. But the Ambassador also remains the chief channel of communication between his own Government and that to which he is accredited.

And then later he quoted Demosthenes, addressing the Athenian assembly on foreign policy, as saying:

> Ambassadors have no battleships at their disposal or heavy infantry, or fortresses. Their weapons are words and opportunities. In important transactions opportunities are fleeting, once they are missed they cannot be recovered...

Christopher only embarked briefly on the time-honoured function of being an ambassador, but what he wrote in his journal for those fifteen days in Dublin seemed to demonstrate a sense of urgency and a compulsion to get down to work and achieve as much as possible. 'Arrival at this *Forsyte Saga* house whose last inhabitant was a Galsworthy. The man from the Protocol Department calls. Then the Diplomatic staff come for a drink.' He went on to describe his early meetings and discussions with Dr Garret FitzGerald, the Minister for External Affairs, concerning European policies and Northern Ireland: 'All this produced material for two telegrams. So I have started swimming at once.' On 8 July: 'Unpacking and getting the feel of the office. The feel is a bit limp.' (It transpired that he had gained this impression through being frustrated, on his first day, from sending a telegram very late in the afternoon, overlooking the fact that a small mission lacks the flexibility of a large one such as Paris. Christopher's total involvement and commitment to his work often made him forget what time it was, and it surprised him that often his PA, wishing to get on with her personal life, understandably did not much like being expected to do the same.)

We found that our heavy luggage, having preceded us from Paris, had already been unpacked by the staff. There were, as Christopher had earlier commented in his journal, a great number of servants. First Brian O'Driscoll, who was the chauffeur; previously he had been the butler, but had wanted a change. Christopher was the butler (we called him Chris to avoid complications); Annie did the cooking, whilst Lizzie and another lady undertook the cleaning, and Ann, Brian's pretty, dark-eyed wife, had helped with the flowers and party arrangements whilst the previous ambassador was still a bachelor. Outside, there were three gardeners.

The first weekend saw us, as on numerous previous occasions, moving all the furniture. 'We must get it looking less oppressive,' Christopher said. 'There really is too much of Boss Croker's ghost around.' The legacy of mahogany panelling and doors certainly gave the interior a dark and heavy look, in spite of my courageous decision taken on our previous visit. This was about the library, which we had been given permission to redecorate. The room had panelling halfway up its walls, with the same dark wood enshrouding the fireplace set back in an alcove. The decision was to paint this dark wood white, and complement the glistening paleness with a darkish, but slightly luminous, green wallpaper and curtains to match. Redecoration plans for Government property are agreed between the chatelaine and the Department of the Environment – such is the system – and I had coaxed approval out of the representative responsible for Glencairn. But only after a few groans. 'I'm a wood man myself,' he complained. I pointed out to him that in my view the house still contained more than enough heavy panelling to satisfy the most demanding of 'wood men'.

Soon we finished reorganizing the furniture and were pleased. The drawing-room looked distinctly better with the spindly gold chairs moved from their orderly positions round the walls, and we had put the handsome, Empire-style circular table in a central position with a massive vase of flowers on it. This was all carried out under the disapproving – although benignly so – eye of the members of the staff. (I later learned that immediately after my departure they put every single item back in its original place!)

'When am I getting my puppy?' said Henrietta. 'You know you promised me one for taking my BEPC (Brevet d'Études Premier Cycle, the French examination closest in line with our O-levels).' Word soon got around that the new British ambassador wanted to buy a dog – it would, of course, have been more appreciated had we wanted a horse – but, on a parallel with *Some Experiences of an Irish R.M.*, we soon realized that we had become the focus for every dog trader in the neighbourhood. Ignoring the fact we had implicitly specified a spaniel puppy, every breed and age of dog was offered us. However, after a couple of days of this, one morning we overheard a slight commotion at the front gate. The security guard permanently stationed there was audibly remonstrating with a visitor. Eventually satisfied, he allowed in a man with a dog on a lead. This was a spaniel – clearly not in its first youth – carefully steering a crablike course, carrying one of its long ears in its mouth. This all tended to give it a bizarre look. 'But I thought we were getting a puppy,' said Henrietta plaintively. The owner, using tones barely comprehensible to our unaccustomed Anglo-Saxon ears, explained that the dog looked older than indeed she was and added – cunningly – that he was perfectly willing for the children to keep her for a few days to get to know her, and there would be no commitment. He was confidently and accurately predicting that the combination of the children's kind hearts and Bracken's piteous look would make things work out his way. 'All right, we'll keep her on a week's trial,' said Christopher; adding prudently, 'But if we *do* decide to have her, how much will you be asking?' 'Ach, she's a valuable dog but as it's for Yer Honour I'll be lettin' her go for one hundred pound.' 'Whew,' said Christopher.

It became obvious even in those first few days that the house and garden created a true paradise for the children. Robin by that time had arrived for the holidays (he was engrossed in writing a journal for a school competition) and Henrietta's friend Virginie was still with us. With a stream of other embassy children they made the most of all the recreations the garden offered. They played tennis and croquet; drove around in the small garden tractor; and Brian took Kate for careful rides on the donkeys who seemed to go with the house. We made plans for riding lessons and sailing expeditions. And then, on top of it all, there was Bracken to look after. I could see they felt liberated after the constrictions of the Paris flat and their obvious happiness did a great deal to diminish my own sense of foreboding and gloom.

On 9 July an official car, flanked by a motorcycle detachment, came to take Christopher, in morning coat and top hat, to present his letter of credence as Ambassador of Great Britain to President O'Dálaigh at Arus an Uachtaran. Kate and I saw him off and took photographs. She and I both felt keenly for one of the outriders – he was very young – whose motorcycle refused to function, and he was left behind desperately trying to kickstart the wretched machine. The noisy cavalcade returned in due course, the audience over.

Christopher looked happy – the photographs still bear witness to that; and so did Kate, posing in his top hat.

Christopher recorded the momentous event thus:

Present credentials. It goes all right though I have an incipient migraine which afterwards drives me to bed. I say to the President that I will do all that I can, all the time, to try to ensure that our two countries whose interests are so closely interwoven shall always have the comfort of truth and trust together, that we shall know one another's minds as true friends do, and that our relationship will be directed to our common future as partners in Europe. President O'Dálaigh responds eloquently but to me, alas, unintelligibly in Irish. He and Garret FitzGerald were extremely affable to me afterwards. O'Dálaigh is a constitutional President. He compared himself in careful French to the Fourth Republic President who said he was there to open chrysanthemum shows. Perhaps for this reason he stayed away from matters of substance, though he kept me there for a long time. He was informal and loquacious and helped me to coffee himself. The only policy impression I gained was a good deal of disquiet at the economic situation.

And on 10 July he recorded the press reaction:

Quite a lot of photographs in the press but also a snide little bit in the *Irish Times* Saturday column suggesting a comedian with a British imperial image [this had obviously been written by a correspondent who had not seen behind the black monocle and prototype diplomatic image]. Fortunately the 'profile' in the *Sunday Independent* by Mary Kenny, as a result of my lunch with her, was much better. ... A few first impressions. It is our beautiful but resentful relation – easy-going but intolerant, and its policies in the North as well are cut the wrong way, horizontally not vertically. There are no ideological politics in North or South.

The security arrangements made on our behalf – or rather on Christopher's behalf – were oppressive. Garda officers roamed the garden night and day, the entire house was brightly illuminated during the darkness hours, and Christopher shadowed by security guards wherever he went on foot or by car. In spite of such unequivocal proof of his being under threat, I did not, in that very short time, come round to accepting this fact. My sense of foreboding never really focused on something happening to him. It was more of a *general* apprehension. But how did he feel? I have sometimes wondered since whether he was frightened during those sixteen days. (After all, physical fear was not unknown to him. What about that time in Algeria at the height of the troubles when, on our way back from the airport with a journalist, our way was barred by a body lying across the road? He used the excuse of parking and re-parking the car to avoid getting out to see what was wrong, until the journalist did it for him. I knew then that he was frightened.)

On 12 July he described a meeting with members of the Garda immediately concerned with his security at Glencairn:

> See two officers of the Garda, to try to learn something of the rationale behind the measures taken to protect me, and what should be done in emergency, about which there seem to be no instructions. They are not very reassuring. They assess that I, but not Jane and the children, am distinctly at risk from the PIRA. They do not seem to have given much thought to the scenario of attack. They thought for some reason that an attack on the car was unlikely ('It hasn't happened yet'). I ask them to keep us informed about any changes in their assessment of the risk ...

He told me about this meeting – but I later realized it was a watered down version after seeing the above extract – and I asked him, not panicking but merely enquiring, if there was anything we ourselves could do towards our security arrangements. He said yes, perhaps, but he hadn't had time to think seriously about it yet. As I reached the door on my way out, I remember stopping and saying, 'But if being in the car is a possible risk, wouldn't it be better and more logical if we lived closer to the embassy offices? As you also like coming back for lunch, it will mean your driving miles and miles each day backwards and forwards.' 'Yes,' he said, 'that's perfectly true. But they say that as this house is particularly well placed and designed with a view to protecting us, we should stay here.' I believed him and went off to play tennis with the children.

On 13 July came an entry in his journal describing the final agreement about the European elections, an issue which had previously preoccupied him so much in his dealings with the French:

> The European Council has agreed about Direct Elections. A compromise on the allocation of seats which entails a larger total than had been

envisaged. Ireland get 15. We and the other big brothers get 81, which would allow three for Northern Ireland (though this does not assure that one of them will be Catholic). Roy Jenkins' appointment to the Presidency has in effect been agreed though the nomination was not formally made. On fish Cosgrave [Irish Prime Minister] seems to have supported us in pressing for a 200-mile economic zone for the EEC to be declared soon. So it looks as if the European Council had a good day.

And for that evening: 'Drinks party for us given by the Gouldens [John Goulden was the able and charming young first secretary at the embassy]. Mostly the press. Try to escape the Bertie Wooster/Blimp image.'

The next extracts describe the courtesy calls which the system requires newly accredited ambassadors to make on other heads of mission, politicians and civil servants. Ambassadors' wives also make these courtesy calls on each other. The journal described another border incursion, but this time one from the south to the north, and the part Christopher played in the representations he was obliged to make to the Department of Foreign Affairs. Then on 16 July:

> The Commonwealth lunch. There are five of us: Canada, India, Australia, Nigeria and ourselves. . . . The Indian was Krishna Menon's private secretary. . . . The Nigerian tells us that he thinks his country will not withdraw from the Olympic Games – just about at the time she was in fact doing so.

This is an example of why so often it is wiser for a diplomat to equivocate than to put forward a definite view.

I was immensely busy during these ten days. I am, and have always been, very adaptable and this chameleon quality has stood me in good stead at various times of my life. In this case it helped me to start putting down roots for our new life which at the same time diminished my longing for Paris. The unpacking had been completed – everything was in place except for the ping-pong table. The perfect place for it was upstairs at one end of the big landing, but this meant it would be too close to the bedroom reserved for visiting ministers. Would they put up with the noise? We didn't dare risk it. But otherwise everyone had – so to speak – set up their bedouin tent again, and the children each established their territorial rights and decorated their small rooms.

Coming from Paris, where food was such a major preoccupation, I had automatically tried to establish some culinary or gastronomic link with Annie, our cook. The ingredients for our meals were impeccable. I knew this from having returned from the butcher myself with the most perfect fresh meat. I also knew the vegetables coming from the garden were fresher by far than those in the *marché* of Paris, and the Irish butter and cheeses are excellent. So I wondered why our meals didn't reflect all this perfection. 'Annie, don't you think per-haps you might start putting things on to cook for lunch a bit later?' 'Well, I loike to be on the safe side – that's why I get everything for lunch on to the stove straight after we've finished breakfast.' The mystery was solved.

There was also a problem with Chris, the butler; it was a matter of sensitivities. He both enjoyed and was accustomed to serving the dishes at everyday mealtimes. But, first, this elaborate procedure did not fit the informal lifestyle we liked and, second, the children became restless during the lengthy process. I found it difficult to find the right words to dissuade him from doing what he considered to be his job and of which he was inordinately proud.

We started drawing up the guest lists for our first big occasion. This was a party given annually by the British ambassador during the August Dublin Horse Show week. (It was really in lieu of a Queen's Birthday Party which – in view of the memories left to the Irish by previous British monarchs – was still too provocative.) We wanted, as in the past, to give a party which was at the same time professionally useful and glamorous. (I was convinced that my list of 'beautiful people' would be well filled in Ireland.) Moreover I was determined to get the house looking as good as possible; I even planned to drive back to London to collect the curtain material chosen and ordered during my visit to the Department of the Environment. It could then be possible to have the curtains, chosen to harmonize with the wallpaper and new white panelling, made up locally in time for the party.

The process of installing ourselves had certainly taught me a few Irish characteristics. 'Chris, do you think we could get those pictures up today?' 'T'be sure, that'ull be done, m'lady – an' no troible at all.' Marvellous, I thought. Next day: 'Chris, I know you're very busy, but do you think you and Brian might manage to get those pictures up today?' 'It'ull be a pleasure, m'lady.' This became a daily ritual. (It was not until later I heard the story, attributed to Conor Cruise O'Brien, which goes like this. Question: Dr Cruise O'Brien, can you tell me if there is a word in the Irish language which means 'mañana'? Answer: No, there's nothing in our language which conveys the same degree of urgency.)

We became drawn into the usual round of diplomatic and other parties. I remember one in particular. It was a National Day party given by one of the Commonwealth ambassadors. The guests, who had not yet met Christopher, were curious to see him for the first time. The British envoy, naturally, is considered a leading figure in the Dublin diplomatic corps, and here was one who had singled himself out even more by writing a book subsequently banned by the Irish censor. He had also been labelled a Bertie Wooster. The guests had spilled over into the garden and standing there on the lawn I saw heads turn as Christopher came out of the house, through the glass doors, into the open air. I like remembering that moment.

The last two entries in his journal were for 17 and 18 July – a weekend. In the first Christopher described the Curragh Oaks. He was not a racing man and had previously only been to one race meeting. This was at Chantilly, where he had enjoyed the Dufy setting and the pretty French girls. But he also enjoyed the Irish occasion. We met Christopher Soames there – and he *was* a racing man. Prior to the races we lunched with Roderic More O'Ferrall at Kildangan. This was one of the few occasions on which we met members of Irish society, and Christopher rather anxiously noted in his journal how involved that society seemed to be with horses and Guinness, in combination. How would he manage, he wondered, as he was frightened of the first and the second gave him bad headaches?

Finally his last entry on 18 July described our lunch with Lord Moyne:

> Lunch at Knockmaroon with Lord Moyne ... who gives us two of his novels, and the children two children's books also from his pen. He takes us next door to see the head Guinness, Lord Iveagh, who has been very ill

and is still frail: he is a member of the Senate and concerned in a reasonable way about the North. Deplores the lack of contact with Northern politicians except the SDLP. Wife gentle and pretty.

And then a summary of his professional activities:

This is our Twelfth Night in Ireland. I have produced five reasonably substantial telegrams: two about the frontier and two about the European Council (one before and one after), and one about FitzGerald on fisheries, and sent a despatch, slight and impressionistic, about presenting credentials. We have made a start with meeting people. The trick will be to get out of the previous low posture without getting into trouble. Over the border affair I felt there was a delicate balance between not giving offence on the one hand and showing that I was not to be taken for a ride on the other. When Paul Keating raised the question of the fire returned by the ship that was shot at from the shore of Carlingford Lough, I said that I hoped he was not asking me to take this up, because if I did those with whom I did so might well take the view that any taking up should be the other way round: 150 shots had been fired at the boat from the Southern shore. Maybe that was about the right exposure of tooth.

Giles Merritt (*Financial Times*) and his wife and Mary Hope come to tea. He confirms that it would be right to pay some attention to the Irish press, whom the Embassy have previously held at arm's length.

We are having the Irish press and the British correspondents to the house on Tuesday: an operation that could be hazardous.

The 20th of July was going to be a busy day; and at the end of it I was taking the night ferry to Liverpool to drive down to London to collect the curtain material – returning on the 22nd. 'Do you *have* to go? The house will look perfectly all right for the Horse Show party without new curtains.' 'But I've got it all fixed now.' 'Oh well, all right, but it does seem a pity; especially, as you know, as Brian Cubbon [PUS of the Northern Ireland Office] is coming to stay tonight and bringing one of the young officers in his department called Judith Cook with him. And you were meant to be having tea with Joan FitzGerald tomorrow.' 'I'm so sorry – I wish I wasn't going.' I agreed with him that everything seemed to have conspired to prevent my going. But I have always found it almost impossible to change my plans once they are made; the process of unravelling them is infinitely difficult for me. They form a straitjacket from which I cannot struggle free. If only I had succeeded in breaking the habit just that once.

The house was starting to look nice: it was as if it had begun to take on our contours. Ann and I had filled every vase with flowers from the vast selection in the garden and greenhouses, and at eleven o'clock the journalists started to arrive. This was a small press conference arranged by Christopher, with the object of making contact with the local press corps and at the same time eradicating once and for all the Bertie Wooster image attributed to him. After we had welcomed them, he stood by the open fire in the drawing-room to make his short speech, the gist of which was as follows:

> I see my role here as an exercise in clarification. I do not believe in the diplomacy of evasion. I very much do not believe in diplomats being cut off from the life of the country in which they live. I realize that, in spite of all the common features and the friendliness with which I have been met here, I am in a country which in a paradoxical way may be harder than most for an Englishman to understand.

And then speaking from a more personal point of view he said:

> British diplomats are in some mysterious way not supposed to have political views. But I suppose they are allowed some personal ideas. Mine are liberal with a small 'l'. My political philosophy belongs somewhere on the centre left.

In order to dispel the notion that he was, as he put it, a caricature created from a cross between Wodehouse and Kipling, he pointed out that the black monocle arose from the loss of his right eye at Alamein and that the comparison with Kipling 'just bloody well won't wash at all'.

He concluded with a remark which in effect formed the core of his approach to the Irish crisis: 'I have one prejudice acquired during the war, and reinforced again in Algeria: a very distinct and strong prejudice against violence for political ends. It is not only evil but self-defeating.'

He performed this delicate job well and I could see the journalists making some rapid mental readjustments. I felt very admiring and was pleased to be there and to talk to the journalists with him afterwards. I remember thinking that our professional partnership was about to take off again in earnest.

After the journalists had gone, Thomas Pakenham came to lunch. He and his wife Valerie had invited us all to stay at their home near West Meath called Tullynally Castle (Robin in his competition diary named it the 'Crumbly Castle').

But the afternoon was taken up with the children's worries about Bracken. 'He has never barked,' said Henrietta, 'except once when Kate trod on his paw by mistake.' 'And he's never ever come when we've called him,' Robin added. I looked at poor Bracken with his head slightly to one side and the passive look in his eyes. 'Perhaps we had better take him to the vet straight away and then we'll really know if there is something wrong with him.' We went then and there and the verdict could not have been worse – I can still see the desolated look on Henrietta's face, who had loved the dog particularly for his frailties. The vet told us that Bracken was almost blind, completely deaf, and could not for long survive the brain disease which afflicted him. Moreover, the 'puppy' was well over two years old. Bracken was sent back to his owner and I tried to comfort the children. We would start looking for another dog the minute I got back from London, I promised them.

That evening Christopher and I went to the cocktail party given in our honour by the McMullens. He was the military attaché at the embassy. I was wearing one of my new dresses (having kept the smartest one, made of peacock blue paper silk taffeta, for our Dublin Show party), and we both felt very relaxed with our kindly hosts and their guests, and grateful that by that time we were even recognizing a few faces.

We arrived home to find that Brian Cubbon and Judith Cook had already been installed in their comfortable rooms by Chris, who, according to practice, would also have unpacked their cases for them. We had planned a small dinner party for them, including the Hickmans (counsellor at the embassy) and the Gouldens. 'What's this I hear, Jane,' Brian said to me, only *half* laughing. 'The minute I get here you're just off.' We turned it into a joke and sat down to dinner. If I remember rightly the first course was smoked salmon (Ireland in my view produces the best in the world) with slices of the good local soda bread, to be followed by the juicy little lamb cutlets which I had bought and handed over to Annie, imploring her to watch the cooking time. And then there was a variety of our own vegetables. It was just one more in the long, long series of parties Christopher and I had given together. He seemed happy and was in excellent joke-telling form. Every now and then – as so often had been the case at our parties – there was a sudden burst of laughter at his end of the table. 'Poor love, you've heard them all so often before,' he used to say apologetically to me of his stories. But I never grew tired of them and often led the laughter out of very genuine amusement.

Just before the end of the meal, as the raspberries and cream were being passed round by Chris, I had to leave, having already cut it a bit fine to catch the ferry. Once again I apologized to everyone and stood up. So did Christopher, and joined me on the way to the door. He looked at me and he still seemed to be saying, 'Please don't go.' He kissed me on the lips and then resumed his place at the table while I went out. In the hall Brian was waiting: 'Hurry, yer ladyship, we haven't got much time.' I quickly changed into my usual old velvet jacket and jeans, and when I came downstairs with my case I asked Brian to ask the ambassador to come out of the dining-room for me to say goodbye to him again. 'But we'll miss the ferry, m'lady.' 'Oh all right, I'll ring him from Liverpool when I get there tomorrow morning.'

We set off at a great speed in the dark blue Jaguar – my own car was already embarked – and out of the two routes which led from Glencairn to the Dublin road we chose the one which immediately passed over a shallow culvert. I was the last passenger to board the ferry.

Next morning – it was still very hot – I didn't ring Christopher because I didn't know the code from Liverpool, and anyway it was very early. It would be better to ring him when I got to London.

While I was speeding down the M6, Christopher was reading the papers in bed, with his breakfast, as he always did. He was joined by Kate (she told me of this later), who helped him open his letters. 'I'm not looking forward to the day,' she said, 'because Mummy's away.' 'I'm not looking forward to it either,' he told her. 'Why not?' 'The same reason as you – because Mummy's away.'

I would have liked to listen to my car radio during the long journey down the motorway, but I couldn't be bothered to stop to put the aerial up. A couple of times I nearly drew in at a petrol station to do this, and also to make the telephone call which was all the time at the back of my mind. 'But he's probably on his way to the embassy by now so I'll ring him at his office from London.'

By that time he had probably finished his coffee and toast, read the newspapers, shaved and dressed. Kate had gone back to her little room, I suppose. He must have come downstairs to meet the two visitors – no doubt looking very immaculate (he had the reputation of wearing the best-cut suits in the Foreign Office, and this was a confidence booster to him at times of self-doubt). The dark blue Jaguar was outside the door with the police escort waiting behind it. They all got in – Christopher and Brian Cubbon behind and the girl in front beside the driver. They must have been driven off at quite a lick – as that was the security rule for the chauffeurs when driving passengers under threat. I have since learned that they were discussing their meeting with Garret FitzGerald. But Christopher interrupted this discussion almost immediately and, pointing at the panel of safety switches on the floor between the two back seats, said half smiling: 'Don't touch that – we're always telling the children. We call that the fatal switch.'

I don't know if the children – only a few hundred yards away in the house — heard the explosion. I've never asked them.

Postscript

Three years ago I was fortunate enough to be made a life peer and the *Hansard* of 3 June 1981, recorded: 'Felicity Jane Ewart-Biggs, having been created Baroness Ewart-Biggs, of Ellis Green in the County of Essex, for life — was, in her robes, introduced between the Lord Goronwy Roberts and the Lord Greenhill of Harrow.'

I decided on Ellis Green for my title because Christopher and I had been so happy in our cottage there but, when I went in the usual way to the College of Arms to discuss it with Garter King at Arms, I had difficulty in persuading him it existed.

'I'm afraid it's only a green with nothing but our cottage on it', I told him.

Looking worried, he said, 'Well, let us imagine I found myself in a neighbouring village and asked someone the way to Ellis Green; would they be able to direct me?'

'Only if you happened to ask someone who had been there to pick blackberries or take their dog for a walk on the Common,' I said apologetically.

Not at all convinced, he turned to the Ordnance Survey map and there, luckily for me, he found a tiny dot which was Ellis Green. So that made it all right. (On another point, Hansard should not, for the sake of accuracy, have recorded 'Was, in her robes, introduced', but instead 'Was, in Lady Sharples's robes, introduced' because as I did not have any, Lady Sharples was good enough to lend me hers. This was the second important event in my life spent in borrowed clothes.)

I shall never forget the happiness I felt when I was told of the honour. My pleasure came not only from the privilege conferred but because I saw it as a public acknowledgement of Christopher's life and death, and a tribute to the work I had been trying to do ever since. I was in the French Alps with two of the children when the list of new peers was published. In the same way that five years before the media had brought me unequivocal proof of an ending, now they told me of a new life starting. I had a dream that night: I dreamt that I was skiing uphill – effortlessly and gracefully. This dream I knew would blank out the one of previous years; the nightmare where I wandered lost on a horse until, directed by men with blackened faces, I arrived at a gigantic crater where I fell from the horse and, slipping over and down into the abyss, managed to clutch at the rim with my fingers. There I hung – every night – until I woke up sweating.

Since working in the Upper House I have often wondered how Christopher would have interpreted a particular issue; so strong is my feeling of sharing the position with him: indeed on many occasions I have longed for the guidance of his superior intellect. Nevertheless, my attitude towards these issues is, I know, in line with the one he would have adopted. Ten days after my introduction I made my maiden speech – petrified, with a parched mouth. It was on an EEC subject which would have been of his choosing and into which I interjected some of his ideas. In spite of the terror this caused me, I persisted and took part in debates about Ireland. I soon realized how expert and highly informed House of Lords speakers are on their subjects and Ireland at least was something I knew a little about. Now I have become interested in issues relating to children, young people and the family and my party has paid me the compliment of making me one of their front bench spokesmen on home affairs. Elwyn Jones and Victor Mishcon are my bosses and very nice ones too.

I most certainly consider my participation in the work of the Second Chamber as the most important development in what I can only regard as my second life.

This second life started at the particular moment in Birdcage Walk when, hearing the newsflash, I screamed my disbelief to the road in front and careered on with a deadened mind towards the Foreign Office and the inevitable confirmation. My memory still carries an almost luminous picture of the next few minutes. I left my car in Horse Guards Parade – I didn't park it but just left it with the door swinging open. The attendant's voice followed me as I ran: 'Hey, you can't leave your car there ...'. All remaining doubt disappeared when I was inside the building because they were waiting for me. The kindly ladies at reception said, 'Oh, Mrs Ewart-Biggs, the PUS wants to see you.' I ran down the broad corridor to his office, 'Michael, what's happened?' The look on his face gave me the answer. There was a mirror behind his desk and I caught sight of my reflection – the face, blue cotton shirt and jeans were all familiar enough. But how could the mirror reflect exactly the same person as the one who had just run in. For during the second in between everything had changed for that person: why had this not been reflected in the mirror?

Apart from the honour and the interesting work, the House of Lords has also provided me with the sense of security that goes with its beautiful physical environment (Kate says she feels safe·there; like in an embassy). This has made it possible for me to stand back and try to look objectively at the intervening years. For it is difficult to make a rational assessment of the grief caused by such a severance when still submerged by it. Those who are fortunate enough never to have experienced the pain of losing a husband, wife or child can in no way recognize the extent of the crisis the survivor faces. It is something which cannot be dealt with whilst maintaining the previous pattern of life, so an interval has to be created to give the person the opportunity to do no more than concentrate on weathering the crisis. During the interval one feels neither part of the dead nor of the living – he or she occupies a no-man's-land between the two. My theory is that the bereaved are not the only ones to occupy this no-man's-land, for it is possible to compare the effect extreme grief has on the life of a person to that which extreme poverty or even a physical disability also have. Grief, poverty or disability all conspire to remove powers of decision or freedom of action from their victims, reducing their aspirations to the minimum: they merely hope to do their best, to get by, to manage. Equally, anticipation and expectation are reduced to the minimum, and a different scale is used to measure progress and success. For instance, simply getting through each moment, hour, day or week is progress, and doing so without giving in to despair is rated as success. Everything is viewed in the short term, for to look into the future gives despair an opening. No-man's-land has the advantage of preventing its inhabitants' minds from tipping over into the future to dwell despairingly on the possibility – or indeed probability – of the permanence of their present pain. Indeed the recognition that the present is the only manageable period of time is important.

Certain metaphors regarding despair occurred to me and helped a little in dealing with it. The 'bricks' metaphor – a well-known one I suspect – contributes towards understanding why grief can so quickly and suddenly erupt over the threshold of tolerance and explode into despair. This metaphor can be applied to grief, pain or poverty, but in the case, say, of a bereaved wife, the basic 'pile of bricks' represents the original sorrow of losing her husband. Soon, and inevitably, additional bricks representing worries and problems growing out of the tragedy will be piled on. Speaking from experience, these extra bricks can represent a multitude of things: disproportionate worry about a child's health; frustration at not being able to fill in a DHSS form; physical tiredness; the anguish which the unequivocal proof of widowhood a visit to the post office to collect your widow's benefit will bring on; the ever growing sense of loneliness; and so on. The weight of these extra 'bricks' starts to overbalance the structure and finally it only takes one last one – perhaps merely a thoughtless word from a friend – to bring the whole edifice crashing to the ground. This collapse, when translated into human terms, is uncontrollable despair.

I dare say this thought is not original, but it helps to clarify the confusion in the mind. Likewise, despair can be compared to the weight of two heavy suitcases, one in each hand: their bearer is never given the chance of putting one down, even momentarily, to relieve the strain. Or like having a high fever and being unable to find a cool place between the sheets or on the pillow as a respite for the throbbing head and body. For me this symbolized my search for a resting-place for my mind; the pursuit of one single comforting thought to bring respite.

I know from experience that caring members of the community will, metaphorically speaking, give a hand with the suitcases or turn the cool side of the pillow over. Nevertheless, I believe that the actual journey out of the no-man's-land can only be undertaken by the individuals concerned and they should try to face up to the fact.

The stages of this journey vary according to the particular person concerned. Speaking personally, I found it difficult initially to deal with the shock to my mind. I thought I might go mad. For, after all, how can a mind hold firm whilst performing the acrobatic feat of moving from a concentration on new curtains to a decision between cremation or burial of the person with whom you have shared your life – all in the passage of half an hour? If the body is shattered, you can take it to hospital and have it bound up – but the mind .... So to stop itself going mad I suppose the mind only half accepts what's happened. I think the full realization, in my case, came – strangely – in the following way. About two weeks after Christopher's death and just before leaving Dublin, I went to dinner with some friends. (Some find it easier to withdraw entirely for a while from the community; but others prefer, from within its orbit, to inhabit their no-man's-land. It was like that for me.) There were a number of other guests at dinner and we were seated at several small tables distributed round the room. From my place on the right of the host – familiar from so many previous occasions – I noticed a pretty girl on the other side of the room. 'I must remember to ask Christopher if he thought her pretty too,' went through my mind. This for some reason served as the trigger to expose the previously obscured reality in a blinding light. I went home immediately and took to my bed for several days – sick.

It is also difficult to realize that other people really care about your personal tragedy, but it is important to do so. It is, I fear, an undeniable truth that Anglo Saxons, above all, find it hard either to look as if they care or say they do. On the surface, death is certainly a topic they prefer to avoid and even try to brush under the carpet, although the kindness and support actually offered give a lie to this. It is different with the Latin and the Celt who find it natural to involve themselves to the full in any emotional disturbance, and soon I felt as if I were being caressed by hundreds and hundreds of soft Irish voices telling me of their concern. The stream of letters increased after a television broadcast I made. Children wrote to me: 'As a little girl who loves her Daddy and family I know how your family must feel.' A card signed by six children: 'Please do not say "goodbye" as even in so short a time we have all come to know and love you. We send to you and your children this little gift of a painting which we did for you.' From a mother: 'When I saw you on television last night I felt like putting my arms round you to try to comfort you', and another 'As an Irish family we bow our heads in shame. As a mother of children – and happy wife – my heart goes out to you in sorrow.' On Robin's birthday – five days after his father's death – a complete stranger sent the three children a present of a little spaniel puppy. From the start she became the most cherished animal on earth – and still is. Another example of how other people felt came when, conscious of looking a wreck and mindful of the priority Christopher placed on appearances, I asked for a beautician to come to Glencairn to repair the ravages to my face, as best she could, before the great service in St Patrick's Cathedral. While I leant back with the pretty girl bending over me applying her lotions I felt a tear on my cheek – but it came from her eyes.

Chris the butler made his own personal act of dedication to show the depth of his feelings. Returning after dark to Glencairn following the cremation in London, the great house from afar appeared to be on fire. But on arrival I realized that it was merely ablaze with light. Chris had switched on every light in the place, had lit all the chandeliers and candelabras, and great peat fires were burning in all the grates. This was the funeral pyre he saw as a fitting tribute to the dead ambassador. I felt a strange elation as I walked from one brilliantly illuminated room to another; in total contrast to the unutterable pain and deadness I felt at the cremation at Golders Green.

So, having overcome the incredulity, come to terms with the reality of death and absorbed the sympathy offered by other members of the community, I wondered what the first practical steps towards building a new life should be. A diplomatic widow, more than any other, is forced to start from scratch. She was wedded not only to her husband but also to his profession. Almost every entry in her well-filled diary would have been related to the Foreign Office. (By a strange irony my own contained one entry, about two weeks ahead which read: 'Lord Mountbatten to breakfast'.)

In our case, the children and I had not lived in England for the last seven years. It felt and was unfamiliar, but at least we had a house and for the last time the huge cases containing all our possessions arrived at the front door. I could not imagine how the tiny house in Radnor Walk would absorb it all. We were so used to spreading ourselves, having lived in huge houses for so long. My cousin, Gillian Waud, came to help me with the unpacking. She made herself responsible for the suitcases containing my own clothes and she filled up one of the two cupboards in the bedroom with the wardrobe of my past life and the other with that of my future life. I do not have to say that one was filled to capacity with evening dresses etc., and the other had hardly anything in it. It seemed to be symbolic. (All Christopher's clothes had been sent to the Foreign Office and I was not to unpack those cases for about three or four years. By that time I found it possible to keep many of his things: Robin had grown closer to fitting them and men's shirts – by then – were what fashion-conscious little girls were wearing.)

Henrietta, by that time fifteen, and Kate, aged eight, had started school at the French Lycée in London, while Robin, then just thirteen – whose departure to the Dragon School three years before had so affected me – suffered the least disruption. I went back to work at the Savoy where Hugh Wontner, the chairman, was good enough to offer me a slot in the department responsible for the furnishing and interior decoration of the hotels in the group. We had the comfort of being surrounded by friends from the original Paris 'mafia' who happened to be serving at home: Derek and Lineke Thomas, who came with a tool kit to hang up the pictures; Robin and Annie Renwick – almost neighbours – who made me feel they were always at hand; Stephen Wall, who helped me launch Christopher's Memorial Fund, and his wife Catherine, and the Palmers, the Hannays, the Daunts, the Lushes and so many others who had previously formed the nucleus of *our* friends and continued as the nucleus of *my* friends. Applying the same method we used when abroad, and to widen the circle, I contacted all the people we had known in different postings who happened to be in London (I knew how to find them as they had all written me letters of condolence). The French Ambassador and Marie-Alice de Beaumarchais and Mohammed Brahimi of our Algiers days were among many others.

Besides my work at the Savoy, I became very involved in the work of reconciliation in Northern Ireland. I gave my support to the Movement for Peace which, led by Mairead Corrigan and Betty Williams, had become active soon after Christopher's death, succeeding in uniting Protestants and Roman Catholics together in condemnation of violence. With them I led a march for peace in London and made a speech in Trafalgar Square. Demonstrations and soap-box speeches were very distant from my former diplomatic life but I suppose I was simply responding to my overwhelming need to build something in the void left by Christopher's death; in some small way to balance the utter negativity of his destruction with something positive and creative. His work would have been for Ireland, so what I tried to build must be for Ireland too. Before leaving Dublin I had launched a Memorial Fund in his name (this was later to be relaunched from London, Paris and Brussels). It was Thomas Pakenham's inspiration and Irish ministers had immediately given it their support. The object of the Memorial was to promote the ideals to which he dedicated himself; peace and understanding in Ireland; stronger links between the peoples of Britain and Ireland and closer cooperation between the partners of the European Community. The Fund was to be used to finance an annual literary prize to be awarded to the writer whose recent work would be considered by a panel of judges to contribute most to promote these ideals. The Memorial was made to fit the man whom it honoured.

Once again proof of how the ordinary people of Ireland felt arrived with the postman, envelopes containing postal orders, single pound notes – even coins – accompanied by letters telling me of the wish of Irish people to respond to the spirit of peace and reconciliation represented by the Memorial: 'and we shall all, individually and collectively, continue in our work for Truth and Peace with renewed purpose'; and, 'It is for the Irish people now to try and follow up his ideals.' For it was, after all, a Memorial designed not only to commemorate a name but also to reflect the tolerance and moderation for which Christopher had stood, and out of which alone a state of reconciliation and peace can be born.

Enough money was raised to award an annual prize of £1,500 and starting in 1977 we have awarded it each year, varying the annual presentation between Dublin, London and Belfast. Literary figures such as Graham Greene, Thomas Pakenham, Seamus Heaney, Dervla Murphy have served or are serving on the panel of judges, and the winning entries have included historical works, television and theatre plays, journalism, etc. I hope in coming years writers of all kinds will continue to send us their work.

Meanwhile, building a new life for the children and myself had not been easy. The total disorganization caused by suddenly becoming a one-parent family increased. I recognized that in respect of money, status, emotions and relationships the old ways of being and doing had been swept away. My metaphor likening grief to a pile of bricks was proved true time and again. The extra brick, causing its collapse, was continually added. Christopher had left no will (I'm sure he had often meant to make one, but because of his preoccupation with living he put it off). Consequently, part of what he left was required by law to go to the children and was, therefore, liable to death duties (or Capital Transfer Tax as it is now called to make it sound less harsh). I found this immeasurably hurtful. Our tenants at the cottage at Ellis Green refused to budge (it was three years before they left). I found it difficult to cope with the things that Christopher had previously dealt with: insurance, money, looking after the car, etc. Our house in Radnor Walk needed structural work – the front wall had a forbidding bulge. Kate developed serious asthma. Henrietta was not happy at the Lycée and Robin missed his father very much. The problems piled up and each time they exceeded the threshold of tolerance, I gave way to serious depression. Depression is pervasive: it filters through and affects everyone around. I must admit to having always had a slightly depressive nature – I am a sort of up and down person – but in my previously safe existence I had always been quickly pampered and cosseted out of the low moments. In fact, I believe that people's basic nature rarely changes regardless of what has happened to them, so that while not turning them into different people, shock and extreme grief can have the effect of accentuating weaknesses or strengths in their characters. In my case, from being an active person I became a super-active one, and from being mildly depressed, I became a serious depressive.

I realized that the tangible problems of life were bound to increase – I couldn't control them. The difficulties of bringing up children as they grow older always increase and, in the same way that it takes two people to conceive a child, so it takes both parents to bring one up otherwise the anxiety, instead of being shared, is concentrated in the single parent and invariably boomerangs on to the children. I even believe it to be possible that children suffer less from the effect of losing one parent than from the accumulated anxiety and despair of the survivor. And there were the increasing problems related to money, property, etc., to be dealt with alone. Moreover, I just could not get round to creating a comfortable home again. I spent the minimum time there – I felt better even driving around in my car – and the house was cold, cheerless and needed redecorating. It was only because Mrs Dutch – whom, with her husband, the children considered their closest friends – came to help us that it did not become shambolic. I kept saying it was not worth doing much to the house because we might move. I now see how much the children suffered from this, and how much it helped them when, three years later, we converted the house and made it look cosy and nice. (What an irony that our house had previously been too smart for the children to invite their friends; then the shabbiness had the same effect.) As I don't believe in self-pity – I never have – I started to think of ways to tackle depression. I called it *le singe noir* and worked out a campaign to defeat this enemy. Whenever I allowed it to win (there it was, perched on my shoulder), this seemed synonymous with letting Christopher down again (after all, I hadn't even said goodbye to him); but when I won, this represented a small victory against the IRA and all the evil it stood for. There could be no stronger incentive for winning.

Gradually I realized that there were certain parts of life over which I did have some control; problems which could be avoided. There was my health, for instance. At first I had not even considered it, but soon I recognized that feeling unwell opens the door to depression. I started to eat properly, take measures to sleep better, and especially through the all-time low periods of 4–5 a.m. There were weekends – and Sunday evenings in particular – to be filled, and the danger areas caused by Christmas and family holidays. I accepted that they could not be regarded in the same light as before, but should be treated as 'projects': events which required careful organization but above all could not be compared with those of the past. I tried to reverse the deep pessimism which permeated my whole outlook. For example, one day the precious little dog was a bit off colour. Seeing her lying motionless on a chair I flew to telephone the vet. Just in time my mother had the good idea of giving the puppy a little shake, where-upon she jumped down, shook herself and wagged her tail. I was like this over everything: my expectations of anything going right were minimal.

I knew I must learn how to cope with the memory of Christopher. Although having him in my mind caused me so much sorrow, I certainly could not survive without thinking of him; even if it were possible not to. So it was a matter of working out the *way* in which to think of him. Realizing it was the physical memory which hurt so much I resisted thinking of him as a walking-about person, someone who left long black shoes all over the bedroom floor, someone who particularly liked avocado pears; but instead focused on his ideas, humour, love of politics and literature, and gentleness. The memory of those qualities and characteristics brought me comfort, interest and even amusement, and little by little I hoped to reflect some of these qualities myself. This is in fact the only rationalization I have ever been able to make for life after death: namely that a dead person goes on living within the person who loved them.

A person left to soldier on alone also has to rethink his or her position *vis-à-vis* the rest of the community. Here I will dare to make a generalization and suggest that over this society sees men and women differently. A widower is regarded as rather a noble figure whilst a widow is thought of as being pathetic. I badly needed to remain part of the community, but could not work out how to avoid feeling hurt when surrounded by people whose lives were still enviably intact. Bereavement brings out a multitude of sensitivities and the nerve ends exposed are such that others cannot be expected to recognize and respect them. First, it is very hurtful to see everyone else's life continue as before: untouched, untroubled. Certain occasions such as parents' evenings at the children's schools, Christmas, family holidays, expose the single parent. One of Christopher's novels was called *The Unkind Light*; the significance of the title being that truth is cruelly exposed by the glare of a bright light. Similarly I felt certain occasions brought out the glaring reality of being alone; other times it could be fudged. I called such occasions the 'Noah's Ark scene' when everyone else went two by two except me. In addition certain words took on an emotive quality – 'we, us, our' – (they appeared to be in perpetual use). Other women always seemed to be telling me of how their husbands were away for a week and wondering how they could bear it. Babies – previously I had loved them – became a source of distress. Symbols of new life, as they were, they accentuated the deadness within me. I couldn't bear talking about them and crossed the street when seeing one advance towards me in its pram. I remembered how Christopher used to tell me how people, prompted by a stirring in their subconscious, often referred to one-eyed phenomena when talking to him. I never quite believed him until I recognized how my presence often appeared to draw conversations inexorably towards some reference to explosions and bombs: 'X is so lazy – he needs a bomb putting under him', or 'My car was making such a funny noise this morning I thought it might blow up', or, when referring to parcels, 'It was such a funny shape I thought it might have a bomb in it.'

Now this could all have been attributed to my super-sensitivities but I'm not so sure – Christopher may have been right and, for psychological reasons, reference to 'one-eyed sailors' was reserved exclusively for him. For my part I was only sorry for the people concerned who looked so miserable the moment the offending words had – as it seemed – been drawn from their lips. Anyhow I became quite used to general references to death permeating everyday talk: I had never even noticed it before. The list of examples is interminable.

In order to gain from remaining within the community it is important to try to become the kind of person with which others want to be. They can't be sorry about someone else's misfortunes for ever – after all they've got their own problems. Moreover it is hard to put up with those who are bitter and bear a grudge against life – however justified this may be. In any case, it doesn't help anyone – particularly not the person bearing the grudge. Moreover, instinctively everyone avoids gloom. I thought I was doing quite well in seeming and looking cheerful, but a good photographer can expose what really lies behind. Jane Bown – in my view the most talented of photographers – took some photos of me for an article and they revealed a face so weighted with misery that no one could have been blamed for avoiding it. I made a big effort after that.

Of course I realized quite soon that people started to treat me differently because I wasn't married any more: they saw me as a different person. I didn't in the least mind being put on embassy lists under the 'single people' section and felt quite flattered – I had kept such lists myself – but I hated it when suddenly women treated me as if I were a threat; I had always, I thought, got on well with other women and it came as a shock. Even more I disliked various husbands seeing me as having become a single person again towards whom they might make the occasional pass. It all seemed so ludicrous when for my part I felt the same as before – firmly and inexorably married to Christopher. (Indeed I never used the word widow – it didn't seem relevant.)

A woman who is left alone dreads one thing above all else – she dreads pity. She would like others to share her loss with her but her pride is very susceptible to pity, and there is a very real difference between 'sharing sorrow' and 'being sorry for'. I imagined people saying, 'that poor Ewart-Biggs woman. Wasn't it dreadful. I wonder what's happened to her now!' (In French it sounded even worse, 'La pauvre. Qu'est-ce qui peut lui être arrivé?' Although in fact whenever I went to France – which was often – my friends succeeded in making me feel that, in their own right, they too were mourning their dear 'Christophe'.)

I remember one occasion when I must have been feeling very vulnerable. It was about a year after Christopher's death – a year during which everything grew steadily worse – and a girl journalist from one of the Sunday papers came to interview me for a short article. I described to her – probably rather aggressively – all my work relating to Ireland and so on and ended by saying even more aggressively: 'And please don't in any way suggest I'm pathetic in your article.' The journalist, by that time cowering in a corner of the room, said, 'But, Mrs Ewart-Biggs, I don't think you're the least bit pathetic.' On the other hand, one of the moments of encouragement came at the end of a weekend in Brussels where I had been staying with the Wakefields. The ambassador's residence – well remembered from when John and Diana Beith were there – was as luxurious as ever and whilst enjoying it I told Felicity about my new life; the struggles and small achievements, and she said: 'Well, I promise you, after hearing all that I'll never say poor Jane again.' It was music to the ears. As religion plays a big part in the life of Ireland, the Irish showed their concern for me by praying for me. It was good of them but one can have enough of it. When one day yet another priest told me how he included me in his prayers I thanked him but added, 'How do you think I look?' 'Wonderful,' he said. 'Well, there you are,' I said, 'it must have worked.'

Whilst all these inner battles were going on, I tried to move on with the practical steps of building a life. I had left the Savoy, having found it impossible to honour my commitment to the hotel, look after the children and deal with my emotional problems all at the same time. This coincided with the start of the selection procedure for candidates for the 1979 European elections, and I added my name to the list of hopefuls who wished to be considered by Labour Party selection committees. It was the first time I had publicly nailed my political colours to the mast and, in our society with its entrenched class system, it brought the anticipated reaction: 'Heavens, Jane, I didn't know you were one of those.' I have never understood why being a socialist evokes surprise and has to be justified whereas being a Tory is entirely acceptable and needs no justification. Further proof of this came later when I realized people thought of there being 'peers' and 'Labour peers'. 'Oh, I suppose we shall just have to put up with that,' said a guest at a diplomatic dinner party on being told that I was the latter.

I knew nothing of the process of seeking selection but, fortunately, was able to enrol Tilli Edelman as my adviser and counsellor. (She had been a major support to her MP husband, Maurice, who visited us in Algiers, in his political career until his tragic death a few months prior to Christopher's.) With her help I equipped myself with a curriculum vitae (it didn't have very much on it) and she pointed me in the right direction. After appearing before the first selection committee, I realized just how brave – or rather foolhardy – I was. The link between the members of the committee and me had been almost non-existent. I knew quite a lot – perhaps too much – about Community policies and nattered on – to their astonishment – about Lomé I and the CAP. But when asked how all this could help them with their housing problem in, say, Kentish Town, I was stumped. Moreover, although I didn't in the least feel they disliked or disapproved of me, I knew they did not regard me as the ideal person to be their standard-bearer (and I rather agreed with them). They seemed to imply that although I was a nice, well-meaning woman, perhaps it would be better if I went back to the life-style that suited me – like getting on with my shopping at Harrods – and left Labour Party politics to them.

However, displaying the most heroic courage of my life, I persisted. (Sometimes I woke at 4 in the morning uneasily thinking: 'Now why have I woken up feeling sick?', before remembering the selection committee of that evening; whereupon I fell into a cold sweat of apprehension and spent hours writing and rewriting my required ten-minute speech.) Although continually turned down, my dogged determination eventually paid off. I was shortlisted for two Euro constituencies in the Greater London area; only to be defeated by a member of the NUM at the final selection conference at Sidcup. He certainly had the edge on me when, asked by his selectors, 'Can you give us one good reason for staying in the Community?', he answered 'No'. (I thought sadly of those heady days in Brussels and Paris when the European ideal had so strongly taken hold in our minds and hearts.)

By this time, in early 1979, I had learned more about the process of building another life. Although still not in any way making precise plans for the future I realized how often one thing had evolved out of another. For instance, although I had never seriously expected to become a European Member of Parliament, my efforts in that direction had drawn me into a circle of people concerned with European affairs, and with many of whom I had made friends. I realized that although there often seemed little or no point in doing a particular thing, it was nevertheless better to do it in the hope that something else might come out of it and, in an indirect way, contribute to the process of building.

It was at this time that I joined the lecture circuit – and this turned out to be a more appropriate setting for me than the hustings. It happened purely by chance when a journalist, realizing that I often gave talks about reconciliation in Northern Ireland, asked if I had ever thought of giving lectures for money. I said I had no idea it was even possible to do this and he said, 'Oh yes, it is. Why don't you get yourself on the Foyle's Lecture Agency list.' Seeing me look doubtful, he said, 'I'll ring them up for you.' This was how my trips round the country started and also the beginning of my happy relationship with Miss Kay Whalley, who runs Foyle's Agency and is one of the most considerate people I have met in years. She sent me off to groups all over the country – Ladies' Luncheon Clubs, Women's Institutes, Soroptimists, Rotary Clubs, Business and Professional Ladies' clubs, Literary Societies, the Guernsey Chamber of Commerce, and so on.

I often found myself on the train going to the north of England (where the institution of the Luncheon Club was, in fact, born) and I learned how in exactly the opposite way to, say, France or Italy, the warmth of the British people increases as one goes northwards. I came to recognize the eager, welcoming face of the Club secretary at the Huddersfield, Scarborough or Manchester railway station, first worried and then so relieved at the safe arrival of the 'speaker'. I learned a little of the geography of my own country which I had previously not known. This ignorance, at first, let me in for much longer journeys than I had anticipated; except for once when, not realizing there were two Newcastles, I was amazed at arriving at my destination so quickly and even more startled when told that the local industry was pottery and not coal. (Luckily I got by without being rumbled.)

I was often asked whether I had done any public speaking during my married life. Of course I had not, but I think the ability to do so comes not only from practice but from a genuine interest in communication. I had always enjoyed 'telling people about things' (hence Christopher's anxious eye fixed on me from across a room) and, after all, conversation is a very central part of a hostess's life. So to my amazement I realized that talking to our guests round the dinner table at rue Francois l^{er} and elsewhere had been a good apprenticeship to addressing, say, a thousand members of the Derbyshire Federation of Womens' Institutes in the vast pavilion in Buxton.

But what did me the most good was the kindness and warmth of the women. There can be no better palliative for desolation and a sense of loss and bitterness (although carefully camouflaged) than warmth and caring openly expressed. Sometimes I was especially spoiled. One day, at the cosy Ashdale Hotel in Helmsley, Yorkshire – with fire burning brightly – I was chatting to the members of the Country Women's Luncheon Club before sitting down to a meal. One of them, not realizing I was the speaker, said, 'And of course you know we *should* have had that man talking about Kentucky horses today, but he cancelled, so I think we're very lucky to have Mrs Ewart-Biggs to talk about those nice "Diplomatic Wives" instead.' I gasped. Taking this as a lack of support from me, she said rather crisply, 'Well, don't you agree we're lucky?'

I can remember being particularly obsessed at that time by the concept of happiness. When meeting all those women – who were total strangers – I asked myself only one question about them: were they happy? And the criteria for happiness, I thought, was being able to look forward with pleasure to an empty weekend, a family holiday or Christmas. Sometimes I felt like asking them, in the hope that their answers might confirm that at any rate the central pool of happiness was well filled, even though I myself might find it so elusive.

The lecture circuit even took me to the west coast of the United States. I spoke in about six or seven cities, and my theme was to dissuade potential American funders of the IRA. I was made aware very early on of the need for my mission. This was on a flight between Seattle and Portland – the first two cities where I was speaking – and inevitably my neighbour became expansive. 'What are you doing over here?' 'Oh, just giving a few lectures.' Relentlessly, 'What about?' 'Ireland'. 'What about Ireland?' Feeling persecuted, 'Oh, well, mainly about support for the IRA.' A flicker of interest: 'Oh, are you for or against?'

Little by little, year after year, my life and that of the whole family started to take some form again. Looking back, I realize now that this did not happen through carefully laid plans and long-term aims, but evolved through one thing leading to another. The secret, I am sure, was never to reject an offer or turn down a suggestion or proposal, however irrelevant, boring or inconvenient it might seem. Finally, all the pieces come together: pieces including your own determination, other people's support and encouragement, a bit of luck; the healing quality of the passage of time; things coinciding or just happening to your advantage, and so on. Finally, returning to my original metaphor, you will find bricks being taken off the pile instead of always being heaped on. Suddenly you find that life is real again and light has appeared at the end of the dark tunnel.

As the postscript of this book was intended to reflect thoughts about the all-important subject of how a person contrives to build another life, it is perhaps not the most appropriate place in which to write about the House of Lords, for it must be said that the process of rebuilding rarely includes hitting such a jackpot. Yet it would be wrong not to make some reference to my good fortune. In a certain way I see it as a framework to continue some of the work I was doing previously. Instead of moving my soap-box around, I have found a respected and influential platform where I can set up a permanent one. I use it to try to help people and to support the things in which I believe. My views on politics have not changed much. I remain a convinced internationalist, believing that the only true frontiers are those we set within society, and, although I am not a doctrinaire Socialist, I believe deeply in the achievement of a more equal society. Not only do I consider equality to be morally right but, from a practical point of view, I feel that countries which have attained a greater degree of equality seem to get on better than we do. I know how difficult it is to bring this about because of the natural cycles which prevail whereby on the one side privilege, wealth, intelligence, etc. are inherited, whilst on the other bad luck, poverty, ignorance or ill-health are passed on from one generation to the next. My interest is in a party which, through its policies, genuinely works towards interrupting these natural cycles to bring about a fairer balance. The Welfare State as put into effect in the 1940s was a rescue operation for people imprisoned within the cycle of deprivation, and I remember how proud we were, when serving abroad, that our country had introduced this radical and humane social policy. Today I might feel there was less to be proud of, as I believe that the present Government policies not only lack a sense of compassion but also deliberately ensure the continuation of both cycles, inequality being seen as necessary in order to stimulate initiative and change. This, in turn, seems to have given a new respectability to reactionary right-wing views and to Victorian values, in spite of all the social injustice they represented. To hear some people talk, it is as if the poor, the sick, the old, the unemployed have only themselves to blame for their problems and that they should 'pull themselves together', learn 'to stand on their own feet' and stop 'sponging off the State'. Indeed, any expression of social concern is often scoffed at in certain circles in Britain today and the moral arguments in favour of a more equal society scorned.

I believe that the materialism and selfishness which at present pervade our country will pass in time, but not before there has been untold suffering among Britain's less fortunate people and a serious blow has been dealt to our sense of national unity.

The Upper House is made up of many remarkable people whom I greatly admire. Through their life's experience they are able to inject much commitment, intelligence and expertise into their work there. Also they are most welcoming and friendly to me and, although, God knows, I'm not exactly young any more, some of them treat me as if I were. About the nicest moment, I think, was when an elderly peer, looking at me pensively one day, said: 'You know, it's really marvellous having you with us – and what's more you're the only person here with a waist!' However, I discovered that parking a car in the forecourt of the Houses of Parliament can have its dangers. Finding her car heavily dented one day, a friend pointed this out to the attendant. He seemed unperturbed: 'You never want to park anywhere near Lord X, my Lady – he drives by touch.'

I have found it hard to participate effectively in debate: my whole background and experience as a diplomatic wife were based on listening, conciliating and seeing other people's points of view. These are valuable political assets in the long run, but they are not much help in the cut and thrust of debate or when searching for an instant verbal retort. Moreover, the extreme shyness of my childhood sometimes seems to reassert itself and my mind goes blank.

I have come to realize the importance attached to a title – once in a humorous light. While I was waiting one day in a queue for the cashier at the bank behind two punks, one of them, apologising for the delay, noticed my name and title printed on the cheque I was holding ready in my hand. 'Cor,' he said admiringly, 'a Lady! I've never met one of those before.' And then he added, 'Biggs. Could it be old Ronald's mum?' With Ronald Biggs's grey hair in mind, I looked rather pained. 'Go on,' he said soothingly, 'I was about to say Ronald's younger sister.'

I do occasionally wonder how it all came about – how the fat, silent child from a very conventional background became a hard-working member of the Upper House, someone who expresses left-wing ideas and, although not an expert in any field, tries to make serious contributions to debates. It's not born of ambition – I know I'm only

ambitious to get things done — so it must be through the continued
need to fill the void Christopher's death left in my life and, as I see it,
in that of the community. It is also a compulsion to go on speaking up
for what we both believed in and resisting what we both thought
wrong. Although my children are still my central preoccupation and I
hope to share my life with somebody again one day, my focus certainly has moved from domestic to professional interests. In doing so,
I have become well aware of the difficulties experienced by women
who want to embrace both the ethos of domesticity and a professional life at the same time. I have even been forced to accept that we
in Britain live in a male-dominated society.

I have quoted many extracts from Christopher's diary in this book,
but my last quotation comes instead from my speech during the
opening debate of the 1982 parliamentary session. Choosing the
family as my subject, I started by reproaching the Government for not
honouring their commitment to be the party which champions the
rights of the family, and I went on to emphasize the plight of many of
Britain's poorer families:

> May I point out to your Lordships how, in my view, the Government
> policies are failing to accommodate changes in the family structure . . . .
>
> First, do the Government really *recognize* what constitutes today's
> family? Do they *realize* that in ever-increasing cases the stereotyped
> family group consisting of the breadwinning father, the full-time house-
> wife mother and at least two or three residing young children is entirely
> misleading in contemporary Britain? Instead, a majority of family house-
> holds in Britain now consist of other combinations: couples (married or
> unmarried) without accompanying offspring; single parent households;
> dual worker families; no-worker families and a variety of kinds of
> 'reconstituted' families.
>
> So, what provision, I wonder, does the Government make for these new
> categories of families? We also wonder whether their social policies are
> really focused on the true needs. First, I should like briefly to look at the
> one-parent family and see how it is faring. Sadly, the number of one-
> parent families in this country has now risen to nearly one million. Of
> these, nine out of ten are headed by a lone woman. Ever increasing
> numbers of separations and divorces account, of course, for a very great
> number. Another group of single-parent households is headed by widows,
> and a further group is headed by young mothers who elect to stay single to

bring up their child or children . . . . Surely there is a gap between the rhetoric used by the Government when talking about the family and their refusal to put money into redressing the balance for our least privileged families and children.

One can refer to social justice and the aspiration of a more equal society in either moral or practical terms; but, using practical terms, may I put it to the Government that, when we hear of an upsurge of violence by white and coloured youths in Brixton, do we not wonder how many of those young people are alienated by the brutality of a deprived childhood? When we hear of the Catholic youth in Belfast's ghettos voting for the Provisional Sinn Fein – in other words, voting in as extreme a manner as possible – do we not wonder what his home was like in a city that is reputed to have the worst housing in Europe? Putting morality aside, is there not a very real possibility that the lack of additional provision for Britain's least fortunate families might well result in even more embittered young people wishing to get their own back on society in a way which is most destructive to that society?

The reason why I have ended by including this extract is not so much to reflect my ideas on this particular issue but rather to symbolize how the survivor of a partnership – and I believe marriage is the most natural and important of all partnerships – can keep alive what was good and positive in the marriage. This will serve at the same time to honour their dead and to carry into their new existence the values they fostered together.

Index

INDEX

235